An Introduction to Curriculum Research and Development

An Introduction to Curriculum Research and Development

LAWRENCE STENHOUSE

HEINEMANN EDUCATIONAL

Heinemann Educational Books Ltd
Halley Court, Jordan Hill, Oxford OX2 8EJ

OXFORD LONDON EDINBURGH
MADRID ATHENS BOLOGNA PARIS
MELBOURNE SYDNEY AUCKLAND SINGAPORE TOKYO
IBADAN NAIROBI HARARE GABORONE
PORTSMOUTH NH (USA)

ISBN 0-435-80851-6

First published 1975
91 92 93 94 95 24 23 22 21 20 19 18 17 16 15

Printed and bound in Great Britain by
Biddles Ltd, Guildford and King's Lynn

CONTENTS

ACKNOWLEDGEMENTS

This book could not have been written if I had not drawn on the knowledge, advice and work of my immediate colleagues, past and present: the staff of the Centre for Applied Research in Education; the teachers working with them on research and development projects; those who worked on the Humanities Curriculum Project; and the staff of the Nuffield Foundation and the Schools Council. Their names are too numerous to mention.

The following have read all or part of the manuscript and have made comments which have led me to rewrite: Clem Adelman, John Elliott, Barry MacDonald, Jean Rudduck, Hugh Sockett, Bob Stake, Gajendra Verma, Rob Walker and Bob Wild. They are accountable neither for its inadequacies nor for my opinions.

John Bull gave me valuable information on his work in school-based, in-service training.

Marion Pick helped me with typing.

FOREWORD

In the last fifteen years or so a major curriculum reform has taken place in the field of educational studies in colleges and university schools of education in Britain. The teaching of education as an undifferentiated field has been largely supplanted by the teaching of constituent disciplines. Philosophy, psychology and sociology are virtually everywhere represented: history and comparative education have been only partly successful in establishing their claims.

This change in curriculum has increased the rigour and the intellectual tone of education courses. It has done little for their relevance to the problem of improving the practice of teaching.

When the revision of the education curriculum was initiated, one of its proponents, R. S. Peters, spoke of the need for 'mesh'. In my view that mesh has not been achieved and relevance to practice depends upon it. I see a possibility of its achievement through the close study of curriculum and teaching, and that is why this book has been written.

A major problem of mounting courses of study in curriculum and teaching has been the lack of a satisfactory British text-book. There are American text-books, but they do not suit our needs. Text-books are useful because they define the field and its problems for both staff and students.

A good text-book would need to be written by someone who was able to combine practical experience of research and development in curriculum and teaching with an extensive knowledge both of the literature and of research and development projects in which he or she had not participated. I am not equipped for this task in the extent of my reading or my knowledge of the work of the many projects carried out in recent years. But it may be that no one is.

Accordingly, I have written this 'book instead of a text-book' in the hope that it will serve until an adequate text-book can be written.

This attempt falls short in that if offers a highly personal view. I believe that a text-book should present a thesis about the field it covers; but one which takes account of a wider range of work and experience than I have been able to master. This book looks outwards from the work of my colleagues and myself consequently its over-representation tends to over-estimate its importance, by implication if not by intention.

Nevertheless, it has, I hope, to a greater or lesser extent, three attributes which are necessary in a text-book. It has a reasonably extensive coverage of issues and problems. It has a reasonably adequate initial bibliography to guide reading. And it demands additional reading and teaching if it is to be adequately understood.

I hope that it will be of use both to those who wish to mount courses in curriculum and teaching and to anyone who is interested in introducing himself or herself to this important area of research and development.

Lawrence Stenhouse
Bintree
1975

I

DEFINING THE CURRICULUM PROBLEM

Definitions of the word *curriculum* do not solve curricular problems; but they do suggest perspectives from which to view them.

In this chapter I shall examine some definitions and then attempt to make clear the perspective from which the present book is written by suggesting what a curriculum ought to do.

The *Shorter Oxford Dictionary* defines *curriculum* as a 'course; especially a regular course of study as at a school or university'. It records its use since the seventeenth century, and this perhaps marks the beginning in this country of systematic and self-conscious attempts to regularize courses of study.

The dictionary offers, among others, the following definitions of *regular*:

> Having a form, structure or arrangement which follows, or is reducible to, some rule or principle; characterized by harmony or proper correspondence between the various parts or elements; marked by steadiness or uniformity of action, procedure or occurrence; conformable to some accepted or adopted rule or standard.

If we do not interpret these attributes too mechanically, I think they represent in a general way what we may ask of a curriculum.

How are we to create curricula which have this quality of form, principle, harmony, steadiness and conformity to standards? There is a classic, though very un-British, answer to this question.

On my desk before me is a book of 350 pages. It is called *Mønsterplan for Grunnskolen* – literally, *Model Plan for the Foundation School* (1971). I was able to buy it in a bookshop in Oslo. It is the curriculum of the Norwegian comprehensive school. It lays down the ground to be covered and to some extent the methods to be used for each subject in each year of the school. It also makes statements about aims. Such a document is not untypical of centralized school systems; and it is the response of such systems to the problem of ensuring regularity in the curriculum. One might call it a specification.

To the British teacher such an approach to the curriculum is quite novel. But in some countries the first thing that comes to mind when mention is made of the curriculum is a book of instructions to teachers. 'Could you please pass me the curriculum,' one might almost say.

Such a view equates the curriculum with a written prescription of what it is intended should happen in schools.

Some, however, equate the curriculum less with the intentions of the school than with its performance. 'Basically the curriculum is what happens to children in school as a result of what teachers do. It includes all of the experiences of children for which the school should accept responsibility.' (Kansas 1958). (The clarity of this position is weakened by later statements in the same document.)

For such a curriculum one does not look at a book but at the school. If curriculum is defined in this way, then the study of curriculum can be reduced to the empirical study of schools. The curriculum is not the intention or prescription but what happens in real situations. It is not the aspiration, but the achievement. The problem of specifying the curriculum is one of perceiving, understanding and describing what is actually going on in school and classroom.

Curriculum study based on this position presumably also leads to the writing of books. So again, as in the case of the Norwegian *Mønsterplan*, we find out about the curriculum by turning to a book. In this case, however, the book is not a statement of the intended curriculum, but an anthropological or sociological analysis of the school as an agency of teaching and learning, based on the interpretation of careful observation. Curriculum study is case study.

We appear to be confronted by two different views of the curriculum. On the one hand the curriculum is seen as an intention, plan or prescription, an idea about what one would like to happen in schools. On the other it is seen as the existing state of affairs in schools, what does in fact happen. And since neither intentions nor happenings can be discussed until they are described or otherwise communicated, curriculum study rests on how we talk or write about these two ideas of curriculum.

In essence it seems to me that curriculum study is concerned with the relationship between the two views of curriculum – as intention and as reality. I believe that our educational realities seldom conform to our educational intentions. We cannot put our policies into practice. We should not regard this as a failure peculiar to schools and teachers. We have only to look around us to confirm that it is part of the human lot. But, as Karl Popper has observed, improvement is possible if we are secure enough to face and study the nature of our failures. The central problem of curriculum study is the gap between our ideas and aspirations and our attempts to operationalize them.

Curriculum development is founded on curriculum study, and is its applied branch. Its object is the betterment of schools through the improvement of teaching and learning. Its characteristic insistence is that ideas should encounter the discipline of practice and that practice should be principled by ideas. The curriculum development movement is an attack on the separation of theory and practice.

In a classic book on curriculum, Ralph Tyler rests his work on four fundamental questions:

1. What educational purposes should the school seek to attain?
2. What educational experiences can be provided that are likely to attain these purposes?
3. How can these educational experiences be effectively organized?
4. How can we determine whether these purposes are being attained?

(Tyler 1949, 1)

With the first of these questions I am only obliquely concerned in this book. Not that it is unimportant – far from it. It is the fundamental question of educational policy. But how can we translate purpose into policy, and then test how far and why practice has fallen short of hopes? Given an aspiration, how should we go about trying to realize it? And what range of choice of aspirations is open to us? These seem to me to be the fundamental questions on which curriculum research and development can throw light.

Such a standpoint might seem barren and pessimistic were it not that exciting educational proposals abound, whereas practice that lives up to them is hard to find. Students in training often notice a gap between the educationalist and the school not unlike that between Haig's headquarters and the mud of Flanders. So many seem elated by the discussion of educational ideas: so few are encouraged by close critical scrutiny of their own classrooms. The gap between aspiration and practice is a real and a frustrating one.

The gap can be closed only by adopting a research and development approach to one's own teaching, whether alone or in a group of co-operating teachers. The framework of a national curriculum project is sometimes helpful. This book can only aspire to provide a foundation on which to build.

I have tried to define the role of curriculum development and curriculum study in a general way, and also to formulate a central problem; but I have not offered a definition of *curriculum*. I suppose I ought to try.

Here are three mainstream American definitions:

> Curriculum is 'all of the planned experiences provided by the school to assist the pupils in attaining the designated learning outcomes to the best of their abilities.'
>
> (Neagley and Evans 1967, 2)

> Curriculum is the planned composite effort of any school to guide pupil learning toward predetermined learning outcomes.
>
> (Inlow 1966, 7)

> In view of the shortcomings of the currently popular definition, it is here stipulated that curriculum is a structured series of intended learning outcomes. Curriculum prescribes (or at least anticipates) the results of instruction.
>
> (Johnson 1967, 130)

In each of these, progressively more strongly in the order in which I print them, is the implication of a particular type of end-means model, which until recently was almost universally accepted in curriculum study. This model starts from a definition of the performance or attainment which students should reach at the end of a course, and proceeds to attempt to design a course which will deliver that permance. Education is a means to an end which is expressed in terms of student attainment, using the terms *intended learning outcome* or *behavioural objective* (i.e. the student behaviour aimed at).

I want to treat that model as problematic: that is, I want to leave open the question whether it is a good one. So I must find a definition of curriculum which does not make so many assumptions.

The definition offered here is a tentative one to get us on our way.

A curriculum is an attempt to communicate the essential principles and features of an educational proposal in such a form that it is open to critical scrutiny and capable of effective translation into practice.

Of course, this definition reflects my own perspective. A curriculum is rather like a recipe in cookery. It can be criticized on nutritional or gastronomic grounds – does it nourish the students and does it taste good? – and it can be criticized on the grounds of practicality – we can't get hold of six dozen larks' tongues and the grocer can't find any ground unicorn horn! A curriculum, like the recipe for a dish, is first imagined as a possibility, then the subject of experiment. The recipe offered publicly is in a sense a report on the experiment. Similarly, a curriculum should be grounded in practice. It is an attempt so to describe the work observed in classrooms that it is adequately communicated to teachers and others. Finally, within limits, a recipe can be varied according to taste. So can a curriculum.

But analogies should be abandoned before they cause indigestion. A curriculum is the means by which the experience of attempting to put an educational proposal into practice is made publicly available. It involves both content and method, and in its widest application takes account of the problem of implementation in the institutions of the educational system.

As a minimum, a curriculum should provide a basis for planning a course, studying it empirically and considering the grounds of its justification. It should offer:

A. In planning:

1. Principles for the selection of content – what is to be learned and taught.
2. Principles for the development of a teaching strategy – how it is to be learned and taught.
3. Principles for the making of decisions about sequence.
4. Principles on which to diagnose the strengths and weaknesses of individual students and differentiate the general principles 1, 2 and 3 above, to meet individual cases.

B. In empirical study:

1. Principles on which to study and evaluate the progress of students.
2. Principles on which to study and evaluate the progress of teachers.
3. Guidance as to the feasibility of implementing the curriculum in varying school contexts, pupil contexts, environments and peer-group situations.
4. Information about the variability of effects in differing contexts and on different pupils and an understanding of the causes of the variation.

C. In relation to justification:

A formulation of the intention or aim of the curriculum which is accessible to critical scrutiny.

In fact, when we apply these criteria, it is clear that neither traditional nor innovatory curricula stand up well under close scrutiny. Education is not in practice very sophisticated or efficient.

2

THE CONTENT OF EDUCATION

Prophets may teach private wisdom: teachers must deal in public knowledge.

Although content and method are inseparably interwoven in the practice of education, it is useful to distinguish them for the purposes of analysis. In this chapter I shall consider some of the problems and issues in curriculum which are best brought out by an approach through content.

A teacher is a man of learning skilled in teaching. He is qualified by virtue of his education and his training. He does not teach what he alone knows, letting his pupils in on secrets. On the contrary, his task is to help his pupils gain entry into a commonwealth of knowledge and skills, to hand on to them something which others already possess.

The school has the task of making available to the young a selection of society's intellectual, emotional and technical capital. It is this capital which I have characterized as 'public traditions'. In our society, schools teach a variety of public traditions. Among the most important are bodies of knowledge; arts; skills; languages; conventions; and values. These traditions, seen from one point of view, exist as social facts; and they are therefore subjects of study for the social scientist.

The anthropologist and the sociologist use the term *culture* to designate what I have called above 'public traditions'. This is a useful term for curriculum studies, but it needs to be explained and explored.

As it is used here, culture does not of course carry the meaning caught in the *Oxford Dictionary* definition: 'the training and refinement of mind, tastes and manners', even though some schools would say that this is what they are about. For the social scientist the concept of culture is intended to be value-free, denoting bad as well as good public traditions.

Culture is a concept used by social scientists when they attempt to explore the social structure of knowledge, skills, customs and beliefs in order to understand how they came about, how they relate to society and how society handles them.

The classic definition of culture is that of E. B. Tylor, the nineteenth-century anthropologist. For him culture is 'that complex whole which includes knowledge, belief, art, morals, law, custom and other capabilities acquired by man as a member of society'. (Tylor 1871, 1) This definition was forged in the study of pre-literate societies. Anthroplogists wanted a word to describe the way of life and thinking which was handed down from generation to generation among the Zulu or the Dyaks.

Talcott Parsons, a modern American sociologist, stresses three attributes of culture: 'first, that culture is *transmitted*, it constitutes a heritage or a social tradition; secondly, that it is *learned*, it is not a manifestation, in particular content, of man's genetic constitution; and third, that it is *shared*'. (Parsons 1952, 15) One can see the relevance of such a concept for curriculum: the content of education is transmitted, learned and shared in this sense.

We face difficulties, however, in applying the concept of culture to our own society because it is pluralist, that is to say, it contains many different and often logically incompatible traditions which are transmitted, learned and shared. It can be argued that it is an over-simplification to talk of the culture of the Dyaks as if all Dyaks shared exactly the same tradition. In our society this difficulty of usage is still greater. No doubt the Rolling Stones, Mary Whitehouse, Jeremy Thorpe, Matt Busby, Henry Moore and Paul Raymond do in some sense share 'British culture'. They can all add up their shopping bills, they all drive on the left side of the road and recognize the tune of 'God Save the Queen'. But their differences are much more interesting than their similarities.

A common way of tackling such differences within a culture is to term them *sub-cultures*. I do not think this is a helpful term in the present context. It tends to suggest a hierarchy of cultures, the higher order ones containing the lower order ones, as in a branching tree pattern. Our multiple cultures are much more fluid than this, and present many alternatives. A person participates in as many cultures as the culturally different groups he mixes in. He carries the currency of these groups – their common understandings and language – rather as a traveller carries a pocket full of coins from each of the lands he has visited.

We need a much more flexible and sinuous conception of culture to do justice to the way in which it is shared and distributed in a society like ours where groups form and dissolve, the members joining new groups in patterns of bewildering complexity. Talcott Parsons states the situation in rather abstract terms. 'Culture . . . is on the one hand the product of, on the other hand a determinant of, systems of social interaction.' (Parsons 1952, 15) We have to relate culture to social interaction of a very fluid kind rather than to group identity, because in cultural terms one person in our society belongs to many groups and the pattern of his affiliation is often surprising. The professor may be the football fan, the steelworker the enthusiast for opera.

In Parsons' terms culture is a product of social interaction. Each person learned each of the cultures to which he has access in contact with a social group, and the cultures were also created in groups. It is by taking part in the communication system of a group that one learns its culture. A school and a class are both groups in this sense. Each has its own culture. But it is the peculiar function of educational groups to represent to their members a culture which exists outside and is not native to the group. Education exists to give people access to cultural groups outside their own.

As well as being a product of social action, culture is also a determinant of it. It determines who can talk to whom about what. We talk to one another by virtue of what is common in the cultures we have learned; we are unable to talk to one another when we lack common experience.

It is possible to view culture as 'the medium through which human minds interact in communication'. (Stenhouse 1963, 120) People who 'can interact without misunderstanding do so on the consensus of meanings manifested in linguistic usage and dependent upon a deeper consensus of values and understandings.' (ibid. 122)

Out of communication systems of this sort, thinking systems are constructed. The culture supports a language which is made accessible to the individual and serves him as an instrument of thinking.

> Once we have learned language, we have command of an instrument which can be used not only for communicating with others but also for communing with ourselves. Language supports our solitary reflection. Given life in communication, it becomes the possession of the individual, who can, as it were, carry it with him into his inner privacy and use it as an instrument of thought.
>
> (Stenhouse 1967, 31)

In the concept of culture we can catch the idea of a multiplicity of traditions, public in the sense that we can learn them by joining the groups which share them. Such culture is transmitted, learned and shared and through the development of language it supports both communication among members and thinking on the part of individuals. In a sense, culture is an intellectual commodity; and it is the commodity in which schools deal, and out of which they quarry the content of education.

Schools make culture available by providing pupils with an opportunity to take part in learning groups. The characteristic and the difficulty of such educational groups is that they have the task of introducing their members to cultures which are not natural to them and which often conflict in certain respects with the cultures of the home and the peer group. The problem is how to get the group to interact co-operatively and richly in terms of the cultures the school offers it so that those cultures gain reality and offer satisfaction. The alternative – to accept the discipline of learning what appears to be useless for the present in the trust that it will serve in the future – appears likely to commend itself to only a small minority of pupils.

This problem influences the schools in their selection of culture. The school cannot transmit the entire culture of our society. As it selects, is it to follow the principle of relevance or interest and try, so far as it can within that principle, to guide pupils towards the ultimately worthwhile? Or is it to choose that which is judged worthwhile and attempt to teach it so well that it evokes interest? Midwinter (1973) tends towards the first line. The alternative is well argued in the chapters on 'Criteria of Education' and 'Worth-while activities' in R. S. Peters' *Ethics and Education* (1966). Although I am myself more inclined to the second view, it is not my purpose to argue the case here. The issue, which will raise itself from time to time throughout the book, cuts across my main thread and purpose.

In practice, most schools tend to emphasize in their curricula the teaching of bodies of knowledge, arts, skills, languages, conventions and values; and I must turn now to review these as elements in culture.

Any subject, as it is taught in schools, is likely to involve several of these elements, but I think it is possible to make distinctions along the lines of these categories even though they are a little rough-hewn. Mathematics, science, history, geography and social science can be thought of as bodies of knowledge (as can many university subjects not taught in schools). Literature, music and visual art comprise the arts. Reading and writing, commercial subjects, domestic subjects, technical subjects and games are primarily concerned with skills or traditions of craft. Languages too are skills in a sense, but their status and position in the curriculum justifies separate treatment. I shall discuss conventions and values as they relate to the curriculum as a whole.

Where do the school subjects come from? Although they may be transformed to some degree by the culture of the school – a possibility to be considered later – they originate outside the school and have an existence independent of it. The school is a distributor of knowledge rather than a manufacturer, and this implies reference points outside the school for the subjects it teaches. These reference points lie in cultures outside the school on which the school subjects depend and to which they refer.

The bodies of knowledge can be called 'academic disciplines' or 'disciplines of knowledge'. In terms of culture, what does this mean?

> The disciplines of knowledge are not clearly described as areas of study or of knowledge, but metaphorically as communities of scholars who share a domain of intellectual inquiry or discourse. In essence these societies of specialists are engaged in a variety of styles of human imagination in which the spirit of inquiry is applied to defined domains of human concern. Each group of intellectual discoursers has a heritage and is striving to bring the development of its domain or field to a continually higher and more fruitful state of knowledge and meaning. The body of intellectual discoursers in a field has one or more characteristic ways of knowing – of warranting knowledge – or it may share modes of inquiry with other disciplines. The group shares the precious resource of a specialised language or other systems of symbols which makes precision of definition and inquiry possible. The body of discoursers has a set of more or less well-related concepts. The community has an inheritance of books, articles and research reports, and a system for communication among the membership. Members of the community share affective as well as cognitive links, with the excitement of discovery and the pleasure of sharing with colleagues as common characteristics. The work of the community emphasizes style and the search for truth. Further, the community has either an explicit or a tacit conception of man. Finally, the discipline is an instructive community.
>
> (King and Brownell 1966, 68)

This is perhaps a somewhat idealized view of the academic community in the picture it draws of human beings. Musgrove (1968, 101) is rather more astringent about social relationships within disciplines.

> . . . subjects are communities of people, competing and collaborating with one another, defining and defending their boundaries, demanding

allegiance from their members and conferring a sense of identity upon them. They are bureaucracies, hierarchically organized, determining conditions of senior membership, establishing criteria for recruitment to different levels, disciplining their members through marks of recognition like honorary fellowships and admission to exclusive inner councils.

Whatever the merits of these two accounts as likenesses, it is clear that they identify academic subcultures as the creators and curators of those disciplines of knowledge which find expression in the school as the group of academic subjects. Disciplines of knowledge have a social existence and are located in groups of scholars, typically in our society working in universities, extending their disciplines by research and teaching them to students.

In the arts the situation is rather different. Visual art, music and literature are not generally created in universities as part of the task of the institutional community. The groups which include and support the individuals who create the arts are less formally marked out and institutionalized, except perhaps in the case of the bureaucratic arts of radio, television and cinema. Nevertheless, even in the individual arts there are groups which are in their own way parallel to the groups of university scholars just described. In visual art and music there are colleges and teaching communities. There are also schools of artists or musicians linked in dialogue about their work. Each art also has its institutions – concerts, galleries and exhibitions, societies.

In the universities the arts tradition is generally, though not invariably, critical or historical. A discipline is created to study and respond to the arts, and at its best and in its own terms this supports creative responses; but the universities do not possess the arts in the way that they do the formal academic disciplines, and precisely because they do not create them.

There are thus two distinguishable cultures in the arts with which the school may identify: the creative tradition and the critical tradition. In practice, the creative tradition has been stronger in the schools in visual art and music than it has in literature. This is probably because the majority of teachers of art or music are or have been practitioners, whereas the majority of English teachers have not in any full sense been writers.

In the third category of our classification of content, that of skills, it seems worthwhile to distinguish three main areas of interest in the schools: basic skills; craft and vocational skills; and leisure skills, including skills in sports and games. Basic skills are characteristic of the majority of people in our culture. There is no clear and closed group outside the school which is identified with them. Vocational skills have reference points in crafts and industries, where again there are groups maintaining traditions and their standards, groups which in structure are not unlike academic groups. Similarly, leisure skills are associated with groups which have their clubs and associations and sometimes their rules committees and training committees.

Our fourth category, languages, has been prominent in the grammar school tradition, so prominent that the very name of the school derives from it. I am concerned here with the teaching of the use of a classical or modern foreign language, and not with philology or linguistics, which are university disciplines.

The origins of the schools' interest in the teaching of languages lie in the teaching of Latin (and to a lesser extent Greek), first as the *lingua franca* of the mediaeval scholarly world and later as a 'discipline to thought' and for the sake of classical literature. Modern languages were at first alternative disciplines for thinking and are now increasingly seen in practical terms. In the case of Latin and Greek, the 'dead' languages, the culture which supported them lay first in the church and later in the university establishment, but in the case of modern languages, the point of reference is a nation of people who speak the language as their mother tongue. It is interesting that there is a threat for the modern language teacher in the existence of a large body of people inferior in education to himself who nevertheless speak the language better than he since it is their native tongue.

Conventions and values are expressed in all the school's teaching and in its organizational arrangements. Disciplines, arts, skills and languages all carry values and conventions within them. Consider the value tones of the two accounts of disciplines of knowledge quoted earlier in this chapter. (King and Brownell 1966; Musgrove 1968). Social class values and conventions are explicitly taught by many schools, especially in the private sector, and are implied in many others. Whether the disciplines themselves rest on a base of social class-linked values is a matter of discussion. Even the day-to-day arrangements of schools, such as streaming and options systems, express values strongly, as of course do the rituals such as morning assemblies and speech days. And in all these cases the school reflects values which are held by sections of society outside the schools.

It is clear, therefore, that over a large range of its curriculum and institutional arrangements the school is teaching a content on which it has a lease rather than a possession. In most cases possession is felt to lie in some group outside the school which acts as a point of reference and a source of standards. How far do these groups outside the school constitute 'reference groups' in the sociological sense?

A standard introductory text in sociology defines a reference group in the following terms:

> For members of a particular group, another group is a reference group if any of the following circumstances prevail:
>
> 1. Some or all of the members of the first group aspire to membership of the second group (the reference group).
> 2. The members of the first group strive to be like the members of the reference group in some respect, or to make their group like the reference group in some respect.
> 3. The members of the first group derive some satisfaction from being *un*like the members of the reference group in some respect, and strive to maintain the difference between the groups or between themselves and the members of the reference group.
> 4. Without necessarily striving to be like or unlike the reference group or its members, the members of the first group appraise their own group or themselves using the reference group or its members as a standard for comparison.
>
> (Johnson 1961, 39–40)

All the above circumstances seem to prevail from time to time or for individual members of the school teaching group, but the essential relationship is best caught in the last, the idea that links standards in the school to their sources in the larger society. And in schools the teachers appraise the pupil group rather than themselves by reference group standards.

It seems to me fair and helpful to describe as reference groups those groups outside the school which create and curate knowledge and skills and values. Reference is indeed made to them as sources of standards both in school subjects and in the conventions of school life. History, it is claimed, is not close enough to the history of the real historian; art is not close enough to the art of the artist; a foreign language is not taught idiomatically, that is, according to the standards of native speakers; vocational subjects do not really equip people to work in the vocational group; and the values and conventions of the school are out of touch with the world.

When accusations of this sort are made, there is an implication that in the pressure of school situations teachers may develop within the educational process cultures which, to a greater or lesser degree, lose touch with the reference group cultures they are meant to represent to the pupils. Ford and Pugno (1964, 4) quote Ralph Tyler:

> From the standpoint of the curriculum, the disciplines should be viewed primarily as a resource that can be drawn upon for the education of

> students. Hence, we want to understand these resources at their best. And we, I think properly, are often fearful that some of the second-hand treatment that we get of these subjects really prostitutes them – does not represent them at their best. Certainly these disciplines at their best are not simply an encyclopaedic collection of facts to be memorized but rather they are an active effort to make sense out of some portion of the world or of life.

And they comment:

> Thus those concerned with the curricula of the schools must in some way maintain close contacts with scholars in the disciplines so that the nature and contributions of the disciplines are accurately reflected.
>
> (ibid. 17)

This is an important line of argument for it catches the spirit of the post-Sputnik curricular reforms in the United States with their emphasis on educationalists working with university scholars in the disciplines. It is a matter of debate how fruitful this approach proved to be.

Are we to accept the view that although knowledge is distorted in the culture of the school, outside the school there are reference groups which set the standards in knowledge, having as it were a purchase on truth? I don't think we can, in that simple form. The concept of reference groups lies in sociology and applies to the dynamics of knowledge in society rather than to truth values. There is no guarantee that the disciplines as represented in the reference groups are true. We are dealing not with epistemology and the theory of truth but with the sociology of knowledge.

The sociology of knowledge treats 'knowledge or "what counts as knowledge" as socially constituted or constructed', and examines 'how "subjects" or disciplines are socially constructed as sets of shared meanings'. (Young 1971b, 5) In short, the acceptance of the idea that 'knowledge' is represented in the culture of groups – the idea I have explored above – implies that 'knowledge' may be socially determined and in particular determined by the needs of the groups and individuals involved.

Not that this influence is a deliberate and intentional departure from truth.

> The sociology of knowledge is concerned not so much with distortions due to a deliberate effort to deceive as with the varying ways in which objects present themselves to the subject according to the differences in social settings. Thus, mental structures are inevitably differently formed in different social and historical settings.
>
> (Mannheim 1936, 238)

It is easy to see that this must be true of sport and of skills – consider domestic science in schools, for example, and compare it with *cordon bleu* cookery – and certainly of language. In these areas the relativism which is apparently implied in the perspective of the sociology of knowledge is fairly easily acceptable; but in the academic disciplines relativism seems much more threatening. Here there is a strong tradition of aspiration towards absolutes, towards some notion of a warranted knowledge. Does the entire tradition rest on a plot to reinforce the status of the academic group, to underwrite a bid of scholars to be philosopher kings?

There is no easy answer to such questions, and they will recur directly or obliquely throughout this book.

I was led to them by a consideration of content as culture, as public traditions. But although it is important to consider those public traditions known as the disciplines of knowledge as elements in culture, it is equally important to consider them not as culture, but in their own terms – as knowledge. Laying on one side for the moment their social location and function, what do they look like in themselves? As culture they are considered in their social location: as knowledge they are considered against tests for truth.

In the study of the curriculum this contrast between the view of knowledge taken by the sociologist and that taken by the philosopher has been an important theme.

Questions of the nature and structure of knowledge have been a matter of philosophical discussion since the time of the Greeks and of course assumptions about the structure of knowledge are implicit in the traditional school curriculum. New impetus has been given to this discussion in the curriculum field, and a strong line of development has stemmed from an elegant crystallization of the issues by Jerome Bruner in *The Process of Education*:

> . . . the curriculum of a subject should be determined by the most fundamental understanding that can be achieved of the underlying principles that give structure to the subject. Teaching specific topics or skills without making clear their context in the broader fundamental structure of a field of knowledge is uneconomical in several deep senses. In the first place, such teaching makes it exceedingly difficult for the student to generalise from what he has learned to what he will encounter later. In the second place, learning that has fallen short of a grasp of general principles has little reward in terms of intellectual excitement. The best way to create interest in a subject is to render it worth knowing, which means to make the knowledge gained usable in one's thinking beyond the situation in which the learning has occurred. Third,

> knowledge one has acquired without sufficient structure to tie it together is knowledge that is likely to be forgotten. An unconnected set of facts has a pitiably short half-life in memory. Organising facts in terms of principles and ideas from which they may be inferred is the only known way of reducing the quick rate of loss of human memory.
>
> (Bruner 1960, 31–32)

Here Bruner's background as a psychologist is evident. He argues in terms of transfer of learning, of motivation and of retention, and though the points he makes are not expressed in a scientific key, they are based on experimental work. He leaps beyond this to assert that the essential quality of learning is the same for all, advancing the bold hypothesis 'that any subject can be taught effectively in some intellectually honest form to any child at any stage of development'. (Bruner 1960, 33) This hypothesis is programmatic. It suggests a line of experiment in teaching likely to push the educational frontier forward.

Bruner sees knowledge as organized into disciplines or subjects each with its own structures and methods. His model man is not so much concerned with the search for truth in an absolute sense as with the desire to understand his world, that is, to give it structure and meaning, both to satisfy curiosity and to form a basis for action. Knowledge should be 'usable in one's thinking'. With the confidence of the scientist Bruner is able to take the step of regarding all knowledge as provisional, all learning as an adventure against the boundaries. The disciplines and their grasp of truth are the best we have as of now. He is, I would say, centrally concerned with the quality of life, Promethean in his attitude to truth and its application – and a risk-taker, prepared to make calculated errors in pursuit of inquiry, seeking a 'disciplined intuition'.

The provisional and changing nature of bodies of knowledge is also stressed by Joseph Schwab, who characterizes the disciplines as resting on structures of concepts:

> The dependence of knowledge on a conceptual structure means that any body of knowledge is likely to be of only temporary significance. For the knowledge which develops from the use of a given concept usually discloses new complexities of the subject matter which call forth new concepts. These new concepts in turn give rise to new bodies of enquiry and, therefore, to new and more complete bodies of knowledge stated in new terms. The significance of this ephemeral character of knowledge to education consists in the fact that it exhibits the desirability, if not the necessity, for so teaching what we teach that students understand that the knowledge we possess is not mere literal, factual truth but a kind of knowledge which is true in a more complex sense. This in turn means

that we must clarify for students the role of concepts in making knowledge possible (and limiting its validity) and impart to them some idea of the particular concepts that underlie present knowledge of each subject matter, together with the reasons for the appropriateness of these concepts and some of their limitations.

(Schwab 1964, 13–14)

Knowledge in this sense consists not of facts, but of facts so structured by theory that they acquire meaning. Whereas facts *per se* – railway timetables or general knowledge – can be mastered by memorization, knowledge with meaning requires understanding for its mastery. And the world of meaning can be likened to the terrestrial world in the sense that it has been discovered gradually. The map of knowledge has changed just as – witness the historical maps printed in atlases – the map of the terrestrial world has changed. And the world of knowledge, like the terrestrial world, can be mapped on different projections.

Bloom, concerned to compile a taxonomy of educational objectives, regards knowledge as 'the recall of specifics and universals, the recall of methods and processes, or the recall of pattern, structure, or setting'. (Bloom 1956, 62–78) He offers the following classification:

Knowledge of specifics
Knowledge of terminology
Knowledge of specific facts
Knowledge of ways and means of dealing with specifics
Knowledge of conventions
Knowledge of trends and sequences
Knowledge of classifications and categories
Knowledge of criteria
Knowledge of methodology
Knowledge of the universals and abstractions in a field
Knowledge of principles and generalizations
Knowledge of theories and structures

This is primarily a psychologist's classification, the logic being related to the possibility of measurement of learning.

Phenix (1964b) approaches the problem with more philosophical concerns, and finds within the map of knowledge *Realms of Meaning*. We are, he believes, 'essentially creatures who have the power to experience *meanings*. Distinctively human existence consists in a pattern of meanings. Furthermore, *general education is the process of engendering essential meanings*.' (1964b, 5) In short, the characteristic intellectual achievement of mankind which is to be transmitted through education is his ability to ascribe meaning to existence. 'Six fundamental patterns of meaning emerge from the analysis of the six possible modes of human understanding. These six patterns may be designated respectively as *symbolics*, *empirics*, *esthetics*, *synnoetics*, *ethics* and *synoptics*.' (1964b, 6)

On this basis he distinguishes nine classes of knowledge in the following way:

> Any epistemic meaning has two dimensions – extension and intension, or quantity and quality. That is to say, knowledge consists in a relation of the knowing subject to some range of known objects, and the import of the relation is of some kind. Extension has three degrees: singular, general and comprehensive. That is, the knowledge is either of one thing, or of a selected plurality, or of a totality. Intensions of knowledge are also of three kinds: fact, form and norm. In other words, the quality of meaning is existential, formal or valuational. Still another way to express the intensional types is to say that all epistemic meanings refer either to actualities, or to possibilities, or to obligations.
>
> (1964a, 54–55)

Phenix offers the following schematic table:

The Generic Classes of Knowledge

Extension	*Intension*	*Designation*	*Disciplines*
Singular	Fact	Synnoetics	Philosophy, psychology literature and religion in their existential aspects
Singular	Form	Aesthetics	Music, visual arts, the arts of movement, literature
General	Form	Symbolics	Ordinary language, mathematics, nondiscursive symbolic forms
General	Fact	Empirics	Physical sciences, life sciences, psychology, social sciences
Singular	Norm	Ethics	The various special areas
General	Norm	Ethics	of moral and ethical concern
Comprehensive	Fact	Synoptics	History
Comprehensive	Form	Synoptics	Philosophy
Comprehensive	Norm	Synoptics	Religion

(Phenix 1964a, 60–61)

I find it difficult to resist the feeling that Phenix has over-tidied a little, but his classification has been much quoted and discussed and is a good, if extreme, example of the genre.

Phenix is quite explicit about the relation of such an analysis of the disciplines of knowledge to the school.

> My theme has been that the curriculum should consist entirely of knowledge which comes from the disciplines, for the reason that the disciplines reveal knowledge in its teachable forms. We should not try to teach anything which has not been found actually instructive through the labours of hosts of dedicated inquirers. Education should be conceived as a *guided recapitulation of the processes of inquiry which gave rise to the fruitful bodies of organised knowledge comprising the established disciplines.*
>
> (Phenix 1962, 133)

Hirst has offered a classification of knowledge, similar in some respects, but rather more speculative. In particular, he stresses the characteristic tests for truth in the various disciplines, their philosophic grounding. He distinguishes:

> (I) Distinct disciplines or forms of knowledge . . . mathematics, physical sciences, human sciences, history, religion, literature and the fine arts, philosophy.
> (II) Fields of knowedge: theoretical, practical (these may or may not include elements of moral knowledge).
>
> (Hirst 1965, 131)

Developed forms of knowledge have certain distinguishing features: central concepts peculiar in character to the form; a distinctive logical structure; expressions or statements which, by virtue of the form's particular terms and logic, are testable against experience; particular techniques and skills for exploring experience and testing their distinctive expressions.

Fields of knowledge are distinguished by their subject matter rather than by a logically distinct form of expression. Given that subject matter, they draw on the disciplines as need be and are thus in a sense inter-disciplinary, though not in the service of some inter-disciplinary principle. Hirst cites geography as an example of a theoretical study of this kind and engineering as an example of a practical study. Curriculum study would fall into this second category.

Hirst is concerned with the nature of a liberal education, and he seeks to define it in terms of knowledge and its nature and significance and 'not on the predelictions of pupils, the demands of society, or the whims of politicians.' (Hirst 1965, 115) It can well be argued – as White (1969) has argued – that curricula which do not face the need to open up knowledge to the pupils are often the staple of an education designed for the underprivileged and reinforcing their exclusion from the education and knowledge most valued and most valuable.

On the other hand, it is often argued that a knowledge-based curriculum too easily becomes an academic curriculum from which pupils are excluded by boredom. I see no inherent reason why this should be. Hirst is certainly attacking rather than defending school subjects as we have them now. He argues for:

> first, sufficient immersion in the concepts, logic and criteria of the discipline for a person to come to know the distinctive way in which it 'works' by pursuing these in particular cases; and then sufficient generalisation of these over the whole range of the discipline so that his experience begins to be widely structured in this distinctive manner.
>
> (Hirst 1965, 132)

A revision of school practice along these lines is certainly worth experimental exploration. At present it has scarcely been attempted except in mathematics and science.

There have been proposed many more classifications of knowledge than I have considered here. They differ in some respects, but share a good deal of common ground. I do not believe that we shall improve our curricular practices by finding the right one and sticking to it. Rather we need to recognize that problems in the structure of knowledge ought to be on our agenda when we consider problems of curriculum. Thought about curriculum is, in one of its dimensions, thought about the nature of knowledge.

Beyond the problem of classification lies that of the status of knowledge. In particular, is knowledge immutable or changing? This is Joseph Schwab:

> The dependence of knowledge on a conceptual structure means that any body of knowledge is likely to be of only temporary significance. For the knowledge which develops from the use of a given concept usually discloses new complexities of the subject matter which call forth new concepts. These new concepts in turn give rise to new bodies of enquiry and, therefore, to new and more complete bodies of knowledge stated in new terms.
>
> (Schwab 1964, 13)

If knowledge is transient and shifting, what is the justification for teaching it? Is it in any sense true?

Phenix asks:

> How, then, can we be sure that the concept of a discipline is definite and significant enough to serve as a basis for the organisation of knowledge?

> [And he replies:] The answer is empirical and pragmatic: disciplines prove themselves by their productiveness. They are the visible evidences of ways of thinking that have proven fruitful.
>
> (Phenix 1964b, 48)

Fruitful for whom?

Let us for the moment shift our usage from *knowledge* back to *culture*. Culture is the sociologist's term. It indicates the same content as knowledge viewed from a different point of concern: how is it socially organized and developed? rather than how is it related to truth? Berger and Luckmann (1966, 15) contend that 'the sociology of knowledge is concerned with the analysis of the social construction of reality', and that it 'must concern itself with whatever passes for "knowledge" in a society, regardless of the ultimate validity or invalidity (by whatever criteria) of such "knowledge" '. On this view epistemology and sociology of knowledge are two universes of discourse, different ways of talking and thinking adapted to the consideration of different problems.

Michael F. D. Young blurs this distinction when he alludes to Hirst's work and comments:

> The problem of this kind of critique is that it appears to be based on an absolutist conception of a set of distinct forms of knowledge which correspond closely to the traditional areas of the academic curriculum and thus justify, rather than examine, what are no more than the socio-historical constructs of a particular time. It is important to stress that it is not 'subjects', which Hirst recognises as the socially constructed ways that teachers organise knowledge, but forms of understanding, that it is claimed are 'necessarily' distinct. The point I wish to make here is that unless such *necessary* distinctions or intrinsic logics are treated as problematic, philosophical criticism cannot examine the assumptions of academic curricula.
>
> (Young 1971a, 23)

I want to sharpen the point being made here and then to argue that Young is being less than fair to Hirst and the tradition which he represents.

The sociology of knowledge (which is, in the terms used in this book, a branch of the sociology of culture) is concerned in part with the way that knowledge is determined by its social context, held by powerful groups as a possession and an instrument of their power and used to validate institutions. On the basis of such an approach, one could argue that some of those concerned with the analysis of the disciplines of knowledge are in fact caught in the prejudices and blindnesses of their own situations. They are consistently underwriting the present organization of knowledge that is the establishment in which they have a vested interest.

Phenix does seem to me vulnerable to this charge. Consider these two passages:

> The richness of culture and the level of understanding achieved in advanced civilization are due almost entirely to the labors of individual men of genius and of organized communities of specialists. A high level of civilization is the consequence of the dedicated service of persons with special gifts for the benefit of all. Every person is indebted for what he has and is to a great network of skilled inventors, experimenters, artists, seers, scholars, prophets, and saints, who have devoted their special talents to the well-being of all.
>
> (1964b, 30)

> The perennial threat to meaning is intensified under the conditions of modern industrial civilization. Four contributing factors deserve special emphasis. The first is the spirit of criticism and skepticism. This spirit is part of the scientific heritage, but it has tended to bring the validity of all meanings into question . . . curriculum should be planned so as to counteract destructive skepticism . . .
>
> (1964b, 31)

I should not wish to claim that Phenix intends a picture of 'the rich man in his castle, the poor man at the gate'; but there is surely an implication of that sort to be drawn. The scholar sees himself as devoting his special talents to the well-being of all, as making a case for the teaching of the culture in which he excels, and as combating scepticism when it escapes from science into values and policy. The poor man in East Harlem or Middlesborough might be forgiven for believing that the scholar's talents contributed most of all to the well-being of the scholar and that he on his part is entitled to some scepticism, even if it be a little destructive.

But if Phenix can be suspected of ideology, of developing ideas which serve as weapons for social interests, this is not to say that the sociology of knowledge implies that all knowledge is ideological. Werner Stark (1958, 1962) saw that the sociology of knowledge must be more than a debunking science, that it must be concerned with the study of the social conditions of knowledge, with the sociology of truth rather than merely with the sociology of error.

Let us return to Hirst. Young is grossly unfair in attributing to him a naïve absolutism. Of course he has noticed that knowledge changes and he actually discusses the point. His search is for some objectivity in knowledge – or to put it another way, some degree of independence of social influences, partial though it be in practice, which enables us to criticize rather than accept what is given. '. . . it is a form of education knowing no limits other than those necessarily imposed by the nature of rational knowledge and thereby itself developing in man the final court of appeal in all human affairs'. (Hirst 1965, 127) Such knowledge is a basis for scepticism and social criticism.

Hirst proposes a concept of knowledge which has

> objectivity, though this is no longer backed by metaphysical realism. For it is a necessary feature of knowledge as such that there be public criteria whereby the true is distinguishable from the false, the good from the bad, the right from the wrong. It is the existence of these criteria which gives objectivity to knowledge; . . .
>
> (Hirst 1965, 127)

The status of this objectivity is in philosophical terms a matter for discussion. It is problematic.

Popper sees truth as a regulative principle and explains this by an analogy.

> The status of truth in the objective sense, as correspondence to the fact s and its role as a regulative principle, may be compared to that of a mountain peak usually wrapped in clouds. A climber may not merely have difficulties in getting there – he may not know when he gets there, because he may be unable to distinguish, in the clouds, between the main summit and a subsidiary peak. Yet this does not affect the objective existence of the summit; and if the climber tells us 'I doubt whether I reached the actual summit', then he does, by implication, recognise the objective existence of the summit. The very idea of error, or of doubt (in its normal straightforward sense) implies the idea of an objective truth which we may fail to reach.
>
> (Popper 1963, 226)

In fact, the content of the actual curriculum of the school would appear to fall short in two respects. It consists of 'constructed realities realised in particular institutional contexts' (Young 1971b, 3) and distorted by those contexts. It fails to realize in practice the best truth available as judged on philosophical grounds. To climb higher up the mountain, we must significantly change the institution.

The viewpoints of philosophy and sociology of knowledge are complementary rather than contradictory. If their contradictions seem sharpened, this may be because sociologists and philosophers are prone to contradict one another 'in particular institutional contexts'.

3
TEACHING

People are learning almost all the time. Children especially are good at learning. They learn to walk, and how to find their way about town. Having learned to talk, they learn the names of everyone in the village. They learn to recognize by their shapes the make of every car on the road, and to get their own way in disputes. They frequently learn how to manage their parents adroitly, and they are often able to predict and sometimes to control the behaviour of their teachers. Children are no fools.

Schools take responsibility for planning and organizing children's learning. They try – not very successfully in many cases – to give it direction and to maximize its effectiveness.

I take *teaching* to denote the strategies the school adopts to discharge this responsibility. Teaching is not merely instruction, but the systematic promotion of learning by whatever means. And teaching strategy is an important aspect of curriculum.

I prefer 'teaching strategy' to 'teaching methods', which has traditional undertones of training the teacher in skills. 'Teaching strategy' hints more at the planning of teaching and learning in the light of principles, and it seems to lay more weight on teacher judgement. It involves developing a policy and putting that policy into practice.

There have been some attempts, particularly in the United States, to devise 'teacher-proof' curricula – packages so well planned and constructed that the teacher cannot undermine them. The evidence does not generally suggest that this is an effective strategy. In any case, it seems odd to attempt to minimize the use of the most expensive resource in the school. In so far as the teacher has shortcomings – and like everyone else, including those bent on teacher improvement, he has – the way ahead is through providing opportunities for teacher development, and particularly for the refinement of judgement.

It is a thesis of this book that curriculum development must rest on teacher development and that it should promote it and hence the professionalism of the teacher. Curriculum development translates ideas into classroom practicalities and thereby helps the teacher to strengthen his practice by systematically and thoughtfully testing ideas.

Almost inevitably, new curricula involve new teaching strategies as well as new content. New teaching strategies are extremely difficult to learn and to set oneself to learn, especially when they cut across old habits and assumptions and invalidate hard-won skills. It is not enough to assume that teachers are in a good position to develop new strategies independently on the basis of common professional skills. Co-operative and well-organized effort is needed, and teachers working co-operatively together have the same right and need as other professionals – such as doctors or engineers – to have access to consultancy and to draw on research.

Nevertheless it is true that strategies can only be developed in the classroom. There are too many variables, including the teacher himself, to allow of the generalization of easy recipes. And our understanding of classrooms and what goes on in them is still very limited.

Thus, the development of teaching strategies can never be *a priori*. New strategies must be worked out by groups of teachers collaborating within a research and development framework. The emergent curriculum which is communicated to the profession at large must be grounded in the study of classroom practice.

Nevertheless, a provisional curriculum specification with its teaching strategy must be offered as a starting point for experiment, however subject it may be to modification in the light of experience. In devising the teaching strategy aspect of curriculum what sources of information and grounds of judgement are available to us?

The principal sources are the psychology of learning, the study of child development, the social psychology and sociology of learning, the logic of the subject and accumulated practical experience, systematic and unsystematic. In creating the initial rationale and framework for the development of a teaching strategy, these need to be fused by educational imagination: the capacity to visualize with verisimilitude imaginary classrooms and to pre-test ideas in them in one's mind.

The psychology of learning has had a bad press from many curriculum workers. King and Brownell, for example, declare that 'Recent curriculum theories which espouse psychology as the "foundation" of curriculum theory, and *learning* as the fundamental process of human behaviour should be confronted with the testimony of psychologists in the last decade or so,' and they quote ten pessimistic comments. Among these are, for example, Hilgard's 'There are no laws of learning that can be taught with confidence', and Estes' 'no convergence is imminent between the educator's and the laboratory scientist's approaches to learning'. (King and Brownell 1966, 106)

Leaving aside programmed learning – to which I shall return later in this chapter – I still feel that this is an unduly negative approach. Indeed, it seems in conflict with King and Brownell's own concept of the disciplines. The psychologists quoted tend to be thinking in terms of the cross application of particular results or predictive theory; but it is the concepts adopted in the psychology of learning which have been of the greatest relevance to curriculum development.

Motivation and *interest* are closely and usefully bound into psychologists' work on learning, and the curricular atrocities sometimes committed under the sanction of these words are attributable to ignoring the work of psychologists, rather than to paying too much attention to it. The distinctions made between blind or *rote learning* and *insightful learning* also derive from psychological work. Psychologists' exploration of the role of *structure* and *meaning* in learning are an underpinning of, if not the foundation of, a curriculum based on disciplines rather than on the encyclopaedic view of knowledge reflected in the typical nineteenth-century school reader. The conceptual schemes of *social learning* and the study of *emotion* in learning are also of clear relevance to work in curriculum. And *transfer of learning* is a fundamental and perpetual concern of curriculum developers.

I concede that there have been some misplaced attempts to derive curricula too narrowly from psychology, but there can be no doubt that the conceptual scheme of the learning psychologist – and hence a general acquaintance with the experimental work in which it is rooted – is a tool in trade of the curriculum worker. So too is a familiarity with some major hypotheses of learning theory. In fact, it is in the context of curriculum development that we are most likely to be able to mount classroom experiments which will take the experimental psychology of learning beyond the walls of the laboratory. The mistake is to see the classroom as a place to apply laboratory findings rather than as a place to refute or confirm them. Curriculum workers need to share the psychologists' curiosity about the process of learning rather than to be dominated by their conclusions. Not enough attention has been given to this line of thinking in the design of curricula.

By contrast, almost all curriculum developers have given close attention to the psychology of child development. In this field Piaget is the father figure. It is his achievement to have attempted a descriptive account of the logics which inform the thinking of children at different stages and also of some of their emotional constructions. His work, and that of the many experimenters who have followed his lead, is concerned with empirical logic, that is, with the logical strategies of observed thinking, rather than the normative logic which is concerned with principles of thinking.

Piaget conceptualizes the development of thinking by means of stages which, it is claimed, are necessarily sequential, but uneven in their application. In one area of his thinking a child may be at one stage, in another area at another stage. In his work it is not the age norms for development that matter – his samples are in any case too small to generalize – but the sequence which marks the child's construction of a logic to deal with his reality.

Following a sensori-motor stage during which the infant is discriminating and relating sensory stimuli and motor responses, the child enters on a pre-operational stage of thinking, characterized by an animism deriving from his difficulty in distinguishing between his internal experience and external reality. His generalizations and grasp of laws are intuitive and the product of trial and error. In a sense he deals in myths rather than in theories. In particular, he cannot grasp the idea of reversability and consequently of conservation.

The next stage of development is a stage of concrete operations, an operation being a pattern of thinking or organizing the world in the mind, of internalizing it. The child develops concepts of reversability, conservation and double-entry relationships. For example, when a piece of clay is manipulated into a new shape the child argues that there is the same amount of clay from the fact that it can be restored to its original shape (reversability) or that what it loses in length it gains in girth (relationship) or that none has been taken away and none added (conservation). Another important advance is the ability to arrange things in classes and series.

But at this stage the child theorizes his concrete experience rather than being capable of speculation in terms of hypotheses. Thus, for example, the child will often find it more difficult to grasp that the weight of the clay is the same than that the amount is the same, the idea of weight being somewhat more abstract. And such operations as the following are not within reach: 'Edith is fairer than Susan. Edith is darker than Lily. Which is the darkest?' The comparative adjectives are taken as straightforward attributes, the notion of a comparative continuum not being grasped. But if Edith, Susan and Lily are present, of course the answer is simple. It is the abstraction which is elusive.

In the succeeding formal operational period these limitations are overcome. Before the formal stage the child cannot accept abstracted hypotheses for examination. Piaget quotes Ballard's nonsense statement: 'I am very glad I do not like onions, for if I liked them, I would always be eating them, and I hate eating unpleasant things.' At the stage of concrete operations the child will criticize (for example) the statement that onions are unpleasant: at the stage of formal operations he will point out the contradiction in the statement, that is, he accepts the statement as a hypothesis to be examined critically. Thus thought is no longer bound to proceed from actual to theoretical. It is not concerned only with objects and experiences, but also with propositions. Thinking becomes speculative and the possibility is opened up of the study of scientific analysis and synthesis, of the grasping of concepts like predictability.

Piaget's schema of the development of thinking is of great significance for curriculum development, so long as it is accepted as a hypothesis rather than as a dogma. In particular, it should be borne in mind that concrete and formal operations are both characteristics of advanced thinkers. Formal operations do not obliterate concrete operations from our repertoire.

Among the psychologists who have conducted research of importance into the development of thinking, Jerome Bruner stands out as having given committed attention to education in general and to curriculum in particular. His handling of problems in psychological development in the context of education is speculative and flexible because he is committed to the adventure of action as well as of theory.

He distinguishes enactive, iconic and symbolic modes of thinking. (Bruner 1966, 10–12) 'In earliest childhood events and objects are defined in terms of the actions taken towards them. . . . An object is what one does to it.' This is the enactive mode. 'What appears next in development is a great achievement. Images develop an autonomous status, they become great summarizers of action.' This is the iconic mode. The third or symbolic system of representation is 'based on the translation of experience into language'.

A child who picks up a stick to lever up a stone defines it enactively as a tool for levering. A child who sorts picture cards to pick out a knife, a spade, scissors and a pen (but not a car) as tools has an iconic grasp of a concept. A child who distinguishes improvized tools from tools by design and considers whether a car or a language is a tool is operating in the symbolic mode.

There is a close parallel with Piaget, but more emphasis on early forms of conceptualization.

Bruner talks of the curriculum in terms of growth and offers

> . . . some benchmarks about the nature of intellectual growth:
>
> 1. Growth is characterized by increasing independence of response from the immediate nature of the stimulus.
> 2. Growth depends upon internalizing events into a 'storage system' that corresponds to the environment.
> 3. Intellectual growth involves an increasing capacity to say to oneself and others, by means of words or symbols, what one has done or what one will do.
> 4. Intellectual development depends upon a systematic and contingent interaction between a tutor and a learner.
> 5. Teaching is vastly facilitated by the medium of language, which ends by being not only the medium for exchange but the instrument that the learner can then use himself in bringing order into the environment.
> 6. Intellectual development is marked by increasing capacity to deal with several alternatives simultaneously, to tend to several sequences during the same period of time, and to allocate time and attention in a manner appropriate to these multiple demands.
>
> (Bruner 1966, 5–6)

It is perhaps worth noting that Bruner's use of *growth* in this context is sharply distinguished by its intellectual content from the use of the same word in many contexts in association with 'child-centred education'; and indeed that his enactive mode is not to be assimilated to activity methods. His is not the tradition attacked by Hirst and Peters and it is significant that the curriculum developed under Bruner's influence is much concerned with 'man's attempt to understand and appreciate the world'. (Hirst and Peters 1970, 31).

In fact, developmental psychology has been applied in two main ways in curriculum development. On the one hand, it has been taken to provide norms, to set limits to readiness, to place restrictions on the possible. In Britain in particular, where educators are depressingly anxious to 'protect' the young or limited from access to challenging ideas, developmental studies have sometimes supplied texts for sermons on the need to temper the wind to shorn lambs. The other application of developmental psychology is to provide an understanding of the developmental processes which will enable us to raise our sights, to attack and overtake present developmental norms by means of education. At the Woods Hole Conference, Professor Inhelder of Geneva, Piaget's associate, 'was asked to suggest ways in which the child could be moved along faster through the various stages of intellectual development in mathematics and physics'.

(Bruner 1960, 40–41) It is this tradition with which Bruner is associated, hence his famous provocative hypothesis 'that any subject can be taught effectively in some intellectually honest form to any child at any stage of development'. (Bruner 1960, 33) Only an understanding of the logic of the development of thinking can enable us to make what Bruner calls 'a courteous translation' of advanced knowledge in order to bring it within the grasp of the child.

I think we should be a little wary of making curricula which are developed by groups of teachers and curriculum workers conformable to developmental norms, not simply because, as I have suggested above, education exists to change such norms, but also because the pupils in any one class are at different stages of development. The most important function of such norms may be diagnostic and individual.

> The teacher can look for the presence or absence of these modes by watching and talking to a child as he goes about his day to day tasks. Occasionally, it might be worthwhile to set up such experiments (as Piaget's) as test situations. Information about a child's mode of thinking which can be gleaned in this way would afford another dimension upon which his intellectual progress could be measured.
>
> (Richmond 1970, 100)

We turn now to social psychology and sociology, and here there are two strands which I wish to discuss as having important significance for the development of teaching strategies. The first is the social psychology of small groups and the second some aspects of the work of sociologists on social class and education.

In an earlier book (Stenhouse 1967) I commented that the underlying model in most of our teaching – at least at the secondary stage – is individual tuition, and that teachers tend to split the groups they teach and deal with their members as individuals, partly because of problems of disciplinary control. The situation is well caught in this excerpt from an interview with a pupil:

> *Question:* Can you speak freely in other lessons?
> *Answer:* No. Because the teacher just stands at the front and asks you questions and if you don't know it you just keep quiet.
>
> (Hamingson 1973, 199)

I argued that the teacher's task might be seen as generating an appropriate sub-culture in the classroom group, and this means setting up a cross-group communication system. In the Humanities Project we developed a style of discussion teaching which laid great stress on the group's accepting responsibility for its work and working co-operatively. Sometimes the results showed up strikingly the way that schools inhibit co-operative working.

Carol: The work we have done already (in the Humanities Project) has given us a greater understanding of each individual member of the class and we are much friendlier towards each other after the lesson.

Linda: Not so much 'friendlier' – it is that we understand each other's point of view.

Sue: In this lesson we listen to their point of view and they listen to ours.

Linda: We have evidence to refer to all the time – that helps.

(Hamingson 1973, 201–202)

Comparatively little attention has been given to making the classroom group a fully interacting sub-culture with educational values, probably because teachers associate class cohesion with problems of disciplinary control.

Mills and Rosenberg have edited *Readings on the Sociology of Small Groups* (1970), *The Small Group* by Golembiewski (1962) is a good standard review of research, and Elizabeth Richardson's *Group Study for Teachers* (1967) is representative of a more interpretative tradition. Among applications may be mentioned Abercrombie's *The Anatomy of Judgement* (1960), Thelen's *Dynamics of Groups at Work* (1954) and *The Humanities Project: An Introduction* (1970).

The sociological work on the relationship of social class to education is in its conclusions familiar to all: children of working-class background are, if we take general trends in large samples, relatively disadvantaged in school as compared to middle-class children. Why? The fashionable answer is that they are handicapped by what Bernstein called the 'restricted code' of their language. This is less than fair to Bernstein, who makes it clear that divergence in habitual linguistic code is a symptom of a much deeper cultural cleavage of values and understandings, in fact, of perception of reality.

This poses a dilemma for the curriculum developer. To what extent is the cultural dissonance of the school, experienced by working-class children, the result of its embodying middle-class values and perceptions of reality and linguistic patterns which are, in the last analysis, irrelevant to education? To what extent is it the result of a gap between everyday culture and the culture of worthwhile learning which is greater in the case of working-class than middle-class children? Should we change the school or should we change the working-class child?

A bit of both I fancy, but I confess that I find it difficult to strike a balance. Some free schools have gone a long way to adjust the school to working-class pupils, and community education has sought roots for education in socially disadvantaged inner urban communities. Midwinter (1973) and Lawton (1973), amongst others, have argued that the gap is perhaps not so dramatic as has been made out, that there are advantages in working-class children developing elaborated codes of language, for example, and that they can do this if the right kind of experience is offered. The Humanities Project attempted to produce conditions in which pupils would be able to use the developing culture of their own discussion group as a secure base from which to encounter formal cultures and elaborated language codes. There was some evidence that striking successes were possible but difficult to achieve against the background assumptions of schools and teachers.

I am inclined to think that the crucial problem is the lack of respect shown by teachers and schools for working-class children and working-class culture, rather than the existence of linguistic and value barriers within the content of the curriculum. It was interesting to find, for example, that school leavers felt that teachers devalued the blue-collar jobs which most of them regarded as preferable to teaching. If respect for the client is of central importance, we need to develop teaching strategies which embody such respect and ensure that if there is to be any translation, it is, in Bruner's terms, a courteous one. A change of posture of this sort towards the pupil cannot be achieved by a change of heart. A change of pedagogy is needed and this is a technical achievement.

One factor in what I have called lack of respect is well-characterized by Esland (1971, 89):

> This view regards the child – by definition – as a deficit system; a passive object to be progressively initiated into the public thought forms which exist outside him as massive coercive facticities, albeit 'worthwhile' ones. It also legitimates a didactic pedagogy – the good pupil is docile and deferential, cognitively, at least – and it provides particular organising principles for the selection and transmission of knowledge.

If knowledge is to be approached as a resource and an open system rather than as an imposition by those who possess it, new styles of teaching need to be evolved, and this is by no means easy. It is one of the central tasks of curriculum research and development to explore this possibility.

I turn now to the question of the significance of subject matter for teaching strategy.

A commonplace view might be: the subject matter is the end, the teaching strategy is the means. Those strategies are best which are most effective in attaining the end. And of course we must be clear about the end if we are to develop the means.

In order to explore the implications of this view I shall look briefly at linear programming and teaching by objectives.

The conception of linear programming was developed systematically by B. F. Skinner, though his work was anticipated in some respects by Sidney Pressey (1927). Basically it is a method of self-instruction.

Linear programming was built on a theory of operant conditioning, which I cannot explore here, though it can be learned by programmed instruction. (Holland and Skinner 1961) The points I wish to make are not dependent on a close understanding of that theory.

In order to prepare an instructional programme, one must be clear about the skills and information the students are to learn by the end of the programme and the skills and information they bring with them on entry to the programme. The programme provides a route from entry point to completion point. This route is not the path of continuous prose exposition, as in a book, but it is broken into a series of small steps, each one self-explanatory and carefully sequenced in relation to the preceding and following ones.

What do such steps look like? Let us take three frames from the second set (chapter) of Holland and Skinner's programme on *The Analysis of Behaviour* (1961):

> The student reads:
> In a reflex, a sufficient explanation of the response is a description of the preceding . . . . . .
> He writes: 'stimulus'.
> The next frame confirms his response as correct, and offers him:
> When food in the mouth elicits the secretion of saliva, the whole series of events is called a(n) . . . . . .
> He writes: 'reflex', and is offered:
> Candy put in the mouth of a child for the first time . . . . . . salivation.

Each step asks for a response from the student, and immediately rewards the response if 'correct'. Steps are intended to be simple enough to make failure rare on the principle, as it were, that nothing succeeds like success. The extent to which you now feel that you would like to fill in the last gap and discover whether your answer is correct is some indication of the capacity of the programme to motivate. The extent to which you are inclined to observe that the use of the word 'sufficient' in the first frame is controversial is an indication of the capacity of the programme to open up speculative thinking.

The linear programme is a fixed sequence and is based on a careful analysis of the subject matter. The willingness of the teacher (programme writer) to discipline himself to analyse his content and achieve this sequence is in a sense a courtesy to the learner, and a courtesy which some inspirational and intuitive teachers do not always pay. On the other hand the assumption that the programmer *knows* in a rather absolute sense might be construed as a discourtesy to the learner if the content is in any sense controversial. There is another important point to be made:

> No attempt is made to provide different treatment for different abilities and aptitudes, but at least each individual works at the rate which suits him best. For the dull and the bright pupil the only difference is that the former will take longer to work through the programme. Both get there in the end and by the same route.
>
> (Richmond 1965, 45)

All pupils are treated impartially if impersonally.

One of the strengths of programming is the clarity it asks of the teacher. There are obvious limitations. Programming tends to treat command of information and understanding as skills and to avoid critical questions. As I have hinted, it is clear in the example quoted that a description of the preceding stimulus can be regarded as a *sufficient* explanation of the response only within the assumptions and universe of discourse of Skinner's behaviourist psychology.

Skinner takes a strong position in the face of criticism:

> The cry will be raised that the child is being treated as a mere animal and that an essentially intellectual achievement is being analysed in unduly mechanistic terms. Mathematical behavior is usually regarded not as a repertoire of responses involving numbers and numerical operations, but as evidence of mathematical ability or the exercise of the power of reason. It is true that the techniques which are emerging from the experimental study of learning are not designed to 'develop the mind' or to further some vague 'understanding' of mathematical relationships. They are designed, on the contrary, to establish the very behaviors which are taken to be the evidence of such mental states or processes. This is only a special case of the general change which is under way in the interpretation of human affairs. An advancing science continues to offer more and more convincing alternatives to traditional formulations.
>
> (Skinner 1953)

He has gone farther than this in subsequent writing. (Skinner 1971)

Clearly, at the extreme, operant conditioning raises value issues of the kind explored in *A Clockwork Orange* (Burgess 1962)

Programmed learning undoubtedly has potential. It seems to me to have three serious limitations. One is that it demands little critical speculation of the learner and thus offers him only the learning built into the design: that is, it does not seek to 'develop the mind'. Related to this is the second weakness. It provides restricted opportunity for the transfer of learning: transfer possibilities must be predefined and built in by the programmer. Finally, though it deals in the tactics of motivation, it does little about the strategy. Why should I want to learn what is in the programme? It is necessary to posit a process of education (or self-education) outside the programme.

Within its limits it has great strengths. Given that I have a general speculative grasp of a field of knowledge and want to extend my skills or information in a particular area, a programmed course may suit me very well.

A more general question about the organization of teaching is worth raising here. Would some of the analytic rigour involved in programming – clarity of objective and analysis of paths to it – improve teaching by more conventional methods? There are indeed many who believe that the answer is 'Yes', and who see great prospect in teaching by objectives.

Briefly, the logic of the position is this. Teaching is intentional behaviour which clearly has some aim. That aim ought to be clear. If the teacher can get his aim clear, generally by spelling out the changes he expects to produce in the students or the performances of which they should become capable, then the path to that aim should be clarified. Moreover, if his aim is clear, he ought to be able to test whether that aim has been attained.

On the other hand, objections can be raised to this way of picturing the job of teaching.

For instance, Philip Jackson, while admitting that benefits have accrued from the approach to teaching through behavioural objectives, observes that 'The business of teaching involves much more than defining curricular objectives and moving toward them with dispatch.' (Jackson 1968, 165) He points to the unpredictability of classroom events and the opportunist response of teachers.

> As typically conducted, teaching is an opportunistic process. That is to say, neither the teacher nor his students can predict with any certainty exactly what will happen next. Plans are forever going awry and unexpected opportunities for the attainment of educational goals are constantly emerging. The seasoned teacher seizes upon these opportunities

and uses them to his and his students' advantage. If a discussion is moving along at full tilt he may decide to forget about a scheduled test and let the discussion continue. If a student makes an unusual error in his arithmetic notebook, he may call the class to attention and warn them against making a similar mistake. If a fight breaks out in the playground, the teacher may decide to cancel the activity planned for the next period and spend the time talking to his students about the meaning of fair play. And so it goes. Although most teachers make plans in advance, they are aware as they make them of the likelihood of change.

Although gross changes in the teacher's plans provide the clearest evidence of the unpredictability of classroom events, the same quality is also revealed through a more microscopic analysis of teacher-pupil interaction. Stray thoughts, sudden insights, meandering digressions, irrelevant asides, and other minor disruptions constantly ruffle the smoothness of the instructional dialogue. Experienced teachers accept this state of affairs and come to look upon surprise and uncertainty as natural features of their environment. They know, or come to know, that the path of educational progress more closely resembles the flight of a butterfly than the flight of a bullet.

(Jackson 1968, 166–167)

Jackson is writing here of the experience of life in classrooms. From the point of view of the curriculum planner or developer, the problem is whether to use the conceptual framework of objectives in designing a curriculum and evaluating it. One aspect of that problem is whether to specify a curriculum to teachers in terms of objectives. That aspect is relevant here.

Unless a teacher internalizes objectives, makes them part of his being and weaves them naturally into his teaching, it is unlikely that they will in fact exercise a controlling force on his teaching. This seems rather rare. But given that, how is the teacher to judge that a classroom transaction offers an 'opportunity' or that an aside is 'irrelevant' without criteria to which he can refer? And what criteria other than objectives might he use?

It may be that the structures of knowledge provide a basis for an alternative approach. This would accord with Hirst's objection to 'the notion that a liberal education can be directly characterized in terms of mental abilities and independently of fully specifying the forms of knowledge involved'. (Hirst 1965, 118)

If there are disciplines of knowledge which are structured and have logical procedures and tests for truth, is not the aim of teaching a discipline to explore the structure, to get some bearings within it? As Hirst says, 'understanding a form of knowledge is far more like coming to know a country than climbing a ladder'. (Hirst 1965, 135)

Let us take another analogy, for the ideas involved here are a little hard to grasp. Chess may be taken as a simple model of a discipline of knowledge about a simplified world of pieces and squares. Certain simple skills are necessary to begin: we must know the basic moves. These can be dealt with through objectives. Standard openings are more difficult. First a learner needs to see a use for them, and then to understand the principles of each. He needs to explore them as they arouse his interest. For much of the time, beyond this, we cannot tell the learner exactly what to do. We can advise him on principles, we can help him analyse his successes and failures and the games of others. But he must move autonomously, he must act under his own direction if he is to learn. And note, sometimes he will beat the teacher, and he can never arrive at the point where he has learnt all.

It is maintained by some that this is the best way to learn a discipline. First find your philosopher. Then begin to do philosophy with him. Ask him to point out to you any obvious areas you ought to explore and to analyse and criticize your work with you.

There are of course some snags. The teacher must know his own subject; and he must be secure enough to rejoice when he is beaten or even overtaken by his pupil. These are not easy conditions. Indeed, though it may well be argued that it is more likely to be possible to absorb a discipline and make it one's own than to possess in the same sense a schedule of objectives, yet it must be confessed that such mastery is not typical of all teachers. Development towards mastery of a subject is, however, a worthwhile and satisfying professional aim for a teacher. Moreover, there is, it is argued, a teaching strategy which invites the teacher to cast himself in the role of a learner in his work so that his life in his classroom extends rather than constricts his intellectual horizons. A good classroom, by this criterion, is one in which things are learned evey day which the teacher did not previously know.

This teaching strategy is called discovery- or inquiry-based teaching. Often the two terms have been used interchangeably. I have tried to draw a distinction which might be useful, but is not generally adopted.

> Instruction-based teaching implies that the task in hand is the teacher's passing on to his pupils knowledge or skills of which he is master. In discovery-based teaching the teacher intoduces his pupils into situations so selected or devised that they embody in implicit or hidden form principles or knowledge which he wishes them to learn. Thus, Cuisenaire rods embody numerical principles. Instruction and discovery are appropriate in the classroom whenever the desirable outcome of

teaching can be specified in some detail and is broadly the same for every pupil.

Where a curriculum area is in a divergent, rather than in a convergent, field, i.e. where there is no simple correct or incorrect outcome, but rather an emphasis on the individual responses and judgements of the students, the case for an inquiry-based approach is at its strongest.

(Stenhouse 1968, 30)

I believe this to be true of the disciplines. The superficialities of the disciplines may be taught by pure instruction, but the capacity to think within the disciplines can only be taught by inquiry. What is characteristic of the advocacy of inquiry-based teaching in this sense is the assertion that one can *think* in a discipline at elementary as well as advanced levels of study.

Schwab has characterized inquiry teaching as an inquiry into inquiries, that is, a learning of the strategies of inquiry in different disciplines. And he characterizes the structure of a discipline as having a syntax. Thus, the key problem for the teacher is the syntactical structure of the disciplines he teaches.

This problem is hidden in the fact that if different sciences pursue knowledge of their respective subject matters by means of different conceptual frames, it is very likely that there will be major differences between one discipline and another in the way and in the extent to which it can verify its knowledge. There is, then, the problem of determining for each discipline what it does by way of discovery and proof, what criteria it uses for measuring the quality of its data, how strictly it can apply canons of evidence, and in general, of determining the route or pathway by which the discipline moves from raw data through a longer or shorter process of interpretation to its conclusion.

(Schwab 1964, 14)

The general position is consonant with that of Hirst and with that of Bruner. It might be said to lead us not towards instruction towards objectives but towards inquiry in the light of what Peters has called 'principles of procedure'. (Peters 1959)

In *Man: A Course of Study*, the social science curriculum with which Bruner was associated, the principles of procedure or 'pedagogical aims' are stated at a high level:

1. To initiate and develop in youngsters a process of question-posing (the inquiry method);
2. To teach a research methodology where children can look for information to answer questions they have raised and use the framework developed in the course (e.g. the concept of the life cycle) and apply it to new areas;

3. To help youngsters develop the ability to use a variety of first-hand sources as evidence from which to develop hypotheses and draw conclusions;
4. To conduct classroom discussions in which youngsters learn to listen to others as well as to express their own views;
5. To legitimize the search; that is, to give sanction and support to open-ended discussions where definitive answers to many questions are not found;
6. To encourage children to reflect on their own experiences;
7. To create a new role for the teacher, in which he becomes a resource rather than an authority.

(*Man: A Course of Study* 1970, 5)

Some people would term these process objectives. I think that principles of procedure is a much better term, both as avoiding confusion with objectives in the normal sense and as stressing the need for teacher judgement and grasp of criteria and principles.

The above statement would stand for most inquiry-based curricula with small alterations.

The Humanities Project, working in the area of the discussion of controversial issues, was very much in this tradition. But lacking the research methodology of a discipline (principle 2 above), it sought to create for educational purposes a discipline of discussion which aimed at understanding rather than consensus. It also laid heavier stress on the role definition of the teacher – as a neutral chairman – in order to provide a sharpness and existential focus to the dilemmas of this style of teaching.

I do not think that any curriculum innovation is likely substantially to improve intellectual power if it is not centrally concerned with the betterment of teaching. The improvement of teaching is a process of development. I mean by this: first, that it is not to be achieved by a change of heart but by the thoughtful refinement of professional skill; and second, that the refinement of professional skill is generally achieved by the gradual elimination of failings through the systematic study of one's own teaching.

Both curriculum development and research into teaching should provide a base for this professionalism. They have begun to do so; but there is much to be done if teachers are to get a research base on which to mount a programme of professional self development.

4

KNOWLEDGE, TEACHING, AND THE SCHOOL AS AN INSTITUTION

In this chapter I shall be concerned with the social construction of reality in schools, and in particular with the way in which the needs of schools as institutions influence the character of the knowledge they offer to pupils.

The culture of the school influences the experience of the pupils and teachers who work in it in unplanned ways. Philip Jackson, having considered the social massing of children in school, their being under constant explicit evaluation and the inequality of power between teacher and pupil, observes that 'the crowds, the praise, and the power that combine to give a distinctive flavour to classroom life collectively form a hidden curriculum which each student (and teacher) must master if he is to make his way satisfactorily through the school. The demands created by these features of classroom life may be contrasted with the academic demands – the "official curriculum", so to speak – to which educators traditionally have paid the most attention'. And he goes on to suggest that 'the two curriculums are related to each other in several important ways'. (Jackson 1968, 33–34)

I want to discuss in this book two ways in which the school as an institution affects curriculum and the process of curriculum development. First it offers content which may contradict or reinforce its expressed curricular intentions but which is not publicly acknowledged. This is sometimes called the hidden curriculum. In some cases it escapes policy control within the school since it is taken for granted. In other cases it is the subject of underground or half-acknowledged policy control. For example, I taught in a school in which certain bottom stream classes were allocated to an old elementary school half a mile away which served as an annex. Teachers arrived late, there were no labs or workshops, the main aim of the teachers was to keep the students quiet. And out there they could not contaminate the main school. Nobody wanted to talk about it, but it was a substantial factor in any analysis of the curriculum offered to those children. It is the way the school sets up its reality and constructs its view of knowledge that I shall discuss in this chapter.

In a later chapter I shall consider the problems a school as an organization may encounter in putting its curricular intentions into practice. The two problems are interrelated, but the first concerns the 'content' of the school's institutional life, and the second is concerned with its capacity for action towards change.

One of the crucial aspects of the school in respect to its values is the gap between pupils and teachers and parents. Now, in one sense, this is to be expected, since teachers represent a value system to which it is intended that the pupils should be exposed, and the school exists because these values are not generally and systematically available in society. However, the problem is whether the values represented by the school accord with intentions we could justify.

The Schools' Council *Enquiry No. 1* surveyed pupils', parents' and teachers' views of school objectives. I want to consider one of their findings. They reported that:

> Both 15 year old leavers and their parents very widely saw the provision of knowledge and skills which would enable young people to obtain the best jobs and careers of which they are capable as one of the main functions that a school should undertake. Teachers, however, very generally rejected the achievement of vocational success as a major objective of education.
>
> (Schools Council 1968, 45)

Then comes the interesting interpretation:

> It is evident therefore that conflict and misunderstanding may arise between the short term viewpoint of parents and pupils who are concerned with starting work in the immediate future and the long term objectives of teachers who see their responsibility as preparing pupils for the whole of their lives.

I have read this statement many times and it still takes my breath away. I should have thought that nothing is more far-sighted than to wish to be a printer or a shipwright rather than a porter or a van-boy or – often enough – unemployed; yet the claim appears to be made that in concerning themselves with such issues parents and pupils show themselves to be less wise and far-sighted than teachers.

But the situation needs close scrutiny. There are two important background facts to be noted. We are concerned here with early leavers; and the commentary is not written by a teacher, but in an official publication.

I should be prepared to claim that vocational success is one of the most powerful factors in the pupils' long-term future. Certainly, in my experience grammar schools and public schools go along with parents and pupils in valuing highly the achievement of such success. But teachers have traditionally known little of the early leavers' world. Probably only a minority of teachers can evaluate the pros and cons of various apprenticeships, or understand the rewards and the stresses of long-distance transport driving, horticultural work or motor car factory work. Teachers in school often understand less than they might the further education sector and its pattern of qualifications. And most teachers are undermined if they face squarely the problems of youthful unemployment. All this is easily understandable and many teachers are deeply concerned about the situation.

However, the comment in *Enquiry No. 1* documents an important climate in the context in which the school has to work. Official policies tend to endorse those teachers who turn away from the practical and vocational realities of their pupils and appeal to higher things. Indeed, one might go so far as to speculate whether the results of the survey are not influenced by the pressure teachers feel to talk about their educational endeavours in terms of the good life rather than in terms of the practical problems of securing a basis on which to live it. Are teachers expected by society to combat the aspirations of leavers and their parents by making it clear that the plentiful supply of cakes the school can offer makes it short-sighted to demand bread?

There is a related point worth making. The power of the British school to define reality and knowledge is increased by the fact that in Britain the teacher is taken to be wise in deciding what his pupils shall learn and not simply knowledgeable in teaching them what they have decided to learn or what society has decided they should learn. Traditionally comparatively little choice of curriculum has lain with the pupil – as compared with the United States for example. And teachers have been rather free of policy constraints on the curriculum – as compared say with Sweden, where most people would regard it as improper that curricular decisions should lie with teachers rather than in the democratic political process. All these factors are potent for the relationship of reality in the school to reality outside it. The British system is well equipped to resist policies of indoctrination being imposed upon it, and this also ensures that it is in a good position to resist the reality at its doors.

The gap between pupils and teachers and the outside world is often rather a large one, and it is often expressed indirectly through the implicit values of the school rather than through its curriculum.

King (1969), in a study of *Values and Involvement in a Grammar School*, provides a list of pupils' interests and activities ordered according to the extent to which they receive teachers' overall approval and disapproval. Here is the ranked list. The higher in the list, the greater the approval. All those activities below the line were more disapproved than approved.

1. Reading worthwhile books
2. Camping
3. Debating
4. Theatre visits
   Swimming
6. Amateur dramatics
   Painting and drawing
   Athletics
9. Playing an instrument
10. Listening to classical music
    Natural history
12. Visiting picture galleries
    Playing cricket
14. Duke of Edinburgh's Award
    Tennis
16. Playing rugger
17. Woodwork
    Keeping pets
19. Being a Scout or a member of the Boys' Brigade
    Girl friend (fifth or sixth form)
    Holiday job
22. Youth club
23. Making radios, etc.
    Photography
    Playing soccer
    Badminton
27. Cycling
28. Choir singing
29. Aero modelling
30. Table tennis
    Doing science experiments at home
32. Joining the A.T.C.
33. Listening to jazz records
34. Fishing
    Crosswords
    Collecting stamps, coins, etc.
    Going to public dances
38. Roller skating

Driving a car
Bridge
41. Reading science fiction
42. Saturday job
Going to the cinema once a week
, Belonging to a youth political movement

---

45. Listening to pop records
46. Twisting or jiving
47. Going to soccer matches
48. Visiting jazz clubs
Scootering
50. Solo
51. Paper round
Wearing the latest teenage fashions
53. Hitch-hiking
54. Ten pin bowling
55. Seeing X certificate films
56. Billiards and snooker
Visiting public houses (legally)
58. Motor bike
59. Reading novels emphasizing sex and violence
60. Smoking

(King 1969, 68–69)

This list could well be used to distinguish goodies from baddies in the public school stories of my youth. Bunter, like Falstaff, was large enough to break the mould.

There are some interesting features. The attitude reflected is pre-MacLuhan. Books are 1 and theatre is 4 but cinema is 42 and television has not been included. You cannot stay tuned to radio 3, for though classical music is 10, jazz is 33 and you could spend your time a lot better than that. It may be, however, that listening to jazz records is construed as an unsupervised peer group activity. All social situations above this and going to dances (34) appear to be supervised by adults. Political awareness seems to be disapproved (42). Rugger rates better than soccer – 16 as against 23 – and going to soccer matches is actually disapproved (47); 59 is not, I think, intended to exclude *Wuthering Heights* or Helen Waddell's *Peter Abelard* or *The Dam Busters*. One is unsure whether it excludes Fielding's *Tom Jones*.

Of course this list cannot be applied to any school, but a similarly organized list could be made. It suggests a substantial hidden curriculum. In this case, it appears to have social class implications, probably divides the staff and is distrustful of autonomy in pupils. It may be compared with the teachers' ranking of values in the same book. (King 1969, 61)

Waller (1932) considers the structure of the separate culture which grows up within the school.

> The social relationships centering in the school may be analysed in terms of the interacting groups in the school. The two most important groups are the teacher-group and the pupil-group, each of which has its own moral and ethical code and its customary attitudes toward members of the other groups. There is a marked tendency for these groups to turn into conflict groups. Within the teach groups are divisions according to rank and position, schismatic and conspirital groups, congenial groups, and cliques centering round different personalities. Within the student groups are various divisions representing groups in the larger community, unplanned primary groups stair-stepping according to age, cliques, political organisations, and specialised groups such as teams and gangs. The social influence of the school is a result of the action of such groups upon the individual and of the organisation of individual lives out of the materials furnished by such groups.
>
> (Waller 1932, 12)

Teachers, like students, are pressed towards conformity to institutional expectations, and the personalities they present in the school are often different from those they present in the social life outside the school. There is a professional *persona*, often the result of tension between the stereotyped role of the teacher and the real person who fills it. And reality may be seen quite differently by the teacher inside and outside school. For example a teacher may both urge his pupils towards reading good literature and away from television and spend most of his evenings watching television.

The job of the teacher in his negotiation with the student group may be seen as an attempt to influence the content through which they interact and the criteria or standards which govern the orientation of their interaction.

> We may say that the core of the teaching process lies in the teachers' judgement of the standards adopted by the pupils. According to his own standards, the teacher deploys his rewards and punishments, encouragement and discouragement in order to influence the standards of the group. These group standards form the basis of the social pressures which in turn influence the individual standards of the group members. The question of the sources of the teacher's standards arises, and we shall expect to find these standards accepted in the groups from which the teacher draws his cultural support.
>
> (Stenhouse 1963, 127)

Many of these groups are reference groups outside the school, whose influence has been instanced in the comments of *Enquiry No. 1*. But a powerful group is the professional group in the school as it reacts both to these external pressures and to the problems encountered within the school itself. Among these problems that of pupil control features largely. There is in many schools a consciousness of the possibility of insurrection by the subject population.

Willower, Eidell and Hoy conceptualized the response to this threat by adapting to the educational situation a continuum of control ideology ranging from 'custodialism' at one extreme to 'humanism' at the other. The poles of the continuum are ideal types in Max Weber's sense, that is, they are pure types not necessarily found in purity in empirical study. Willower and his colleagues developed the following prototypes of custodial and humanistic orientations towards pupil control.

> The rigidly traditional school serves as a model for the custodial orientation. This kind of organization provides a highly controlled setting concerned primarily with the maintenance of order. Students are stereotyped in terms of their appearance, behaviour, and parents' social status. They are perceived as irresponsible and undisciplined persons who must be controlled through punitive sanctions. Teachers do not attempt to understand student behaviour, but, instead, view it in moralistic terms. Misbehaviour is taken as a personal affront. Relationships with students are maintained on as impersonal a basis as possible. Pessimism and watchful mistrust imbue the custodial viewpoint. Teachers holding a custodial orientation conceive of the school as an autocratic organisation with rigidly maintained distinctions between the status of teachers and that of pupils: both power and communication flow downward, and students are expected to accept the decisions of teachers without question. Teachers and students alike feel responsible for their actions only to the extent that orders are carried out to the letter.
>
> The model of the humanistic orientation is the school conceived of as an educational community in which members learn through interaction and experience. Students' learning and behaviour is viewed in psychological and sociological terms rather than moralistic terms. Learning is looked upon as an engagement in worthwhile activity rather than the passive absorption of facts. The withdrawn student is seen as a problem equal to that of the overactive, troublesome one. The humanistic teacher is optimistic that, through close personal relationships with pupils and the positive aspects of friendship and respect, students will be self-disciplining rather than disciplined. A humanistic orientation leads teachers to desire a democratic classroom climate with its attendent flexibility in status and rules, open channels of two-way communication,

and increased student self-determination. Teachers and pupils alike are willing to act on their own volition and to accept responsibility for their actions.

(Willower, Eidell and Hoy 1967, 5–6)

Now it seems quite clear that the general picture of reality and the conception of knowledge transmitted to pupils in schools approximating to these models will be radically different. In the first, knowledge, like control, depends upon the hierarchical authority of persons: the expert is not there to be questioned, but to instruct and to test. He is a source rather than a resource.

In another paper Willower (1965, 44) hypothesizes that the employment of external controls by teachers will be positively related to the displacement of instructional objectives. Educational goals give way under the pressure of control goals. He observes that 'if acceptance within the teacher group is based upon commitment to and competence in the use of external controls rather than competence in instruction; then instructional goals will be pushed into the background, that is, displaced'.

This is a shrewd, but a rather abstract statement. Let me give two observed examples. A teacher of history gives a test on half sheets of paper when pupils enter the room. He finds this settles the class and contributes to control. As he tears the paper for the test these effects are visible in the children. In order to do this he has to teach a kind of history which is extremely closed and positive, and which thus lends itself to one-word or short answers. This is not the kind of history he would defend in conversation with a historian. Its main justification is that it is a good kind of history through which to dominate and control his class.

This is an example of curriculum content being influenced through control ideology. A second example is of influence on teaching strategy. By and large learning is most likely to be promoted by asking questions of those who can give interesting and informative answers. But the stress of control and the associated motivational problems induce most teachers to address a very high proportion of their questions to pupils who, they are well able to predict, will not know the answers. The questioning is punitive rather than elucidatory.

The most thorough and systematic treatment of the influence of the school's organization and value system on its curricular organization of knowledge is that of Bernstein. His paper, 'On the Classification and Framing of Educational Knowledge' (1971), is extremely tightly written. I cannot do justice to it in a summary and must restrict myself to an account sufficient to sustain the present argument.

Bernstein distinguishes two types of curricula, a collection type in which the various content elements are clearly bounded and insulated from each other; and an integrated type where the contents stand in an open relation to each other. It is possible to identify these types with subject-based and integrated types of curricula and to some extent Bernstein appears to do this; but I think that such identification needs to be guarded, as I shall explain later.

Two concepts are also introduced, namely classification and frame. Classification refers to the degree of boundary maintenance between contents. Frame refers to the degree of control teacher and pupil possess over the selection, organization and pacing of the knowledge transmitted and received in the pedagogical relationship.

Educational knowledge codes are defined at a general level by the relationship between classification and frame. Specific examples are given which help to explain what is at stake. European broad subject-based curricula have strong classification and exceptionally strong framing, i.e. central direction of the selection, organization and pacing of knowledge. The English specialized curriculum involves exceptionally strong classification with strong boundaries between specialist options, but it is much weaker in framing than is common in Europe. I have already remarked on the English teacher's comparative freedom from the direction of central policy. Of the American situation Bernstein writes:

> The course-based, non-specialised U.S.A. form of the collection, I suggest, has the weakest classification and framing of the collection code, especially at the secondary and university level. A far greater range of subjects can be taken at the secondary and university level, and these are capable of combination; this indicates weak classification.
>
> (Bernstein 1971, 235)

Integration, as Bernstein uses it, refers minimally to the subordination of previously insulated subjects or courses to some relational idea. Integration can be handled by one teacher or by a group of teachers. It is here that I would want to return to my earlier note of caution about the identification of integration with the word used to stand for actual practices in the school. First, if the relational idea is not strong enough or not sufficiently powerful in the teacher's thinking, then the integrated study may not integrate. Hamilton (1973) has produced a close empirical study of the way in which classification is in fact maintained in a group of teachers handling Scottish integrated science. Second, if integrated units exist side by side in a school, they can readily become a new collection code of 'subjects'.

In fact, it is arguable that integration as Bernstein discusses it depends on the capacity of those involved to hold on to a particular open attitude to knowledge. It depends upon the abandonment of the idea of knowledge as a possession and a source of power to be dispensed grudgingly to those who accept the system hierarchy and are prepared to defer satisfaction. For the collection code holds the hierarchy in place.

> Any collection code involves an hierarchical organization of knowledge, such that the ultimate mystery if the subject is revealed very late in the educational life. By the ultimate mystery of the subject, I mean its potential for creating new realities. It is also the case, and this is important, that the ultimate mystery of the subject is not coherence, but incoherence; not order, but disorder; not the known, but the unknown. As this mystery, under collection codes, is revealed very late in educational life – and then only to a select few who have shown the signs of successful socialization – then only the few *experience* in their bones the notion that knowledge is permeable, that its orderings are provisional, that the dialectic of knowledge is closure and openness. For the many, socialization into knowledge is socialization into order, the existing order, into the experience that the world's educational knowledge is impermeable. Do we have here another version of alienation?
>
> . . . The key concept of the European collection code is discipline. This means learning to work *within* a received frame. It means, in particular, *learning* what questions can be put at any particular time.
>
> (Bernstein 1971, 240–241)

In short, the pressure upon the school to maintain its own order through a hierarchical relationship leads to the generation of an ideology whose function is social control. This ideology does not conform to knowledge as it is *used* in society, but rather to knowledge as it is possessed. As Bernstein has it, the emphasis is on states of knowledge rather than ways of knowing. The effect is that the control problem in the school tends to shape knowledge in such a way that only those who enter the establishment can innovate. Acceptance rather than speculation is the product.

Bernstein's analysis is theoretical and he comments that it stands in need of empirical testing. The Humanities Project, which was concerned with students' access to knowledge and ability to utilize it, particularly as this problem relates to the authority of schools and teachers, was engaged in exploring Bernstein's area of interest, though not in the light of his theory.

By selecting as content controversial human issues the project was able to work in a curriculum area where teachers could not claim authority on the basis of their subject training. Since the project was flexible in its application, it had different patterns of implementation in different schools. A common one was to introduce humanities as a subject within a collection code. One unusual feature of humanities was that the teacher groups handling it crossed subject qualifications drawing commonly on specialists in English, history, geography, religious education and social science and less commonly on specialists in mathematics, science, physical education and domestic science. It weakened traditional classification boundaries in the staff room, though experimenting teachers often created a tight group, casting themselves as innovators, identifying themselves with the project as a possession and thereby trying to protect themselves from the institutional pressures they experienced within the school.

Framing was very weak, the structure being provided less by commonality of selection, organization and pacing of knowledge than by the acceptance of a common teacher role, that of neutral chairman. This role was extremely difficult to implement in practice, partly because it cut across the assumptions of the traditional pedagogy, partly because it involved technical problems, which meant that teachers experienced incompetence. (MacDonald 1973a) Both the tension in implementing the role and the effects observed suggest that Bernstein may have underestimated pedagogical role as a means of altering the perspective from which pupils encounter knowledge in school. In this case there was a shift of teacher's status base from their subject affiliation towards professional identification with pedagogical skills and the capacity to mount experimental innovation.

The evaluation study suggests that a range of results of a kind which might be predicted on the basis of Bernstein's theory did take place. There was rather extensive evidence of an increase in speculative confidence in students and also of increments in reading comprehension, vocabulary and pupil self-esteem, among other variables.

In some cases the project had an influence which spread in the school. Schools which wished to contain it did seem in many cases to react by tightening classification, creating a humanities department and stabilizing the composition of the teacher team involved.

On the whole, however, when the ethos of the project became established, it seemed to survive better than in some integrated code curricula. With complex integrated curricula, team teaching often appears to lead to tight framing; teachers facing the uncertainties of open endedness without a firm role close down on possibilities and obtain security and power by teaching pupils what questions can be put at any particular time; and the custodial function of the school is reinforced by strong developments on the pastoral side.

These are of course only empirical impressions, but it is clear that within the relevant curriculum projects data does exist for the empirical testing and further development of Bernstein's theory. Certainly, there is considerable evidence of ideologies in schools which constitute institutionally reinforced impediments to the realization of curricula embodying open views of knowledge.

5

BEHAVIOURAL OBJECTIVES AND CURRICULUM DEVELOPMENT

In the past three chapters I have reviewed some aspects of the nature of knowledge, of teaching and of schools which have central relevance to curriculum development. In the next five chapters I turn to problems in the design of curriculum development. Most of the discussion will be relevant both to development in a single school and development through the agency of a curriculum project working with many schools.

The organization of the discussion is somewhat unusual in that I propose to treat the problems of curriculum development separately from those of curriculum evaluation, to which I turn in Chapter 8, after having reviewed two strategies for development. In Chapter 9, I shall consider the prospect of synthesizing development and evaluation.

In any consideration of design in curriculum one must, I think, start from the classic model which is based on objectives. This can be traced in its modern form to the two books of the American, Bobbitt: *The Curriculum* (1918) and *How to Make a Curriculum* (1924). Believing that 'Human life . . . . consists in the performance of specific activities', Bobbit held that 'Education which prepares for life is one that prepares definitely and adequately for these specific activities.' (1918, 42) Kliebard (1968, 243) in a review of Bobbitt's work comments:

> Bobbitt undertook the specification of those activities *as* educational objectives. By setting out the range of man's adult activity in detail, he hoped to introduce a practicality and scientific objectivity into the uncertainty and speculation that surrounded the question of the purposes of schooling.

In one form or another the idea of objectives was current in American writing on the curriculum from Bobbitt onwards; but the most lucid and straightforward account of the use of objectives in curriculum development remains that of Tyler (1949).

The school is a purposive institution, education an intentional activity. Tyler starts from the question: what educational purposes should the school seek to attain? and he equates a purpose with an objective or goal. Education is a means towards ends.

The objectives of education are to be formulated as a result of a consideration of the learners themselves, contemporary life outside the school (Bobbitt's original emphasis), the nature of subjects, the psychology of learning and a philosophy, or set of values. Then the question arises how best to formulate one's purposes as a practical guide to action, and Tyler considers the problem of 'stating objectives in a form to be helpful in selecting learning experiences and in guiding teaching'.

He reviews three ways of approaching the problem, and proposes a fourth.

First, one may specify things the instructor is to do. Among his examples are to demonstrate the nature of inductive proof and to present the Romantic poets. Tyler argues:

> The difficulty of an objective stated in the form of activities to be carried on by the teacher lies in the fact that there is no way of judging whether these activities should really be carried on. They are not the ultimate purpose of the educational programme and are not, therefore, really the objectives.

Second, one may list 'topics, concepts, generalizations, or other elements of content that are to be dealt with'. He regards such specifications as unsatisfactory objectives 'since they do not specify what the students are expected to do with these elements'.

Third, one may specify generalized patterns of behaviour such as 'to develop ciritical thinking' or 'to develop social attitudes'. Tyler argues that it is unlikely that such patterns of behaviour generalize and that it is necessary to specify the content to which the behaviour applies.

The third approach is right, however, in concentrating on student behaviour.

> Since the real purpose of education is not to have the instructor perform certain activities but to bring about significant changes in the students' patterns of behaviour, it becomes important to recognise that any statement of the objectives of the school should be a statement of changes to take place in students.
>
> (Tyler 1949, 44)

On the basis of these arguments, Tyler offers his own formula.

> The most useful form for stating objectives is to express them in terms which identify both the kind of behaviour to be developed in the student and the content or area of life in which this behaviour is to operate. If you consider a number of statements of objectives that seem to be clear and to provide guidance in the development of instructional programmes, you will note that each of these statements really includes both the behaviour and the content aspects of the objective.
>
> Thus, the objective, 'To Write Clear and Well-organized Reports of Social Studies Projects', includes both an indication of the kind of behaviour – namely, writing clear and well-organized reports – and also indicates the areas of life with which the reports are to deal.
>
> (Tyler 1949, 46–47)

> One can define an objective with sufficient clarity if he can describe or illustrate the kind of behaviour the student is expected to acquire so that one could recognize such behaviour if he saw it.
>
> (Tyler 1949, 59–60)

This is the classic definition of a 'behavioural objective'. This sense of the word *objective* is a basic linguistic tool of curriculum studies and throughout this book *objective* will be used to signify an aim specified in terms of student behaviour. In curriculum studies the alternative synonymous phrase to behavioural objective is *intended learning outcome*, sometimes shortened to I.L.O. *Goal* is also found in the literature but usage is more inconsistent.

Hilda Taba (1962) draws a widely accepted distinction between *aims* and *objectives*. Aims are broad statements of purpose and intention – to transmit culture or to develop a democratic way of life. 'The chief function of stating aims on such general levels is to provide an orientation to the main emphasis in educational programmes.' (Taba 1962, 196)

The process of systematic curriculum development rests on the analysis of general statements of aim into more specific behavioural objectives. Great store is set by precision.

> In spite of the lip service that objectives have received over the past several hundred years, few teachers have derived many instructional dividends from expressing their goals because, ordinarily, the objectives have been stated in terms too loose to allow the teacher to proceed effectively from them.
>
> (Popham and Baker 1970, 19)

The process of systematic curriculum development rests, then, on the analysis of general statements of aim into more specific behavioural objectives.

> The general aims can be satisfied only if individuals acquire certain knowledge, skills, techniques, and attitudes. These latter represent a more specific platform of goals. The outcomes on this more specific level are usually referred to as educational objectives . . .
>
> (Taba 1962, 196)

> The chief function of the more specific platform of objectives is to guide the making of curriculum decisions on what to cover, what to emphasize, what content to select, and which learning experiences to stress.
>
> (Taba 1962, 197)

> Since education does not consist solely of mastery of content, objectives also serve to clarify the types of powers, mental or otherwise, which need to be developed. The definition of these powers determines how subject matter is selected and how it is handled in the classroom. In teaching literature, it makes a good deal of difference whether the intent is to familiarize students with the content of literary masterpieces, to sensitize them to a greater range of human values, to develop a familiarity with the forms of literature, or to develop a personal philosophy of life.
>
> (Taba 1962, 198)

> A platform of objectives is needed also to provide a common, consistent focus for the multifarious activities we call the curriculum. The programme of the school is managed by many people. There are many subjects, classes and teachers. Some unity in emphasis, some common focus is needed to make these efforts converge on certain common, consistent goals.
>
> (Taba 1962, 198)

> Finally, the objectives serve as a guide for the evaluation of achievement.
>
> (Taba 1962, 199)

Within this conceptual framework, Taba tentatively suggests an orderly procedure aimed at a more thoughtfully planned and a more dynamically conceived curriculum:

> Step 1: Diagnosis of needs
> Step 2: Formulation of objectives
> Step 3: Selection of content
> Step 4: Organization of content
> Step 5: Selection of learning experiences
> Step 6: Organization of learning experiences
> Step 7: Determination of what to evaluate and of the ways and means of doing it.
>
> (Taba 1962, 12)

I have chosen to define this model of curriculum development by drawing on Tyler and Taba because in my view Tyler offers the clearest statement of the basic principles involved and Taba the best exposition of the relation of those principles to the study of education and to the practice of curriculum development. But much of the literature of curriculum studies in all countries is concerned with this model. Moreover, the model draws on experience gained in training personnel such as radar operators and gunners during the Second World War and on a long established tradition of objective testing of student attainment. Within the scope of this book it is not possible to do more than alert the reader to the existence of this large body of literature and network of related studies.

I propose now first to consider the power of the objectives model as a system of organizing thinking about curriculum, then to review some developments in formulating objectives and in applying the model to practice. Finally, I shall consider the concept of mastery learning, the development of the objectives model in systems theory, and the idea and implications of performance contracting.

The organizing power of the objectives model seems to derive from its origins as an applied tradition of educational studies and behavioural science. The process of diagnosis of needs and statement of aims provides a focus for the consideration of high-level values, for an analysis of society's demands upon the schools, and for a consideration of the nature of knowledge and culture. The debate at this stage invites the participation of those interested and qualified in ethics, epistemology, sociology of knowledge and social philosophy.

As the implications of these aims are worked across into practical form with constant reference back to principles by means of the formulation of objectives, the selection and organization of content, and the selection and organization of learning experiences, other relevant studies can be orchestrated into the work. Epistemology and psychology are brought into relationship, particularly in the Piagetian tradition of empirical study of the development of concepts, logics, knowledge and affective responses, the child's reconstruction of the world in the mind. Learning theory, systematic pedagogy and social psychology inform the selection and organization of learning experiences. And when the curriculum which is the product of this synthesizing process emerges as a product, it can be tested, evaluated and improved by the application of the relatively refined techniques of psychometrics and educational measurement.

In short, the objectives model of curriculum development provides a systematic focus for the various branches of the study of education. Bloom (1963) has expressed the aspiration towards the use of the objectives model as such a focus in a paper on 'The role of the educational sciences in curriculum development'.

If you imagine a large faculty of education staffed with philosophers, sociologists, learning theorists, child and developmental psychologists, methods experts, systems analysts, psychometricians and others, invited to give a consultancy in curriculum to a school system, then the objectives model is a means of integrating their contributions. Just as Taba argues that objectives 'provide a common, consistent focus for the multifarious activities we call the curriculum', so the objectives model provides a logical pattern of co-operative action and intellectual synthesis for those engaged in educational research and the academic study of education. It is a means of translating the study of education into the practice of education.

One of the major contributions to the study of objectives is the attempt to produce a taxonomy of educational objectives which arose from 'an informal meeting of college examiners attending the 1948 American Psychological Association Convention'. (Bloom 1956, 4) It illustrates rather well how psychologists and psychometricians tackled the problem and made their contribution within the objectives tradition.

This taxonomy is in two volumes, the first covering the cognitive domain and the second the affective domain (Bloom 1956 and Krathwohl 1964). A third volume covering the psycho-motor domain has not appeared. The taxonomy has attracted widespread attention, and it is worth quoting the authors at some length.

> As achievement testers and educational research workers, the major phenomena with which we are concerned are the changes produced in individuals as a result of educational experiences . . .
>
> We are of the opinion that although the objectives (aims) and test materials and techniques may be specified in an almost unlimited number of ways, the student behaviours involved in these objectives (aims) can be represented by a relatively small number of classes. Therefore, this taxonomy is designed to be a classification of the student behaviours which represent the intended outcomes of the educational process . . .
>
> It should be noted that we are not attempting to classify the instructional methods used by teachers, the ways in which teachers relate themselves to students, or the different kinds of instructional materials they use. We are not attempting to classify the particular subject matter or content. What we are classifying is the *intended behaviour* of students – the ways in which individuals are to act, think or feel as the result of participating in some unit of instruction . . .
>
> The emphasis in the Handbook is on obtaining evidence on the extent to which desired and intended behaviours have been learned by the student . . .
>
> It should also be noted that the intended behaviours specified by

educational objectives do not include many of the behaviours which psychologists are interested in classifying and studying. One reason is that the intended behaviours represent the social goals imposed upon youngsters by their society or culture. Thus, the intended or desired behaviours included in educational objectives usually do not include undesirable or abnormal behaviours which are socially disapproved. . .

(Bloom 1956, 12–13)

The following is an excerpt from the taxonomy itself:

1.24 *Knowledge of Criteria* – Illustrative Educational Objectives
Familiarity with criteria for judgement appropriate to the type of work and the purpose for which it is used.
Knowledge of criteria for the evaluation of recreational activities.
Knowledge of the criteria by which a valid source of information in the social sciences can be recognized.
Knowledge of the criteria by which the nutritive value of a meal can be judged.
Knowledge of the basic elements (balance, unity, rhythm, etc.) which can be used to judge a work of art.
Knowledge of the criteria by which some economists judge the relative proportions of income distributed for different purposes by a family.

(Bloom 1956, 73)

1.24 *Knowledge of Criteria* – Illustrative Test Items.
Directions: In the following, select the *one best* completion.
In the preface to the second edition of the *Critique of Pure Reason*, Kant discusses the problem of placing metaphysics upon the secure path of a science. By science in this context he means

A. a body of generalizations whose truth is guaranteed by observation of facts.
B. demonstrations of conclusions from assumptions which must always retain a hypothetical character.
C. dialectic in the Platonic sense.
D. a body of knowledge corresponding closely to the intellectual virtue called 'scientific knowledge' by Aristotle.

In the view of John Ruskin, the greatest picture is

A. that which imitates best.
B. that which teaches us most.
C. that which exhibits greatest power.
D. that which conveys the greatest number of the greatest ideas.

The criterion Darwin uses to distinguish the more variable species from the less variable species in Chapter II is

A. number of individuals in the species.
B. frequency of individual differences in the species.
C. number of varieties in the species.

D. number of closely related species.
E. number of different climatic conditions tolerated by the species.

(Bloom 1956, 84)

In this example, the student behaviour is first characterized as knowledge of criteria and then progressively given more precision, first in application to a content area – for example, 'knowledge of the basic elements which can be used to judge a work of art' – and then in the formulation of a particular test item. It is clear too that this type of analysis does lay out the objectives for criticism. Philosophers, psychologists and psychometricians are all provided with data which can be discussed critically in the light of their own fields of study. Notionally at least, the taxonomy is open to progressive improvement and refinement, as are the taxonomies of biology. But it should be noted that it is more open to development through criticism of experts in particular fields of study than through criticism based on the observation of classrooms. Its origins are not in the empirical study of teaching, though it could be regarded as empirical in the sense that it is an ordering of goals which are in fact expressed or an observation of 'the social goals imposed upon youngsters by their society or culture.' This also implies that the taxonomy has a conservative cast, though this need not necessarily be true of all taxonomies.

As I have already mentioned, the work on objectives has been extensive. One line has been concerned with precision, clarity and specificity. The following are examples:

Given a human skeleton, the student must be able to correctly identify by labeling at least 40 of the following bones; there will be no penalty for guessing (list of bones inserted here).

(Mager 1962, 49)

The student will be able to evaluate various interpretations of the causes of the Civil War by applying evaluative criteria which were employed in the course for evaluating interpretations of other wars.

(Kibler, Barker and Miles 1970, 94)

The student will write a 500-word essay with a topic sentence, development by example, and a concluding statement. The topic of the essay will be Negro contributions to the culture of the United States.

(Popham and Baker 1970, 52)

Appreciates good literature.

1. Describes the difference between good and poor literature.
2. Distinguishes between selections of good and poor literature.
3. Gives critical reasons for classifying a selection as good or poor.
4. Selects and reads good literature during free-reading period.

5. Explains why he likes the particular selections of good literature that he reads.

This last is a teacher quoted as being generally on the right lines by Gronlund (1970).

The above attempts to increase the specificity of objectives show some of the strengths and limitations of this development. The second takes the course rather than the discipline as a criterion by which to judge work in history. The third seems to me to stereotype undesirably the pattern of the essay. The final one appears absurd. Leaving out 4, the objectives might be shortened to: 'Solves the central problems of literary criticism at which professional critics have been working throughout the centuries!'

Criticisms of such objectives do not invalidate the approach; but they do indicate that it is beset by pitfalls. And it is important to note that the objectives above are quoted from prominent workers in the field and are not, I think, unfairly chosen simply to catch them nodding.

There has been some reaction against too precise specification of objectives within the assumptions of the objectives model. One of the most interesting examples of this trend comes from Sweden. We must bear in mind that in Sweden we are concerned with a centralized system and hence with the problem of framing legally binding curricula for the whole school system.

In the introduction to an official publication on 'goal description' (equivalent to specification of objectives), Marklund sees goal specification as playing down content and stressing teaching principles. Since in Sweden there had previously existed centralized curricula laid down in terms of content, objectives represented a possibility of freeing the teacher rather than tightening the specification to which he works.

> The advantage of this form of goal description was that it was not binding on teachers and producers of learning aids. But experience soon showed that this freedom would not automatically result in the transformation of methods and means envisaged by the new goals. Concrete examples were needed of how the teaching principles enjoined on teachers were to be translated into means and methods. Now as previously, the most concrete help came from learning aids, at the same time as it was found that these did not automatically have exactly the results intended.
>
> A more rigid steering towards the goals came as a result of the so-called learning systems, in which the teacher is only part of a prefabricated teaching plan which also includes organization and methods. So far the learning system has proved something of a mixed blessing. One of its

advantages is that organizational frames have for the first time been devised whereby the general and overall goals of the school system can be more consistently provided for, e.g. through co-operation in varying groups, independent tasks and individualized studies. But the teachers, who have realized the value of these new developments, have often remarked on the rigid steering which learning systems involve. Thus the criticism has sometimes been made that the choice of a particular learning aid must of necessity mean studying according to a particular method.

There is no simple and obvious way out of this dilemma . . .

(Marklund 1972, 6–7)

The response is to suggest that teachers, learning aid designers and evaluators should be stimulated to goal description. In Sweden this implies a degree of decentralization. In the United States and Britain the objectives model is often seen as limiting teacher initiative either by tying them down or keeping them up to scratch. Against the Swedish background it is seen as having some potential for increasing teacher freedom and initiative, albeit against a background in which an extremely precise and systematic application of an objectives model has been found restricting.

It is interesting to find the Swedish MPP physics project producing the following statement which is analytic but quite distinct from the American tradition of objectives:

The teaching of physics should:

A1 arouse the pupils' interest in physical phenomena

A2 create understanding of the application of physical phenomena in technology and everyday life

A3 give pupils an idea of the way in which human living conditions depend on the manner in which physics and techology are utilized

A4 relate to the pupils' experience and interests

A5 observe that certain fundamental concepts, phenomena and relations are a precondition of the pupils being able to comprehend other, more complex relations

A6 aim at letting pupils establish and get to know the relation between cause and effect regarding the phenomena to be studied on the basis of their own observations

A7 lead to conclusions which can provide a basis for universal relations

A8 accord a central position to experimentation.

It is true that the project goes on to specify pretty clear objectives in terms of pupil behaviour, but there are two significant shifts of emphasis. First, the high-level goals are treated as more 'real' than the behavioural objectives which are clearly subordinated to them and instrumental. They are no longer regarded as 'not really the objectives' (Tyler 1949, 44). And second, the high-level goals contain specifications of pupil learning – 'understanding', 'an idea of' – which appear to demand teacher judgement, to demand marking or rating rather than measurement.

In England, although many curriculum projects have discussed objectives, and the North West Development Project encouraged teachers to formulate them, only *Science 5–13* has adopted a developed objectives model.

The principles from which the project starts indicate the need for flexibility, since they stress the responsibility of individual teachers and responsiveness to children's interests.

> In general, children work best when trying to find answers to problems that they have themselves chosen to investigate.
> These problems are best drawn from their own environment and tackled largely by practical investigations. Teachers should be responsible for thinking out and putting into practice the work of their own classes. In order to do so they should be able to find help where they need it.
> (*Science 5–13*, 1972, 4)

Starting from a general aim of science teaching, namely, 'developing an enquiring mind and a scientific approach to problems' (ibid. 21), the project arrived at eight broad aims, which they expressed diagrammatically as follows:

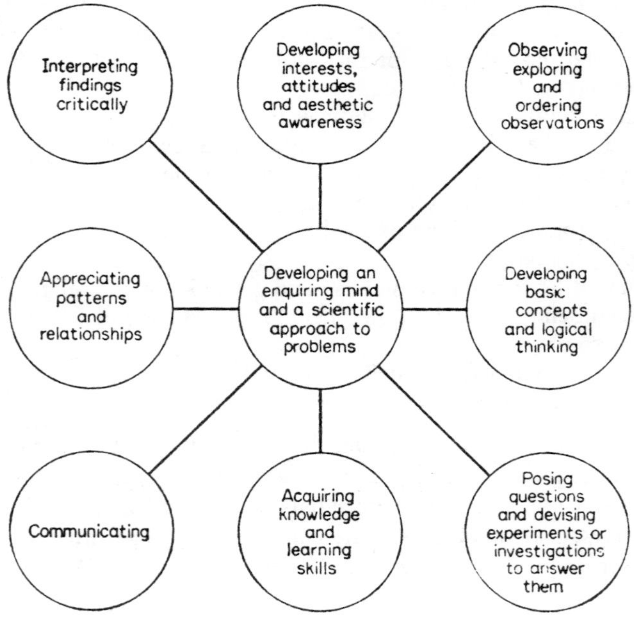

Then, on a Piagetian base, they distinguished three stages of development, the first stage being subdivided. Briefly, these were as follows:

Stage 1a transition from intuitive to concrete operations.
Stage 1b Concrete operations. Early stage.
Stage 2 Concrete operations. Later stage.
Stage 3 Transition to stage of abstract thinking.

Each broad aim was worked into objectives considered appropriate to each stage. And each objective was numbered. Thus 1.34 indicated Stage 1, broad objective .3 (Developing basic concepts and logical thinking), sub-objective 4. The full set of objectives for this broad aim is given below.

1.30 Developing basic concepts and logical thinking:

Stage 1 (a)
1.31 Awareness of the meaning of words which describe various types of quantity.
1.32 Appreciation that things which are different may have features in common.

Stage 1 (b)
1.33 Ability to predict the effect of certain changes through observation of similar changes
1.34 Formation of the notions of the horizontal and the vertical.
1.35 Development of concepts of conservation of length and substance.
1.36 Awareness of the meaning of speed and of its relation to distance covered.

Stage 2
2.31 Appreciation of measurement as division into regular parts and repeated comparison with a unit.
2.32 Appreciation that comparisons can be made indirectly by use of an intermediary.
2.33 Development of concepts of conservation of weight, area and volume.
2.34 Appreciation of weight as a downward force.
2.35 Understanding of the speed, time, distance, relation.

Stage 3
3.31 Familiarity with relationships involving velocity, distance, time, acceleration.
3.32 Ability to separate, exclude or combine variables in approaching problems.
3.33 Ability to formulate hypotheses not dependent upon direct observation.

3.34 Ability to extend reasoning beyond the actual to the possible.
3.35 Ability to distinguish a logically sound proof from others less sound.

(*Science 5–13*, 1972)

These objectives, though not highly specific, are carefully worked out and well defined. The project argues that such objectives help 'the teacher to take advantage of the potential elements of science which are in any of their activities'. Curricular suggestions are based on them, but it is also clear that they are meant to support responsive as well as pre-planned elements in teaching; though, pushed too far, the project's dictum that 'working with objectives takes some of the insecurity out of discovery situations' (26) might restrict responsiveness.

It is, I think, dangerous to judge all but the crudest elements in a curriculum without trying out the strategies it suggests in the classroom. But *Science 5–13* strikes me as an intelligent, moderate, modest and practical attempt to use the general framework of the objectives model in curriculum design. It will repay more detailed study and elements of it can be mounted experimentally in the classroom without great expense or difficulty.

A more radical, systematic attempt to follow through the implications of the objectives model for curricular and instructional problems is associated with the concept of 'mastery learning', in the development of which Bloom has been influential.

The basic premise of mastery learning is that students' aptitudes are predictive of the rate at which they can learn rather than of their possible level of achievement. If aptitude is normally distributed in a group and all are given the same instruction, it is argued that achievement will be normally distributed. As Bloom comments:

> The most wasteful and destructive aspect of our present educational system is the set of expectations about student learning each teacher brings to the beginning of a new course or term. The instructor expects a third of his pupils to learn well what is taught, a third to learn less well, and a third to fail or just 'get by'. These expectations are transmitted to the pupils through school grading policies and practices and through the methods and materials of instruction. Students quickly learn to act in accordance with them, and the final sorting through the grading process approximates the teacher's original expectations. A pernicious self-fulfilling prophecy has been created.
>
> (Bloom 1971, 47)

Suppose, however, that although all the students are distributed normally on aptitude, each learner receives the optimum quality of instruction and the time he needs to complete the learning task. Then there would be little relationship between aptitude and achievement: most students would attain mastery. For example, one study reports: 'Whereas in the previous year only 30% of students received an A grade, 80% of the sample achieved at or above the previous year's A grade score on a parallel exam and thus received A's.' (Airasian 1967, 98)

The reader may well blink! At first sight it may seem as though we shall all know everything. It's not quite like that, of course. The students involved in this course were studying test theory at graduate level and most of the confirmatory experiments are either with groups of this kind within relatively narrow aptitude bands or at the level of learning the elements of a subject. In many cases also individualized instruction is involved so that in the long run students with greater aptitude learn more. But students of modest ability attain mastery within limits rather than failure over an extensive field. This is in itself of great importance and may well have positive effects on morale which go far beyond the context in which mastery learning takes place.

Block (1971, 64–67) discusses the possibilities and limitations of mastery learning. Application is claimed to be most effective where students need either minimal prior learning or previous learning which most learners already possess, where the subject to be learned is sequential and where the subjects are closed and emphasize convergent rather than divergent thinking.

Mastery learning depends upon the clear definition of objectives and sub-objectives in subjects of this sort, the communication of these objectives to students and the passage of students through the learning system only as they attain mastery of a given stage or level. The following points are fundamental and must be communicated to the students:

1. The student will be graded solely on the basis of his final . . . examination performance.
2. The student will be graded on the basis of his performance *vis a vis* a predetermined standard and not relative to his peers.
3. All students who attain the standard will receive appropriate grade rewards (usually A's) and there will be no fixed number of awards. . . .
4. Throughout the learning, the student will be given a series of ungraded, diagnostic-progress tests to promote and pace his learning.
5. Each student will be given all the help he needs to learn.

(Block 1971, 75)

One of the important aspects of an objectives approach is brought out in 2 and 3 above. An objective or series of objectives provides a basis for criterion-referenced rather than norm-referenced testing. Many teachers (and many standardized tests) operate on the assumption of a normal curve, giving for example 10% A's, 15% B's, 50% C's, 15% D's and 10% E's. Such a procedure is desperately demoralizing to students. Only a tiny minority have any indication of having reached a desired level of attainment. For the rest the goal seems to move out of reach as one stretches for it. Objectives are in principle attainable by all; percentile scores or not!

I have not had the opportunity to study mastery learning procedures in practice, but it certainly seems possible to accept that many of the tasks encountered by students in schools and universities are not unduly demanding in terms of aptitude. The assumption adopted by the educational institution may well be that many more tasks involve differential achievement according to aptitude levels than may in fact need to do so. The adoption of marking and grading assumptions which across the board make the assumption that the performance required is one which allows high fliers to fly high and holds others to a low ceiling, may have depressing effects in areas where reasonable mastery should be attainable by most.

Mastery learning is in the view of its adherents of limited application. The most thorough-going attempt to apply objectives to curriculum is the systems approach, which depends upon an analysis of the educational process in the light of general systems theory. General systems theory has been used to gain understanding in the physical sciences, biology, and the behavioural sciences and has been applied extensively in engineering and more recently in management.

General systems theory developed originally from the difficulties encountered by scientists in conceptualizing and expressing the characteristics of complex entities. As Bertalanffy expresses the dilemma:

> If we look at a living organism, we observe an amazing order, organization, maintenance in continuous change, regulation and apparent teleology. Similarly, in human behaviour goal-seeking and purposiveness cannot be overlooked, even if we accept a strictly behaviouristic standpoint. However, concepts like organization, directiveness, teleology, etc., just do not appear in the classic system of science. As a matter of fact, in the so-called mechanistic world view based upon classical physics, they were considered as illusory or metaphysical.
>
> (Bertalanffy 1962, 29–30)

> . . . in modern physics and biology, problems of organized complexity,

> that is, interaction of a large but not infinite number of variables, are popping up everywhere and demand new conceptual tools.
>
> (ibid. 30)

Systems theory is concerned with the study of organized complexity.

'A system is an organized or complex whole: an assemblage or combination of things or parts forming a complex or unitary whole.' (Kast and Rosenzweig, 1970, 14) A crude distinction can be drawn between empirical systems theory which aims at models to advance understanding and 'engineering' systems theory which aims at models to control action. The second perspective is the one which concerns us in this chapter.

The basic argument rests on the proposition that a variety of different systems can be analysed and made amenable to planning by the use of a general theory.

> A system might be described as an array of things in which we are concerned particularly with the way they relate to, and interact with, each other. Systems analysis is a method of understanding the way a system works preparatory to influencing or controlling it.
>
> (Birley 1972, 30)

Systems analysis as applied to policy areas such as education is essentially problem-oriented.

> Amongst the policy-makers' tasks are these:
> 1. defining the problem;
> 2. thinking of possible ways of solving it; and
> 3. weighing the merits of the various ways, both in terms of quantitative assessments and of value judgements.
>
> (Birley 1972, 30)

But how do we know we have a problem?

> It is reasonable, and useful, to take the apparently chaotic universe to be a complex of intereacting systems. If a system has definable objectives then we may hope to be able to engineer it in order that they are achieved. Even if this systems engineering is not possible, the systems view still provides the best framework for relevant debate concerning the problems which arise in the real world.
>
> (Checkland 1971, 51)

We must have criteria for judging the effectiveness of a system and the existence of problems within it, and these criteria are provided by specifying objectives. Problems are problems of efficiency in reaching these objectives, and efficiency involves value for money or cost-effectiveness. Given objectives, this can be conceptualized as output budgeting.

Traditionally, budgets have categorized expenditure by the type of resource on which it is to be spent – staff, buildings, materials and so on – rather than by the purpose for which it is to be spent. The aims of an output budgeting system may briefly be stated as being to analyse expenditure by the purpose for which it is to be spent and to relate it to the results achieved. It is a formal system for establishing:

i) What a department is aiming to achieve – what its *objectives* are – in the areas of policy for which it is responsible;
ii) Which *activities* are contributing to these objectives;
iii) What resources, or *inputs*, are being devoted to these activities;
iv) What is actually being achieved, or what the *outputs* are.

(Department of Education and Science 1970)

I argued earlier that the objectives model of curriculum development provides a focus for the application of the various fields of educational study to curricular problems. In the application of general systems theory it leads through output budgeting, management by objectives and planning-programming-budgeting system to a relating of curriculum design to the management, planning and politics of education. How does this systems approach look at the curriculum development end?

A school or a school system is a system in the general systems theory sense, Feyereisen, Fiorno and Nowak (1970) adopt the following model for the management of curriculum and instruction:

1. Identification of the problem.
2. Diagnosis of the problem.
3. Search for alternative solutions.
4. Selection of the best solution.
5. Ratification of that solution by the organization.
6. Authorization of the solution.
7. Use of the solution on a trial basis.
8. Preparation for adoption of the solution.
9. Adoption of the solution.
10. Direction and guidance of the staff.
11. Evaluation of the effectiveness of the solution.

(Feyereisen, Fiorno and Nowak 1970, 61)

And they immediately comment: 'These steps involve the assumption that the school system has a statement of objectives. If this is not the case, then a preliminary step is the definition of the objectives for the school system.' (62) Later, they consider Problem Identification (Step 1) and observe: 'Problems associated with the actual statement of objectives do not have to be measured by a strict set of criteria: The only criterion these problems must satisfy is a dissatisfaction with the stated objectives.' (64) In short, objectives are not problematic *within* the system. The system depends upon the existence of agreed objectives and does not contribute such objectives.

A systems approach rests on the formulation of objectives, but does not provide a method of defining such objectives. It is concerned with efficiency rather than direction. Systems theory demands objectives as given, as basic data. It contributes only the idea that all personnel in the system should be involved in the formulation of objectives and this in itself is argued more on the grounds of the motivational force of involvement of people in purposes than on the grounds that the purposes are thereby likely to be more 'correct'.

In short, systems theory does not assist us in determining our objectives (except in terms of their realism, as judged by success or failure in implementing them) nor does it contribute to the content of education or to its methods. Rather it is concerned with the identification of problems, with decision-making and with the monitoring of solutions. It is concerned with efficiency, rather than with truth. That is not to be despised. But it should be noted that its concern with efficiency in the sense of value-for-investment provides an emphasis on value rather than values.

From such a base it is possible, though by no means inevitable, to take the step that leads to performance contracting.

Performance contracting basically means payment by results, and in any consideration of the modern American movement, the nineteenth-century British experience should be taken into account. In Britain, Her Majesties Inspectors visited schools and examined children according to certain pre-specified 'standards'. Government grants were paid to the School Board according to the children's performance. In the United States some school systems have contracted out sectors of the educational system to profit-making learning system companies whose profits depend on their capacity to achieve objectives pre-specified in terms of the children's performance on standardized tests.

This 'objectives or bust' policy is the other extreme from 'with objectives in mind' (*Science 5–13*).

6

A CRITIQUE OF THE OBJECTIVES MODEL

No issue has been more contentious in curriculum theory than the objectives model. At the 1972 Chicago Convention of the American Educational Research Association, participants displayed car bumper stickers reading HELP STAMP OUT BEHAVIORAL OBJECTIVES! or HELP STAMP OUT SOME NON-BEHAVIORAL OBJECTIVES! And the history of this sticker war has been amusingly and instructively presented by Popham (1971).

In writing this book, I face the problem of maintaining a balanced view, since my own work in research and development has been in reaction to what I regard as the shortcomings of the objectives model. In the last chapter I have tried to give a general account of the model, relatively free of explicit criticism. I set it out as a theory of and policy for curriculum development which needs to be tested. Now I propose to review some of the criticisms of it, to add critical comments of my own, and finally to review the strengths and weaknesses of the approach to curriculum design through objectives as they seem to emerge from the discussion.

First, however, I want to provide a context by reviewing briefly the nature of theory as it applies to this issue.

In action areas or 'policy sciences' like curriculum study, theory has two functions. It serves to organize the data, the facts we have, in such a way as to provide an understanding. In so far as it does not go beyond our knowledge to rest upon doubtful assumptions, it is 'well grounded'. In so far as it embraces a wide range of data and considerations, it is comprehensive or 'high level'. The second function of theory in a policy science is to provide a basis for action. Understanding must provide the basis for acting: the theory must have an executive as well as a contemplative slant.

The objectives model of curriculum development is an ambitious and comprehensive theory in the sense that it provides a means of organizing and relating a large range of variables, problems and activities. Such ambitious attempts at theoretical synthesis are necessary and important for the advancement of understanding. But in the policy sciences such is our lack of firm knowledge of the workings of the institutions with which we are concerned that ambitious theories and models are inherently precarious. They go far beyond the established data. They reach eagerly for coherence and sacrifice firm grounding. In short, they are highly speculative.

And we must be especially cautious with them because they have implications for action.

Now it is one of the problems of theorizing that our minds are beguiled by systematic tidiness and by comprehensive breadth. Hence, many people believe that the more systematic a theory is, the more likely it is to be correct. In curriculum studies – though perhaps not in the physical sciences – the reverse is likely to be the case. Our firm knowledge of the educational process is very limited. Large-scale theories have great utility as staging points in the advancement of knowledge, but the more logically satisfying they are, the less likely they are to be adequate. They can easily become the lotus isles of our scientific journey.

From the point of view of the progress of our knowledge, it is excellent that such adventurous and speculative theories should exist; but in a policy field it is important that they should not be too confidently advocated or adopted as a basis for large-scale action. We must beware of believing that in the objectives model – or in any other model or theory – we have a systematic solution to our curricular problems, much less an educational panacea. And the tone of some of the literature suggests that this is not an imaginary danger. The function of such a theory is not to command allegiance, but to attract the criticism and experimental testing which will lead to its refutation or refinement.

This is a criticism, not of the objectives model as such, but of the vein of advocacy and certitude of some of its proponents.

Another important point to bear in mind is that the objectives framework is a conceptual scheme, not a thing. We must not reify it. We do not *have* objectives: we choose to conceptualize our behaviour in terms of objectives – or we choose not to. What are the pros and cons of using such a conceptual scheme in curriculum development?

In this chapter I want to consider the issues from the point of view of the designers rather than of the evaluators of a curriculum. Designers of curricula are not just Schools Council project people or university and college teachers. They may be the staff of a curriculum project but typically they are teachers in schools. In the first case, there is a problem of large-scale communication. This is replicated on a smaller scale in a school team. As staff change, the curriculum has to be communicated to newcomers.

The model offered to designers is broadly as follows: agree broad aims and analyse these into objectives; construct a curriculum to achieve these objectives; refine it in practice by testing its capacity to achieve its objectives; communicate it to teachers through (among other things) the conceptual framework of objectives.

I propose to begin my review of criticisms of the objectives model by considering a paper by Popham (1968), 'Probing the Validity of Arguments against Behavioral Goals'. Popham attempts in this paper to defend the objectives model against eleven criticisms.

The first objection he considers is: 'Trivial learning behaviours are the easiest to operationalize, hence the really important outcomes of education will be under emphasized.' Atkin, among others, has levelled this criticism.

> There is a strong tendency in the literature about behavioural objectives in curriculum design to make the assumption that the objectives that can be defined behaviourally, the objectives that can be readily assessed, are the important objectives for a school programme. The corollary also seems to be accepted. If it seems impossible to detect and assess a specific learning outcome, it probably isn't important.
>
> (Atkin 1969, 17)
>
> If identification of all worthwhile outcomes in behavioural terms comes to be commonly accepted and expected, then it is inevitable that, over time, the curriculum will tend to emphasize those elements which have been thus identified. Important outcomes which are detected only with great difficulty and which are translated only rarely into behavioural terms tend to atrophy. They disappear from the curriculum because we spend all the time allotted to us in teaching explicitly for the more readily specifiable learnings to which we have been directed.
>
> (Atkin 1968b, 28)

Kliebard (1968) and Hogben (1972) point to the problem that many worthwhile aims of education might express themselves behaviourally only in the long term or in the face of certain contingencies.

In trying to meet these criticisms Popham argues 'that explicit objectives make it far *easier* for educators to attend to *important* instructional outcomes' by exposing the trivial which is often lurking beneath the high-flown. There is a danger of trivial objectives, but there is always a danger of triviality, and the discipline of expressing our objectives precisely helps to detect it.

Popham obviously considers some of Mager's work a liability in this argument and points out that almost all of Mager's examples deal with cognitive behaviours at the very lowest level.

I believe that the question at issue here is an empirical one. On the basis of experience rather than systematic study, I think that the criticism is justified in many complex fields within the disciplines of knowledge, but it is not justified when no great weight need be claimed for the ultimate worth of the objectives. There are many passages of learning in sciences and languages in particular where an important goal is clearly seen to be both limited and instrumental. On the other hand, it is common experience that conventional examinations can have just the effect feared by Atkin, and it is generally judged that payment by results did.

The second criticism is: 'Prespecification of explicit goals prevents the teacher from taking advantage of instructional opportunities unexpectedly occurring in the classroom.' Jackson (1966, 1968) has argued this at length on the basis of empirical studies of the teaching process. Popham replies that opportunism is always welcome, but it should always be justified in terms of its contribution to the learner's attainment of worthwhile objectives. Again, the question is largely an empirical one. I should guess that objectives formulated at the level of those in *Science 5–13* could well support and discipline opportunism and responsive teaching, but I am by no means certain that such objectives would be precise enough to satisfy Popham.

The third objection Popham faces is: 'Besides pupil behaviour changes, there are other types of educational outcomes which are important, such as changes in parental attitudes, the professional staff, community values, etc.' Popham replies that 'all modifications in personnel or external agencies should be justified in terms of their contribution toward the promotion of desired pupil behaviour changes'. It seems very doubtful whether this can be done in practice. Moreoever, the principle seems questionable. One could well argue that the abolition of corporal punishment could be justified even if it had no effect on outcomes. However, in principle there is no real objection to the extension of the objectives approach to take in other kinds of outcomes, and only the most extreme enthusiasts for objectives would oppose this, so long as pupil outcomes were also specified.

Popham is optimistic about the objection that 'Measurability implies behaviour which can be objectively, mechanistically measured, hence there must be something dehumanizing about the approach', since he believes that 'it is currently possible to assess many complicated human behaviours in a refined fashion' and 'Developmental work is under way in those areas where we must now rely on primitive measures.'

It seems to me that Popham is too optimistic here. Among many criticisms of the position that mental measurement offers refined instruments to the curriculum field, I find that of Stake (1971) the most compelling. In particular, Stake points out that standardized tests involve particular hazards. Writing in the context of objectives-based performance contracting he has this to say:

> To the person little acquainted with educational testing, it appears that performance testing is what educational tests are for. The testing specialist knows better. General achievement tests have been developed to measure correlates of learning, not learning itself.
>
> Such tests are indirect measures of educational gains. They provide correlates of achievement rather than direct evidence of achievement. Correlation of these test scores with general learning is often high, but such scores correlate only moderately with performance on many specific educational tasks. Tests can be built to measure specific competence, but there is relatively little demand for them. Many of those tests (often called criterion-referenced tests) do a poor job of predicting later performance of either a specific or a general nature. General achievement tests predict better. The test developer's basis for improving tests has been to work toward better prediction of later performance rather than better measurement of present performance. Assessment of what a student is now capable of doing is not the purpose of most standardized tests. Errors and hazards abound . . .
>
> (Stake 1971, 583)

Of course, criterion-referenced tests can be used, but they tend to be best adapted to the curriculum when they are detailed. This means that they are best given regularly at short intervals. Retention is not measured. If we measure for retention in a terminal or yearly test, we have to sample from our objectives again. And teaching for the examination enters the picture with all its potential for distorting the curriculum.

In spite of all these problems, I do not think we can rule out the objectives model on the basis of measurement problems. What we can do is question the range of its applicability if the measurement element is stressed, and judge that caution is always needed.

The fifth objection which Popham considers is that 'It is somehow undemocratic to plan in advance precisely how the learner should behave after instruction.' I believe that this objection impinges on the most important shortcoming of the objectives model, but is wrongly conceived as it stands. I shall, therefore, consider it later.

Objection six is attributed by Popham to Jackson. 'That isn't really the way teaching is: teachers rarely specify their goals in terms of measurable learner behaviours; so let's set realistic expectations of teachers.' Popham makes short work of that one. 'They ought to!' I think this response is quite unacceptable from the point of view of the designer for the following reasons.

First, there is a strong case for the close study of teachers at work on the basis that a good many of them know what they are doing. Atkin (1968, 339–340) puts it rather well.

> For the moment, let us call teaching a craft to enable the construction of an analogy, an analogy with the craft of metallurgy. For centuries, and continuing today, skilled craftsmen have been making metals. They have learned to add a little of this substance and a little of that, then heat the batch for a certain length of time until it reaches a certain colour, then let it cool at a certain rate. The craft has been continually developed through the centuries, apprentices learning from masters. Meanwhile, 'scientific' approaches to metallurgy have not succeeded in fully explaining all that the master craftsman does . . .
>
> Isn't it possible that teaching is at least as complex as metallurgy? The theories of psychologists, anthropologists and sociologists – taken singly – do not permit us to deduce an educational programme any more than a physicist's theories lead directly to fabrication of new metals. It doesn't seem unreasonable to follow the route of metallurgy.

In short, curriculum study should be grounded in the study of classrooms. Popham's cavalier assumption that the teacher must be wrong is unjustifiable because it is basically *a priori* rather than empirical. 'Rational curriculum planning must take account of the realities of classroom situations. It is not enough to be logical.' (Stenhouse 1970, 78). 'There appear to be no studies establishing an actual relationship between increased clarification of educational objectives and improved discrimination in the selection of classroom learning opportunities for students.' (Goodlad 1960, 192) This situation appears still to hold.

There is thus actually slender justification for Popham's 'ought'. Classrooms cannot be bettered except through the agency of teachers: teachers must be the critics of work in curriculum, not docile agents.

Moreoever, there is some evidence that curriculum projects have failed to influence schools where they have attempted to enforce the concept of objectives against teacher opposition. The evidence that there may be other ways of organizing one's teaching than through objectives and that some teachers may find these ways more effective needs careful attention from curriculum workers.

It is interesting that at this point Popham's paper changes style. It becomes an attack on the schools. Thus, objection seven: 'In certain subject areas, e.g. fine arts and the humanities, it is more difficult to identify measurable pupil behaviours', gets the response: 'Sure, it's tough. Yet, because it is difficult in certain subject fields to identify measurable pupil behaviours, those subject specialists should not be allowed to escape this responsibility.'

We go on (eight) to: 'While loose general statements of objectives may appear worthwhile to an outsider, if most educational goals were stated precisely, they would be revealed as generally innocuous.' To this Popham responds: 'The unfortunate truth is that much of what is going on in the schools today is indefensible.' Which leads naturally to objection nine: 'measurability implies accountability: teachers might be judged on their ability to produce results in learners rather than on the many bases now used as indices of competence' – evoking: 'Teachers might actually be judged on their ability to bring about desirable changes in learners. They should be.'

Facing the objection that objectives are difficult to generate, Popham looks forward to a time when teachers will teach shorter hours and observes:

> Perhaps we should *give* him objectives from which to choose, rather than force [sic] him to generate his own. Many of the federal dollars currently being used to support education would be better spent on agencies which would produce alternative behavioural objectives for all fields at all grade levels.

I don't think that Popham achieved his objective on shorter hours for teachers, but he made it on the objective bank.

> Tired of hearing teachers complain they were too busy to write out measurable objectives for their instruction, it seemed that we might reasonably expect them to be selectors, not generators, of precise goals. Hence, while returning from an administrators' workshop in Fresno, I decided to try to set up an operation analogous to an 'objectives bank' so that educators could draw out collections of behavioural objectives, then select those which were appropriate for their local instructional situations. The Instructional Objectives Exchange was established as a project of the U.C.L.A. Center for the Study of Evaluation later that year and is now operating as a nonprofit educational corporation. While the vast majority of the objectives currently distributed by the Exchange are behaviourally stated, there are a number of general, non-behavioural goals which are used as descriptors of large groups of more specific objectives.
>
> (Popham 1971)

Rounds six to ten of Popham's fight with his imaginary opponent are instructive. One wonders whether the referee will step in and stop the contest. It is certainly very punitive to teachers. Much of their teaching is not simply bad – it's indefensible. I believe there is a tendency, recurrent enough to suggest that it may be endemic in the approach, for academics in education to use the objectives model as a stick with which to beat teachers. 'What are your objectives?' is more often asked in a tone of challenge than one of interested and helpful inquiry. The demand for objectives is a demand for justification rather than simply description of ends. As such it is part of a political dialogue rather than an educational one. It is not about curriculum design, but rather an expression of irritation in the face of the problem of accountability in education. I believe that politicians will have to face the fact that there is no easy road to accountability via objectives. Payment by results showed that.

The final objection which Popham faces is in many ways more crucial for the evaluator than the developer, at least as it is stated. 'In evaluating the worth of instructional schemes it is often the unanticipated results which are really important, but prespecified goals may make the evaluator inattentive to the unforeseen.' Popham agrees that unanticipated results are important; 'But what can you tell the would-be curriculum evaluator about this problem? "Keep your eyes open," doesn't seem to pack the desired punch. Yet, it's about all you can say.' As I shall argue below, this reveals serious weaknesses in the objectives model. An adequate theory should be advancing our knowledge of the situation so that unanticipated results become susceptible to anticipation. You ought to be able to say much more than 'Keep your eyes open', and if the objectives model doesn't help you to do so, that is a serious weakness.

Consider the position of the curriculum designer. He is offered a model which fixes his eyes so firmly on his destination that he doesn't notice the pond in his path until he is waist deep in it. One of the examples Popham gives of unanticipated outcomes is that some new curricula in science reduced the number of students who chose science in the option system. One can understand that this possibility might be missed, but as soon as one encounters it, one recognizes its importance. For various reasons, not least conservatism, students may not like new curricula, at least at first. The curriculum designer needs a theory which helps him to anticipate such difficulties, and the objectives model does not contribute to such a theory.

Eisner, who is recognized by Popham (1971) as one of the most influential critics of the behavioural objectives model, has attempted a reformulation, which involves drawing a distinction between instructional and expressive objectives. Although I do not think it meets the criticism just outlined, it may help us on our way towards an answer.

In 1967 Eisner published a paper, 'Educational Objectives: Help or Hindrance?', whose argument he summarizes as follows:

> I have argued in this paper that curriculum theory as it pertains to educational objectives has had four significant limitations. First, it has not sufficiently emphasized the extent to which the prediction of educational outcomes cannot be made with accuracy. Second, it has not discussed the ways in which subject matter affects precision in stating educational objectives. Third, it has confused the use of educational objectives as a standard of measurement when in some areas it can be used only as a criterion for judgement. Fourth, it has not distinguished between the logical requirement of relating means to ends in the curriculum as a product and the psychological conditions useful for constructing curriculums.
>
> (1967b, 258–259)

In a later paper (1969) Eisner goes on to distinguish between two concerns of education, that of giving mastery of the cultural tools already available and that of making possible creative responses which go beyond what is available and help to develop it and individualize it. On this basis he distinguishes *instructional objectives*, suitable to the first purpose, and *expressive objectives*, suitable to the second.

Instructional objectives are essentially the same as behavioural objectives.

> The effective curriculum, when it is aimed at instructional objectives, will develop forms of behaviour whose characteristics are known beforehand and, as likely as not, will be common across students – if not at the identical point in time, at some point during the school programme.
>
> (15)
>
> Expressive objectives differ considerably from instructional objectives. An expressive objective does not specify the behaviour the student is to acquire after having engaged in one or more learning activities. An expressive objective describes an educational encounter: it identifies a situation in which children are to work, a problem with which they are to cope, a task in which they are to engage; but it does not specify what from that encounter, situation, problem or task they are to learn. An expressive objective provides both the teacher and the student with an invitation to explore, defer, or focus on issues that are of peculiar interest or import to the inquirer. An expressive objective is evocative rather than prescriptive.
>
> The expressive objective is intended to serve as a theme around which

skills and understandings learned earlier can be brought to bear, but through which those skills and understandings can be expanded, elaborated and made idiosyncratic. With an expressive objective what is desired is not homogeneity of response among students but diversity. In the expressive context the teacher hopes to provide a situation in which meanings become personalized and in which children produce products, both theoretical and qualitative, that are as diverse as themselves. Consequently, the evaluative task in this situation is not one of applying a common standard to the products produced but one of reflecting upon what has been produced in order to reveal its uniqueness and significance. In the expressive context, the product is likely to be as much of a surprise to the maker as it is for the teacher who encounters it.

Statements of expressive objectives might read:

1. To interpret the meaning of *Paradise Lost.*
2. To examine and appraise the significance of *The Old Man and the Sea.*
3. To develop a three-dimensional form through the use of wire and wood.
4. To visit the zoo and discuss what was of interest there.

What should be noted about such objectives is that they do not specify what the student is to be able to do after he engages in an educational activity; rather they identify the type of encounter he is to have. From this encounter both teacher and student acquire data useful for evaluation. In this context the mode of evaluation is similar to aesthetic criticism; that is, the critic appraises a product, examines its qualities and import, but does not direct the artist toward the painting of a specific type of picture. The critic's subject-matter is the work done – he does not prescribe a blueprint of its construction.

(Eisner 1969, 15–16)

I believe that Eisner has grasped fundamental points here, but that he has made two errors which have prevented him from driving them home. In the first place, he has continued to use the term *objectives* in his expressive mode. This has both burdened him with an unwelcome inheritance of assumptions and prevented a fresh analysis of what is at stake. And secondly, as is perhaps natural in one who found the objectives model intractable in the context of his own project in visual arts, he has identified the creative-expressive mode too closely with the arts.

In the remainder of this chapter I shall attempt to set out what I regard as the fundamental objections to the universal application of the objectives model, and to distinguish the areas in which I believe it will often serve us reasonably well. These objections are:

1. That it mistakes the nature of knowledge.
2. That it mistakes the nature of the process of improving practice.

I want to distinguish several functions of the school. I draw the distinctions for the purpose of analysis, recognizing that the functions are interwoven in practice; and I acknowledge some problems in the use of terms – I have done my best to minimize the arbitrariness of my choice.

Education as we know it in schools comprises and necessarily comprises at least four different processes. I shall call these: *training*, *instruction*, *initiation*, and *induction*. Training is concerned with the acquisition of skills, and successful training results in capacity in performance. Examples are making a canoe, speaking a foreign language, typing, baking a cake and handling laboratory apparatus. Instruction is concerned with the learning of information and successful instruction results in retention. Examples are retention of the table of chemical elements, of dates in history, of the names of the countries of Europe, of German irregular verbs and of the recipe for making pastry. Initiation is concerned with familiarization with social values and norms and successful initiation leads to a capacity to interpret the social environment and to anticpate the reaction to one's own actions. Induction stands for introduction into the thought systems – the knowledge – of the culture and successful induction results in understanding as evidenced by the capacity to grasp and to make for oneself relationships and judgements. These terms generally conform to at least one common usage except perhaps for the last. For 'induction' many people would substitute 'education', as it is sometimes used in contrast with training.

Initiation takes place as a by-product of living in a community. Some schools, such as English public schools, promote particular social norms and values consciously and often rather successfully. In so far as they operate in the light of an ideal of man, in the sort of tradition represented by Castiglione's *Book of the Courtier*, they could express their purposes in terms of objectives. In most schools initiation is part of the hidden curriculum, often with a surface myth. They may have an intention, but it is extremely difficult to achieve a congruence between the socialization which pupils in fact undergo and the intentions of the school: there are influential reference points outside the school, in the community and in the peer group.

I am concerned here mainly with training, instruction and induction.

In the case of training, the objectives model gives reasonably good fit, and this is reflected in its successful use in training in the armed forces and in industry where objectives are precise. The aim is performance, that is, behaviour, and this is naturally expressed in terms of behavioural objectives. There is a limitation when style is important, but it is often a marginal one. However, while at the elementary stages, training in playing a musical instrument is easily assimilated to the objectives model, in a master class it is problematic, since it becomes important to evoke personal interpretation, that is, we are more concerned with the musical criteria for the use of skill than with skill in a straightforward sense.

Again, in instruction the objectives model is appropriate. Five verbs by Thursday! Retention can readily be tested behaviourally and at different levels, for example, recall and recognition.

However, it is important to bear in mind that skills and information are often learned in a context of knowledge, which is, in one of its aspects, an organization of skills and information. I have given as examples handling laboratory equipment and retaining the table of chemical elements. Many would argue that the skills and information learned in knowledge contexts are among the most important and further that in knowledge areas skills and information should be subordinate or instrumental. This could either mean that they are picked up incidentally or that training or instruction is offered when the learner sees a need for it. In the first case, it is difficult to use the objectives model. In the second case, the objectives model fits well, but describes only a subordinate unit within the curriculum which plays a service role. Examples might be Latin for mediaeval historians, statistics for social scientists or prosody for students of literature.

The great problem in applying the objectives model lies in the area of induction into knowledge.

At this point, it is worth returning to a criticism of the objectives model which we have already encountered. Popham, you will remember, cites as a criticism: 'It is somehow undemocratic to plan in advance precisely how the learner should behave after instruction.'

Kliebard (1968, 246), among many others, puts this view strongly:

> . . . from a moral point of view, the emphasis on behavioural goals, despite all of the protestations to the contrary, still borders on brainwashing or at least indoctrination rather than education. We begin with some notion of how we want a person to behave and then we try to manipulate him and his environment so as to get him to behave as we want him to.

Certainly, much of the literature of behavioural objectives does reflect a concern for the achievement of socially approved goals, and this might be seen as a threat to democracy. But the point seems to be wrongly taken. It seems to assume that we are free and there is a threat that education will chain us. But in fact our freedom is limited. By standards as near to absolute as we can conceive, men are relatively predictable, limited and uncreative. It is the business of education to make us freer and more creative.

Education enhances the freedom of man by inducting him into the knowledge of his culture as a thinking system. The most important characteristic of the knowledge mode is that one can think with it. This is in the nature of knowledge – as distinct from information – that it is a structure to sustain creative thought and provide frameworks for judgement.

Education as induction into knowledge is successful to the extent that it makes the behavioural outcomes of the students unpredictable.

Consider the marking of history essays. The examination marker has a large number which he must monitor.

As he reads them he often becomes aware that there is a depressing similarity about them. This is because the majority of teachers have been working to a behavioural objective – to produce just such an essay. They don't talk about objectives because they feel they are rather disreputable, but they are using them. From the pile of essays a few leap out at the marker as original, surprising, showing evidence of individual thinking. These, the unpredictable, are the successes. In the university setting, they are the ones who get the firsts.

In any area of knowledge or art the most important product in terms of student performance is the essay – in the broadest sense of that word, that is, a trial piece or endeavour. An essay in this sense would mean not merely a written piece, but also an oral performance or a painting or the playing of a piece of music or designing and making a standard lamp. It is in such efforts that a student tests his powers. They must be criticized, cannot be ignored, and the criticism of them is a much more important evaluation than that derived from an objective test.

An essay should be individual and creative and not an attempt to meet a prespecification. It takes account of the indeterminacy in knowledge which arises because the structures of knowledge are not mere classification and retrieval systems but constitute a raw material for thinking.

The evaluative response to an essay involves the teacher in a claim to make judgements of quality about student work, guided by his understanding of the nature of his subject. An essay is not right or wrong. It is to be judged qualitatively in the light of criteria appropriate in its field.

Now of course this implies that the evaluation of an essay is not objective, and indeed it is an index of the quality of a teacher that he is capable of thoughtful and productive evaluation which helps the student to improve his work. This sets problems in public examining, but there is no escape from them. The quality of a teacher is inseparable from the quality of his judgement of students' work.

In addition to formalizing and thereby weakening standards of quality, the objectives approach also tends to make knowledge instrumental. Literary skills are to be justified as helping us to read *Hamlet*. *Hamlet* must not be justified as a training ground for literary skills. We know only too well how easy it is to turn intrinsically worthwhile content into a mere exercise. We must be careful that we do not allow 'the use of methods to distort content in order to meet objectives'. (Stenhouse 1970, 76)

Knowledge is primarily concerned with synthesis. The analytic approach implied in the objectives model readily trivializes it.

Basically, the objectives approach is an attempt to improve practice by increasing clarity about ends. Even if it were logically justifiable in terms of knowledge – and it is not – there is a good case for claiming that it is not the way to improve practice. We do not teach people to jump higher by setting the bar higher, but by enabling them to criticize their present performance. It is process criteria which help the teacher to better his teaching.

In curriculum development on the large scale the use of objectives laid down from the centre is a kind of teacher proofing. The curriculum is to tend in the same direction whatever the knowledge and talents of the individual teacher and indeed of the individual student.

But there can be no educational development without teacher development; and the best means of development is not by clarifying ends but by criticizing practice. There are criteria by which one can criticize and improve the process of education without reference to an end–means model which sets an arbitrary horizon to one's efforts. The improvement of practice rests on diagnosis, not prognosis. It is not by concentrating on the analysis of health that we cure our ills.

7
A PROCESS MODEL

It is idle to criticize the objectives model as a strategy for the design and development of curriculum if no orderly alternative can be found. In this chapter I shall attempt to explore the possibilities offered by a strategy of curriculum design which attempts to arrive at a useful specification of curriculum and the educational process without starting by pre-specifying the anticipated outcomes of that process in the form of objectives.

The issue is: can curriculum and pedagogy be organized satisfactorily by a logic other than that of the means–end model? Can the demands of a curriculum specification as I set them out in Chapter 1 (page 5) be met without using the concepts of objectives?

First I must ask, can there be principles for the selection of content other than the principle that it should contribute to the achievement of an objective? There seems no doubt that there can. Peters (1966) argues cogently for the intrinsic justification of content. He starts from the position that education 'implies the transmission of what is worthwhile to those who become committed to it' and that it 'must involve knowledge and understanding and some kind of cognitive perspective, which are not inert'. (45) Believing that education involves taking part in worthwhile activities, Peters argues that such activities have their own built-in standards of excellence, and thus 'can be appraised because of the standards immanent in them rather than because of what they lead on to'. (155) They can be argued to be worthwhile in themselves rather than as means towards objectives.

In Peters's view the most important examples of activities of this kind are the arts and the forms of knowledge.

> Curriculum activities . . . such as science, history, literary appreciation, and poetry are 'serious' in that they illuminate other areas of life and contribute much to the quality of living. They have, secondly, a wide-ranging cognitive content which distinguishes them from games. Skills, for instance, do not have a wide-ranging cognitive content. There is very little to know about riding bicycles, swimming, or golf. It is largely a matter of 'knowing how' rather than of 'knowing that', of knack rather

than of understanding. Furthermore what there is to know throws very little light on much else. In history, science, or literature, on the other hand, there is an immense amount to know, and if it is properly assimilated, it constantly throws light on, widens, and deepens one's view of countless other things.

(Peters 1966, 159)

I have already argued that skills are probably susceptible to treatment through the objectives model, which encounters its greatest problems in areas of knowledge. Peters is claiming that these areas of knowledge are essential parts of the curriculum and that they can be justified intrinsically rather than as means to ends. They can be selected as content on grounds other than the scrutiny of their specific outcomes in terms of student behaviours.

It is interesting that Peters moved later – and I think wrongly – from education as initiation into knowledge to the notion of the educated man, thereby letting objectives in again, as any founding of education on an ideal of man, rather than of knowledge, must do.

Within knowledge and arts areas, it is possible to select content for a curriculum unit without reference to student behaviours or indeed to ends of any kind other than that of representing the form of knowledge in the curriculum. This is because a form of knowledge has structure, and it involves procedures, concepts and criteria. Content can be selected to exemplify the most important procedures, the key concepts and the areas and situations in which the criteria hold.

Now it might be thought that this is to designate procedures, concepts and criteria as objectives to be learned by the students. This strategy could, of course, be followed, but it would, I believe, distort the curriculum. For the key procedures, concepts and criteria in any subject – *cause*, *form*, *experiment*, *tragedy* – are, and are important precisely because they are, problematic within the subject. They are the focus of speculation, not the object of mastery. Educationally, they are also important because they invite understanding at a variety of levels. The infant class considering the origins of a playground fight and the historian considering the origins of the First World War are essentially engaged in the same sort of task. They are attempting to understand by using the concepts of causation; and they are attempting to understand both the event and the concept by which they seek to explicate it.

It is the building of curriculum on such structures as procedures, concepts and criteria, which cannot adequately be translated into the performance levels of objectives, that makes possible Bruner's 'courteous translation' of knowledge and allows of learning which challenges all abilities and interests in a diverse group. (See Raths' point 5, page 87)

The translation of the deep structures of knowledge into behavioural objectives is one of the principal causes of the distortion of knowledge in schools noted by Young (1971), Bernstein (1971) and Esland (1971). The filtering of knowledge through an analysis of objectives gives the school an authority and power over its students by setting arbitrary limits to speculation and by defining arbitrary solutions to unresolved problems of knowledge. This translates the teacher from the role of the student of a complex field of knowledge to the role of the master of the school's agreed version of that field.

What is the nature of historical causation? Can the concept of causation be used successfully to understand complex situations? How might one attack the origins of the First World War by using the concept, and how successfully? These are the kinds of question raised by adopting *cause* as a key concept in history. There is no generally acceptable and pre-specifiable answer to them. The use of the objectives model has led to the provision of arbitrary answers in the form of specifications of the causes of the First World War which can be tested and marked and this necessarily distorts the knowledge included in the curriculum.

It is quite possible to evolve principles for the selection of content in the curriculum in terms of criteria which are not dependent on the existence of a specification of objectives, and which are sufficiently specific to give real guidance and to expose the principles to criticism. Raths (1971) offered an interesting list of criteria 'for identifying activities that seem to have some inherent worth'. (716) For the purpose of the present argument it is not necessary that his criteria be accepted. What is at issue is whether we find them meaningful and accessible to our judgement, and whether we can produce counter-proposals in a similar form when we disagree with Raths.
Here is the list:

1. All other things being equal, one activity is more worthwhile than another if it permits children to make informed choices in carrying out the activity and to reflect on the consequences of their choices.
2. All other things being equal, one activity is more worthwhile than another if it assigns to students active roles in the learning situation rather than passive ones.
3. All other things being equal, one activity is more worthwhile than another if it asks students to engage in inquiry into ideas, applications of intellectual processes, or current problems, either personal or social.
4. All other things being equal, one activity is more worthwhile than

another if it involves children with realia (i.e. real objects, materials and artefacts).
5. All other things being equal, one activity is more worthwhile than another if completion of the activity may be accomplished successfully by children at several different levels of ability.
6. All other things being equal, one activity is more worthwhile than another if it asks students to examine *in a new setting* an idea, an application of an intellectual process, or a current problem which has been *previously studied.*
7. All other things being equal, one activity is more worthwhile than another if it requires students to examine topics or issues that citizens in our society do not normally examine – and that are typically ignored by the major communication media in the nation.
8. All other things being equal, one activity is more worthwhile than another if it involves students and faculty members in 'risk' taking – not a risk of life or limb, but a risk of success or failure.
9. All other things being equal, one activity is more worthwhile than another if it requires students to rewrite, rehearse, and polish their initial efforts.
10. All other things being equal, one activity is more worthwhile than another if it involves students in the application and mastery of meaningful rules, standards, or disciplines.
11. All other things being equal, one activity is more worthwhile than another if it gives students a chance to share the planning, the carrying out of a plan, or the results of an activity with others.
12. All other things being equal, one activity is more worthwhile than another if it is relevant to the expressed purposes of the students.

These criteria are less explicity related to epistemology than those I discussed earlier in the chapter, but numbers 1, 3, 5, 6, 8 and 10 provide a link in that it is argued that the arts and forms of knowledge are characterized in part by the fact that they meet such criteria. Others of Raths' criteria are linked to propositions regarding the ethics of education or the principles of pedagogy.

This is an important point. The formulation of a schedule of behavioural objectives helps us little towards the means of attaining them. The analysis of the criteria for worthwhile activities and of the structure of the activities deemed to be worthwhile appears to point much more clearly to principles of procedure in teaching.

Peters (1959) drew a clear distinction between aims and principles of procedure.

> To illustrate more clearly the distinction which I am drawing between 'aims' and 'principles of procedure', let me take a parallel from politics. A man who believes in equality, might, like Godwin, be lured by a

positive picture of a society in which differences between people would be minimised. He might want to get rid of differences in wealth and rank, even to breed people in the attempt to iron out innate differences. He might even go so far as to advocate the abolition of institutions like the army or the Church in which some men were given opportunities of lording it over others. Another social reformer, however, might employ the principle of equality in a much more negative sense without any concrete picture to lure him on his journey. He might insist, merely, that whatever social changes were introduced, no one should be treated differently from anyone else unless a good reason could be produced to justify such unequal treatment. The Godwin type of man would rightly be regarded as pursuing equality as a very general aim; the more cautious liberal would have no particular aim connected with equality. He would merely insist that whatever schemes were put forward must not be introduced in a way which would infringe his procedural principle.

I think this is an illuminating parallel to the point I am trying to make about the aims of education. For, in my view, most disputes about the aims of education are disputes about principles of procedure rather than about 'aims' in the sense of objectives to be arrived at by taking appropriate means. The so-called 'aims' are ways of referring to the different valuations which are built into the different procedures like training, conditioning, the use of authority, teaching by example and rational explanation, all of which fall under the general concept of 'education'.

(Peters 1959, 89–90)

I find Peters's concept of 'principles of procedure' a helpful one, though his use of it here strikes me as a little odd. His 'more negative sense' seems to imply that principles of procedure are constraints upon the way in which aims are pursued, whereas the adoption of such an aim as induction into a field of knowledge – an aim apparently congenial to Peters – seems to give a basis for positive principles of procedure derived from the aim itself.

It does seem to be true, however, that principles of procedure are often most easily formulated negatively, even when they derive from such an aim. It is more difficult to define what the pursuit of a particular field of knowledge comprises in principle than what it excludes in principle. This is because the principles which obtain for knowledge within a field are problematic within that field. It is part of the nature of knowledge that such principles should always be in some sense provisional and open to debate. Consensus is thus more easily achieved in excluding certain procedures as invalid than in discriminating among those which have claims to validity.

The way in which principles of procedure struggle to separate the valid from the invalid is well exemplified in an attempt by Griffin

(1942, reported in Metcalf 1963) to advance principles for the teaching of history in the light of Dewey's reflective theory of teaching (Dewey 1933): 'Reflective thought is the active, careful and persistent examination of any belief, or purported form of knowledge, in the light of the grounds that support it and the further conclusions toward which it tends.' (Metcalf 1963, 934) Griffin attempted to justify the development of reflective thinking on the grounds of the democratic ethic, and one can see clearly how he works towards his positive principles through the exclusion of non-democratic alternatives and how his positive proposals are more controversial than his exclusions.

> Democracies also need order, stability, unity, purpose, and continuity. For them the solution cannot take the form of instilling specific beliefs in all children. Democracies cannot justify the suppression of knowledge, and if they consider doubt to be the beginning of all knowledge, they must positively encourage occasions for doubt. A reliance upon knowledge rather than hallowed belief, becomes the central, all-embracing value.
>
> All culture patterns, democratic or authoritarian, have central and directing values. Democracy is not so much concerned with the specific character of the directing values as with the way in which central values are maintained and modified.
>
> The earliest beliefs of children are not and cannot be acquired reflectively, although some writers have urged that they can be. Early beliefs are taken on uncritically and are often the consequence of conditioning or animal preference. The uncritical acquisition of early beliefs takes place in all societies, democratic or authoritarian, and a child need be no more ashamed of those beliefs than he is of his ancestry. Both are beyond his capacity to choose.
>
> The development of children into adults who can steadily modify their beliefs in terms of their adequacy for explaining a widening range of experience requires two things: (1) improving and refining the reflective capacities of children, and (2) breaking through the hard shell of tradition which encases many deeply rooted and emotionally charged beliefs.
>
> (Metcalf 1963, 934–935)

The principles are reached by the exclusion of other possible positions, and they are more contentious when they emerge than the exclusive steps taken to arrive at them. Metcalf is arguing that history should be the means by which children criticize rather than accept the traditions and values handed on to them.

I believe I have cited enough evidence to support the view that sections A and C of the specificational requirements of a curriculum which I set up in Chapter 1 (page 5) can be met without the use of objectives. But the points I have made are at a high level of generality. Can one in fact plan a curriculum on the basis of principles of procedure? Will a process model work in practice?

In arguing for the use of behavioural objectives in curriculum design, Tyler (1949) mentioned and dismissed two other possibilities. I now want to take those up.

The first was that we might specify what the teacher is to do. And you will remember that he argues (see page 53) that if an objective is stated in the form of activities to be carried on by the teacher, there is no way of judging whether these activities are justifiable, since they are not the ultimate purpose of education. These ultimate purposes are, he avers, changes in the students. And they need to be prespecified, spelled out in advance. We have noted the shortcomings of an ends–means model in education, and looked towards the specification of principles of procedure which refer to teacher activity.

The second possibility which Tyler dismissed was that one might specify the content to be dealt with. This too he regards as unsatisfactory as it does not tell us what the students are to do with the content. I have argued that where a form of knowledge exists, a specification of content does imply how it is to be handled.

I now want to consider by reference to practical cases whether we can reasonably set about curriculum design by attempting to define the classroom process in terms of what the teacher is to do at the level of principles and what the content is. In such a case our statement about a curriculum would be an answer to the question: how is the teacher to handle what? I shall of course have to consider this approach in relation to changes in the students.

I propose to examine two curricula, *Man: A Course of Study* and the Humanities Curriculum Project, both of which are designed on a basis other than that of behavioural objectives.

Man: A Course of Study is an American social science curriculum mainly for the 10–12 year-old age range. It is film-based and is rich in materials. It was directed by Peter Dow with Jerome Bruner as chief consulting scholar, and the force of Bruner's ideas was powerful throughout the process of development.

A brief specification of the content of the course does not reach the heart of it. It consists of a rather detailed study of the Pacific salmon, the herring gull, the baboon and the Netsilik eskimo with a running comparison with the students' own society and experience. The method is comparative, and the curriculum is based in the behavioural sciences and anthropolgoy.

Bruner writes:

> The content of the course is man: his nature as a species, the forces that shaped and continue to shape his humanity. Three questions recur throughout:
>
> What is human about human beings?
> How did they get that way?
> How can they be made more so?
>
> (Bruner 1966, 74)

The ambiguities in these questions and the shift to a value implication in the last one (where strictly speaking 'humane' might be more appropriate than 'human') are intended. They invite teacher and students to speculate about humanness in the broadest sense as they study the materials of the course.

A good deal more than this could be said about content, but that is enough for the present purpose. The content is speculation about humanness through a study of behavioural science in a context of value questions. The teacher then is asked to be, for the purpose of the course, a speculative behavioural and social scientist alive to the value issues raised by his work.

Bruner notes the problem which immediately hits the teacher when he is confronted with such a demand:

> The first and most obvious problem is how to construct curricula that can be taught by ordinary teachers to ordinary students and that at the same time reflect clearly the basic or underlying principles of various fields of inquiry.

He notes the need for powerful and intelligent materials and for adjustment to students of different abilities. He discusses in detail the demands on the teacher implicit in the position he takes.

Either the teacher must be an expert or he must be a learner along with his students. In most cases, the teacher cannot in the nature of the case be an expert. It follows that he must cast himself in the role of a learner. Pedagogically this may in fact be a preferable role to that of the expert. It implies teaching by discovery or inquiry methods rather than by instruction.

The teacher is not free to cast himself in the role of the learner without regard to the learning of his students for which he must accept responsibility. What is required of him to make him a senior learner capable of offering something of worth to the junior learners with whom he works? Skills in finding things out, of course. But more than that: some hold on, and a continual refinement of, a philosophical understanding of the subject he is teaching and learning, of its deep structures and their rationale. The teacher needs to take on to his agenda a desire to understand the nature of social science, the value problems it raises and its relation to the questions at the centre of the course. Only when he has gone some way towards structuring his own understanding of these issues can he adopt the pedagogy of the course.

The principles behind this pedagogy have been expressed as pedagogical aims:

1. To initiate and develop in youngsters a process of question-posing (the inquiry method);
2. To teach a research methodology where children can look for information to answer questions they have raised and use the framework developed in the course (e.g. the concept of the life cycle) and apply it to new areas;
3. To help youngsters develop the ability to use a variety of first-hand sources as evidence from which to develop hypotheses and draw conclusions;
4. To conduct classroom discussions in which youngsters learn to listen to others as well as to express their own views;
5. To legitimize the search; that is, to give sanction and support to open-ended discussions where definitive answers to many questions are not found;
6. To encourage children to reflect on their own experiences;
7. To create a new role for the teacher, in which he becomes a resource rather than an authority.

(Hanley, Whitla, Moo, Walter 1970, 5)

And the authors comment: 'It is clear that these goals centre around the process of learning, rather than around the product.' They are in fact principles of procedure, and they are spelled out more fully in the course materials, and particularly in the teachers' handbook on *Evaluation Strategies*.

Let us take stock. *Man: A Course of Study* is a curriculum designed on a specification of content – objects of study and some master concepts and the point of view of social science – and a specification of what the teacher is to do expressed in terms of principles of procedure. It is not designed on a pre-specification of behavioural objectives. Of course there are changes in students as a result of the course, but many of the most valued are not to be anticipated in detail. The power and the possibilities of the curriculum cannot be contained within objectives because it is founded on the idea that knowledge must be speculative and thus indeterminate as to student outcomes if it is to be worthwhile. And it is a practical and orderly course in use in a large number of schools.

Man: A Course of Study sustains coherence within a process model partly at least because of its reliance on the structures of knowledge. It is often argued that education should be founded on the disciplines of knowledge because they provide a framework of criteria and principles of procedure and a means of justifying these. I believe that if the advantages of this framework are to be gained, a process model should be used rather than an objectives model.

Does this mean that the process model implies the disciplines of knowledge as a framework? Are they the only source of process criteria?

In its experimental design the Humanities Project is an attempt to explore this problem. The content selected, controversial human issues, has in common with knowledge in the disciplines a necessary indeterminacy of student outcomes, but there is no disciplinary structure.

The argument runs thus. Controversial issues are defined empirically as issues which do *in fact* divide people in our society. Given divergence among students, parents and teachers, democratic principles are evoked to suggest that teachers may wish to ensure that they do not use their position of authority in the classroom to advance their own opinions or perspectives, and that the teaching process does not determine the outcome opinions and perspectives of the students. It is important that there is no epistemological base to this argument. The position is that, given a dispute in society about the truth of a matter, the teacher in a compulsory state school might wish to teach the dispute rather than the truth as he knows it. A similar position could be taken on different grounds in almost any area of knowledge.

However, without the support of a discipline of knowledge as a base – though disciplined knowledge is an ingredient – it proved possible to operate a design on the process model.

The Humanities Curriculum Project (1970, Stenhouse 1971a, 1971b) concentrated its research on the technical problems of operating a discussion-based form of teaching in which the group critically examined evidence as it discussed issues under the chairmanship of a teacher who submitted his work to the criterion of neutrality.

The pedagogical (as opposed to the research) aim of the Project is to develop an understanding of social situations and human acts and of the controversial value issues which they raise. (Retrospectively, I think it would have been better to delete 'value', since as it stands the aim may appear to imply that the only controversial issues are value issues or even that value issues are necessarily controversial.)

Two implications of this aim are worth pointing out. First, it is implied that both students and teachers develop understanding, that is, the teacher is cast in the role of a learner. Second, understanding is chosen as an aim because it cannot be achieved. Understanding can always be deepened. Moreover, there must always be dispute as to what constitutes a valid understanding. The teacher and the group have to accept as part of their task an exploration of the nature of understanding.

The hypotheses and suggestions offered to teachers by the Project were largely based on the observation of classrooms and had two principal logics. One logic was that of group dynamics. For example, the arrangement of chairs may be important for encouraging discussion across the group, and slow-paced discussions may broaden participation. Such hypotheses are virtually independent of content. Other hypotheses about procedure, however, are content-linked. For example, understanding of controversy is better achieved by listening to a range of views carefully and using questions to elicit amplification rather than by arguing against opponents and attempting to resolve divergence.

In the Humanities Project we were hammering out in collaboration with teachers a procedural discipline like that of 'procedure at meetings' or parliamentary procedure with the important distinction that we were concerned not with a decision-making group, but with a learning group aiming to develop understanding. And the very existence of such forms as procedures at meetings, the mediaeval disputation and indeed the epic or the novel, should indicate that such procedures can have logical structures which are not dependent on epistemological structures. Controversiality is a particularly interesting theme in this respect, since it contains a paradox. Since the controversy involves (for all but the relativist) competing claims to truth, it implies the notion of some non-controversial standard of truth to which appeal is being made.

The process model of curriculum development raises problems for the assessment of student work. They may be difficult in practice, but they are not difficult to understand. The objectives model is closely related to the American movement towards examination reform. Discontent was felt at the subjectivity of marking and there was a pressure towards objective tests, the criteria for which were supplied by statements of objectives.

Now, of course, compromises could be made between the objectives and the process models in practice, but in its logically pure form I think that the process model implies that in assessment or appraisal

the teacher ought to be a critic, not a marker. The worthwhile activity in which teacher and students are engaged has standards and criteria immanent in it and the task of appraisal is that of improving students' capacity to work to such criteria by critical reaction to work done. In this sense assessment is about the teaching of self-assessment.

Such assessment is not purely subjective since it appeals to public criteria, but it is concerned with difficult judgements and hence performance will vary from teacher to teacher. Critical assessment of work is an activity which exposes the strengths and weaknesses of teachers very clearly. This presents problems. If I as a student trust my teacher's judgement, I want criticism rather than marking. If I do not trust his judgement, I want marking rather than criticism. In the classroom there is no way of compensating me for the loss I suffer in working with a teacher whose judgement I do not trust. But I do want to be protected when it comes to public examination.

There is a conflict of demand between appraisal as teaching and appraisal as grading. In appraisal as teaching, the differing abilities and strengths of teachers are acceptable. That is why a singer may choose to be taught by several teachers in succession. The capacity of the limited teacher to limit us is the price we pay for the capacity of the profound teacher to extend us. But since grading counts for so much, we want to be assured that the limitations of our teachers do not seriously penalize us in examinations. The more objective an examination, the more it fails to reveal the quality of good teaching and good learning. By objective tests Michelangelo and Russell Flint both get distinctions, yet it is the difference of quality between them that is of fundamental importance in art.

The process model is essentially a critical model, not a marking model. It can never be *directed* towards an examination *as an objective* without loss of quality, since the standards of the examination then override the standards immanent in the subject. This does not mean that students taught on the process model cannot be examined, but it does mean that the examination must be taken in their stride as they pursue other aspirations. And if the examination is a by-product there is an implication that the quality the student shows in it must be an under-estimate of his real quality. It is hence rather difficult to get the weak student through an examination using a process model. Crammers cannot use it, since it depends upon commitment to educational aims.

Unfortunately, examinations are so important in our society that most teachers, faced as they often are with choosing between education and opportunity for a substantial proportion of their pupils, opt for the latter. Their aim is to get their pupils through examinations they do not deserve to pass. And it is quite possible to get 'O' or 'A' level passes in chemistry or history or literature (not to mention a respectable degree) without really understanding the subject in the sense of grasping its deep structures and the concerns of scholars in it. The process-based curriculum pursues understanding rather than grades when the two conflict, and since grades are attainable without understanding, this penalizes the limited student in terms of opportunity even though it is educationally advantageous to him.

This tension between educating and examining is, of course, at the centre of most teaching from the third year of the secondary school onwards. Conflicts have to be resolved by compromises. The quality after which the process-based curriculum reaches is to some extent sacrificed by the acceptance of the public examination as a legitimate social objective, though it is recognized as an arbitrary educational goal.

It may be that process models are of great importance in areas of the curriculum where understanding and criteria are central, precisely because such models counteract the pressure of the examination as an objective and deny that knowledge can be defined by the examination.

The major weakness of the process model of curriculum design will by now have become apparent. It rests upon the quality of the teacher. This is also its greatest strength.

The process model is committed to teacher development. If teachers are to pursue understanding, develop and refine their criteria of judgement and their range in their subject, they must be able and they must have time and opportunity for professional development. The conditions of teaching at present too often make survival a more urgent concern than scholarship. And more research and development is needed to forge teaching procedures which embody survival techniques compatible with the personal and intellectual development of both pupils and teachers.

The objectives model applied to knowledge areas seems to me to concentrate on improving teaching as instruction without increment to the wisdom or scholarship of the teacher. It is, as the designers of payment by results believed, a way of increasing standards of formal attainment in restricted areas while accepting the limitations of the teaching force. It is a means of bettering students' performance without improving teachers' personal and professional quality.

Any process model rests on teacher judgement rather than on teacher direction. It is far more demanding on teachers and thus far more difficult to implement in practice, but it offers a higher degree of personal and professional development. In particular circumstances it may well prove too demanding.

In this chapter I have considered the process model of curriculum design and development, arguing that, largely on logical grounds, it is more appropriate than the objectives model in the areas of the curriculum which centre on knowledge and understanding. The objectives model appears more suitable in curricular areas which emphasize information and skills.

Much of the advocacy of the objectives model has, however, come not from those who are engaged in curriculum design and development, but from those concerned with curriculum evaluation. Their problems will be considered in the next chapter.

8

THE EVALUATION OF CURRICULUM

I have argued in the last chapter that from the developer's point of view it is possible to make a systematic and orderly approach to curriculum innovation without using the objectives model. It is, of course, open to the developer to use the objectives model if it appears to suit his needs. My point is simply that promising alternatives do appear to exist.

However, much of the pressure on the developer to use the objectives model has been based on the premise that it is necessary to adopt it in order to make evaluation possible. In this chapter I shall review the field of evaluation. Are there alternatives to the objectives model when the problem of curriculum innovation is seen from the point of view of the evaluator?

Let me begin by picking up a phrase I have just used – 'the field of evaluation'. Is there a field of evaluation?

Now the answer is, I think, that there is a highly developed specialist area of evaluation in educational research in the United States and in Sweden, but only the beginnings of such a development in Britain. Any review of the state of the art is bound to depend heavily on American or Swedish work; and the differing conditions of education in these countries needs to be taken into account if we are to apply their work to our situation.

Cronbach (1963), 673) distinguishes three types of decisions for which evaluation is used:

1. Course improvement: deciding what instructional material and methods are satisfactory and where change is needed.
2. Decisions about individuals: identifying the needs of the pupil for the sake of planning his instruction, judging pupil merit for the purposes of selection and grouping, acquainting the pupil with his own progress and deficiencies.
3. Administrative regulation: judging how good the school system is, how good individual teachers are, etc.

We are here mainly – though not exclusively – concerned with the first of these. But the second reminds us that in the United States evaluation has been closely associated with the tradition of mental measurement. And the third reminds us that in the United States, and indeed in Sweden, the administrative sphere is seen differently from the way it has traditionally been seen in Britain. Within the British system decisions in all these three areas are traditionally seen as falling within the province of the teacher and the school. This is much less so in both the United States and Sweden.

In the United States, curricula are subject to state adoption, or at least to school board adoption. This means that explicit decisions about the worth of curricula have to be made at an administrative level outside the school by supervisors who see themselves, much more explicitly than do the personnel of British local authorities, as in positions of educational leadership. So curricular decisions in the United States are more focused on the question of what curricula to recommend others to use, less on what curriculum to use oneself, than they are in Britain. The contrast is of course not so sharp as it sounds here.

In Sweden the curriculum is centralized. The Swedish Ministry of Education has the task of making curricular decisions for the whole school system.

Now both these situations seem to me to have the effect of making a curricular decision more important than I would conceive it to be. It is at least arguable that curriculum is not in any direct way the major variable in the school's situation; but it is more difficult to argue that in the United States or Sweden. And further, since a curriculum which is widely recommended requires to be justified, there is a pressure to make much more ambitious claims in the United States and Sweden. I probably exaggerate the difference, being on the extreme teacher-centred wing in this country. But certainly, while it seems just possible here to recommend a curriculum as having interesting potential, in the United States and Sweden there is a real pressure to make stronger claims. And this is the context of evaluation.

Within this context, the question posed by the evaluator who uses the objectives model is a straightforward one: 'What one really wants to know about a given curriculum is whether it works.' (Gagné 1967, 29) In order to answer this question it is important to be clear about what a curriculum is trying to do. Clarity is to be achieved by demanding that the developer of a curriculum state the aims of the curriculum in terms of behavioural objectives, each of which 'must describe an observable *behaviour* of the learner or a *product* which is a consequence of learner behaviour'. (Popham 1969, 35) 'Evaluation is concerned with securing evidence on the attainment of specific objectives of instruction.'* (Bloom 1970, 28)

This approach to evaluation is essentially one of measurement.

> The essence . . . is to make explicit the changes in behaviour accruing through instruction, beginning with the writing of behavioural objectives for student learning and followed by measuring changes in behaviour toward these objectives.
>
> For evaluating learning this approach has obvious advantages. . . . The most important one is not the popular notion of writing behaviourally defined objectives before beginning to instruct learners; instead it is a logical result of writing these objectives – the use of an absolute rather than a relative standard for measuring learning.
>
> (Wittrock 1970, 13)

In measurement-based evaluation, it is argued, the function of objectives is to make it possible to develop criterion-referenced, rather than norm-referenced, tests. Norm-referenced tests tell us how an individual performs as compared with a group: criterion-referenced tests tell us how an individual performs in relation to a standard.

The teacher or curriculum developer is invited to nominate, by stating his objectives, the standard by which he wishes his work, to be assessed, provided that the standard is couched in behavioural terms which make it possible to develop criterion-referenced tests. He can opt for how the curriculum is to be measured, but not for how it is to be judged. He cannot, for example, ask that it be judged on its internal logic or by the judgement of teachers or of students. It is to be judged in the light of the measurement of the performance of students on criterion-referenced tests.

Glaser (1970) has distinguished six different educational needs (the first phrase in each of the numbered statements below), and has suggested 'the considerations for evaluation and measurement that each raises'.

> 1. With respect to the specification of learning outcomes, the following are required: (a) behavioural definition of goals, evaluating progress toward these goals, and clarifying these goals in the light of evaluated experience, (b) prior evaluation of educational procedures, insuring they are in effect before assessing educational accomplishment, and (c) development of techniques for criterion-referenced measurement.

---

* The American term *instruction* is a difficult one for British readers to interpret. Translate as *teaching* or *education* until a sense of its connotation has been built up.

2. For the diagnosis of initial state, what is required is determination of long-term individual differences that are related to adaptive educational alternatives.
3. For the design of instructional alternatives, a key task is to determine measures that have the highest discriminating potential for allocating between instructional treatments.
4. For continuous assessment, discovery of measurements of ongoing learning that facilitate prediction of the next instructional step is required.
5. For adaptation and optimization, the instructional model requires: (a) the detailed analysis of individual-difference by instructional-treatment interactions and (b) the development of procedures like the optimizing methods so far used in fields other than education.
6. For evolutionary operation, we require a systematic theory or model of instruction into which accumulated knowledge can be placed and then empirically tested and improved.

(84–85)

The first of Glaser's six statements covers what I have just written about behavioural objectives and criterion-referenced testing, but adds an important point. If we are to measure a curricular proposal, we must find some way of monitoring classrooms in order to verify that the curriculum is in operation. This is, in fact, no easy task, particularly if we are dealing with many classrooms. Moreover, the measurement of effects in classrooms where the curriculum is implemented takes no account of the possibility that it is important to evaluate how difficult the curriculum is to implement. Perhaps reality cannot be brought to conform to the specification except in exceptionally favourable circumstances.

The second point regarding the diagnosis of initial state or entering behaviour (as it is sometimes called) means that we must test people before they enter upon the curriculum. This has wider implications, however, than the pre-test/post-test experimental model, for it points towards a diagnostic procedure by which students are switched on to particular curricula or on to particular units or routes within a differentiated curriculum. Glaser's third point is concerned with the development of these instructional alternatives and the need to produce diagnostic measures which discriminate between these alternatives in such a way that we know which alternative to choose on the basis of the test of entry behaviour. Further (point 4) diagnostic measures of this sort need to form part of a continuous assessment procedure which allows us to predict the next unit of instruction on the basis of where the pupil stands now. And it is possible to work towards the optimization of a decision procedure 'which defines an instructional strategy and is determined by the functional relationship between (a) long- and short-range history and (b) student performance at each stage and at the terminal stage'. (Glaser 1970, 82) Finally, Glaser looks towards a model or theory which allows work within this pattern to become cumulative towards a theory of curriculum and instruction.

Glaser's theory is somewhat in advance of practice. The nearest I know to a realization of this type of strategy is the Swedish Individualized Mathematics Teaching – I.M.U. (U. = *undervisning*, Swedish for teaching). It is designed for the unstreamed and ungraded Swedish comprehensive school.

I.M.U. (upper level) is built of nine modules which together cover the upper level course in mathematics, normally a three-year course. The course has been described as follows:

> Starting with a common curriculum for all pupils, the subject material is then structured according to the degree of difficulty within each module. The following diagram outlines the principles on which a module is based. Each module comprises four parts, components, the

Fig. 2 Diagram showing principles of a module in I.M.U. Upper level – version 3.

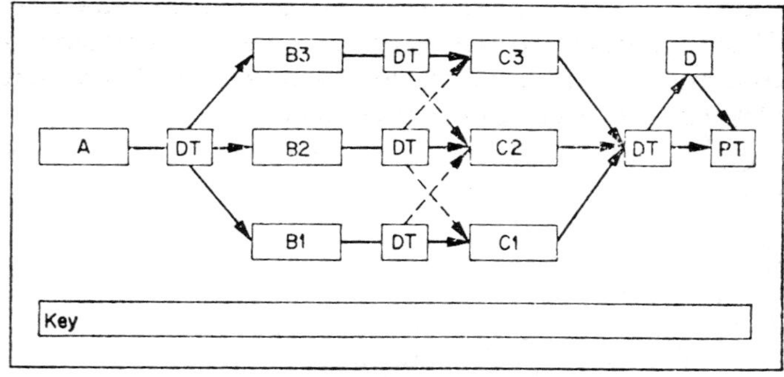

> first three of which belong to the basic course. They are called components A, B and C. Component A is common for all pupils. The B and C components are divided into levels of difficulty, hereafter called booklets. For the B component there are 2 or 3 booklets, called B1, B2, B3 or B1, B2–3. The C component comprises 3 booklets, C1, C2 and C3. The degree of difficulty is easiest in the B1 and C1 booklets, while B2–3 or B3 and C3 are the most difficult. The different booklets cover roughly the same material but the way in which the instructions are presented and the number of extra tasks vary. The D component is not part of the basic course. It exists only in one level and comprises both revision tasks and certain tasks of a more independent nature. Each component except the D component is completed with a diagnostic

test (DT). The number of tasks in this test varies depending on which booklet has been studied within the component. As a rule the number of tasks is greater for the more difficult booklets. Each component also includes diagnostic tasks that the pupils correct themselves. Each module finishes with a prognostic test (PT) which exists in three parallel versions.

The material is individualized in both the rate of work and the degree of penetration. As a result pupils within one grade can reach different points in the material. The intended 'normal rate of study' is three modules per year.

In principle the pupils are free to choose which booklet they like. The idea is that the pupils should, together with their teacher, go through what they have achieved earlier and on the basis of this and other experiences choose a suitable level. It is possible and permissible to change level both within and between modules. The constructors of the material have indicated certain figures for guiding the spread between the different levels in a component, but neither pupils nor teachers are obliged to follow these figures.

(Larsson 1973, 16–17)

I have given this account of I.M.U. because it is a good example of a curriculum which accepts and is permeated by the view of evaluation developed by Glaser. But its evaluation as such was much broader than Glaser appears to be grasping for. In the main evaluation study the effects on both pupils and teachers were studied. There were also the following studies within the evaluation:

Goal testing study
Material study
Job analysis study
Parent study
Observation study
Study of anxious pupils
Studies of different ways of presentation
Studies of the work of project consultants
Study of 'single' pupils

The evaluation report is well worth reading as an example of a highly developed design with the objectives model at its core.

Within the American tradition, Scriven (1967) points out the importance of evaluating goals rather than simply seeing evaluation in terms of goal achievement. The curriculum must be attempting something worthwhile as well as achieving what it attempts. He distinguishes between 'intrinsic' evaluation – of the content, goals, grading procedures, teacher attitude, etc. – and 'pay-off' evaluation – of the effects of the teaching instrument on the pupil. He notes that defenders of pay-off evaluation support their approach by arguing that all that really counts in education is its effects on the pupils, but he believes 'that an evaluation involving some weighting of intrinsic criteria and some pay-off criteria might be a worthwhile compromise' (54) and he discusses the way forward towards such a procedure.

An important point begins to emerge here. Glass (1970, 58) has urged that 'The goal of evaluation must be to answer questions of selection, adoption, support and worth of educational materials and activities.' It is the business of the evaluator, not merely to accumulate data, but to judge. This is Scriven's assertion. Stake (1967a, 527) believes that evaluation must entail judgement, but observes:

> Whether or not evaluation specialists will accept Scriven's challenge remains to be seen. In any case, it is likely that judgements will become an increasing part of the evaluation report. Evaluators will seek out and record the opinions of persons of special qualification. These opinions, although subjective, can be very useful and can be gathered objectively, independent of the solicitor's opinions. A responsibility for processing judgements is much more acceptable to the evaluation specialist than one for rendering judgements himself.

Westbury (1970, 241) comments: 'The evaluator thus becomes a person directing an evaluation. But this subterfuge will not do.' He points out that 'Evaluation may (and probably must) involve description, but description does not necessarily involve evaluation'. But if the evaluator is to judge, how are we to evaluate his judgement? MacDonald (verbal communication, 1972) has gone so far as to suggest that it is the mark of a good evaluation report that it is inconclusive in the sense that it will support divergent judgement.

Scriven's paper (1967) is also notable for introducing the important distinction between 'formative' and 'summative' evaluation. In formative evaluation the evaluation exercise serves as 'feedback and guide', influencing the shaping of a curriculum through the successive revisions of the developmental phase. Summative evaluation is concerned with the appraisal of the emergent curriculum as it is offered to the school system.

In an objectives-based programme of curriculum development formative evaluation is normally of two types. There is the continuous assessment of goal or objectives achievement which enables the curriculum to home in on its goals. And there is a process of diagnosing and feeding back information about barriers to the achievement of goals which lie within the instructional system but are not directly oriented to the goals. For example, failure to achieve the goals of an integrated team-taught science curriculum could be due to the difficulty of getting the teachers to work together effectively as a team on the basis offered to them by the curriculum specification.

A good account of a formative evaluation procedure at work within the objectives model, liberally interpreted, is given by Wynne Harlen (1973b) in her report to the Schools Council on the evaluation of *Science 5–13*. In this particular project the evaluation enterprise exercised a strong formative influence on the work of development, both at the stage of initial planning and at that of revision and refinement.

It is interesting too that Harlen casts doubt on the role of measurement in this context.

> From the first set of trials it was learned that information coming from children's test results was tentative and not readily usable for guiding rewriting without being supplemented by other data. The results played a useful part in confirming that the general approach of the material was effective in promoting achievement of its stated objectives, and the development of tests also had side-benefits for the production of Units. But for indicating changes which would make the Units more effective they were of much less use than information from other sources. The tests were also by far the most expensive item in the evaluation, both in direct cost and in man/woman hours. Whilst it could not be said that the test information was without value for this Project, it can be said that where resources are limited and it is necessary to concentrate upon gathering information to give the greatest return on money, time and human energy, then the choice would be for teachers' reports and direct observations in the classroom and not for tests of short-term changes in children's behaviour.
>
> (Harlen 1973b, 91–92)

This is a rather shattering judgement, given the American emphasis on testing. But perhaps the difference is a difference between the climate and assumptions in the two countries. In the United States the curriculum appears to be seen as a directive placed upon the teachers. Therefore, the question seems to be: 'Will it work?' In Britain, the curriculum is seen more as a tool in the hands of the teacher. The questions are: 'Can this curriculum offer something worthwhile?' and 'Am I as a teacher likely to be able to get the benefits out of it?' Since the teacher is to a great extent free to choose the curriculum, the evaluation must be addressed to him. And he trusts teacher judgement, which has more meaning to him than test results.

If this position were adopted within an objectives model, then the best form for stating objectives would no longer be that which helped towards criterion-based testing, but that which most strengthened and structured teachers' judgements, which are preferred as data. So far as I know, no one has followed up this line of thinking.

Given this emphasis on the teacher as the most important audience of evaluation, I can see another reserve about the American tradition, which can be illustrated from the quotation from Glaser above (pages 100–101). Not only are Glaser's six points difficult to understand, but the paper, of which they are a concluding summary (Glaser 1970), is, if anything, more difficult. It seems to me that the more sophisticated in his mode the American objectives-type evaluator becomes, the less easy it is to communicate his evaluation to teachers. Of course, if there is no remedy, we must put up with the disease, but an evaluation strategy more accessible to practitioners would certainly have important advantages.

These reserves about objectives-based evaluation are not the main line of attack on the tradition in the field of evaluation itself. In order to examine that, it is necessary first to consider evaluation in the context of decision-making.

Wiley (1970) cites two definitions of evaluation, that of Harris (1963), who defines evaluation as 'the systematic attempt to gather evidence regarding changes in student behaviour that accompany planned educational experiences', and that of Cronbach (1963), who defined it as the '. . . collection and use of information to make decisions about the educational programme'. Wiley collapses the two definitions into one: 'Evaluation consists of the collection and use of information concerning changes in pupil behaviour to make decisions about an educational programme.' (261)

Then the question is invited: 'Does data about pupil behaviour give us a good basis for making decisions about an educational programme?'

Once that question is answered in the negative, the floodgates are opened on the meadows of objectives-based evaluation. That is what has happened in the American educational landscape.

An early index of the impact of the line of thinking implied by such a negative answer is an important paper by Stake (1967).

Stake argues for a fuller 'countenance of educational evaluation'. He aspires to an evaluation 'oriented to the complex and dynamic nature of education, one which gives proper attention to the diverse purposes and judgements of the practitioner'. Noting the deficiencies for an evaluation so conceived of traditional tests which stress reliability of individual students' scores and predictive validity, he suggests that 'attention to individual differences among students should give way to attention to the contingencies among background conditions, classroom activities, and scholastic outcomes'.

A distinction is drawn between *antecedent*, *transaction* and *outcome* data. 'An antecedent is any condition existing prior to teaching and learning which may relate to outcomes. . . . Transactions are the countless encounters of students with teacher, student with student, author with reader, parent with counsellor – the succession of engagements which comprise the process of education. . . . Outcomes, as a body of information, would include measurements of the impact of instruction on teachers, administrators, counsellors and others,' as well as, of course, on students.

This is an immense expansion of the data range of evaluation if one starts from the objectives model as a benchmark. How is such a range of observations to be organized?

Stake makes a rather odd move in adopting the term, *intent*. After stating that he considers 'goals', 'objectives' and 'intents' to be synonymous, he includes among intents effects 'which are anticipated, and even those which are feared'. A collection of intents is 'a priority listing of all that may happen'. It would seem most natural to use the word hypothesis here. And yet intentionality appears more prominent in Stake's analytic scheme than it appears to be in his definition of intent.

He offers the diagram on the following page.

In this scheme the key relational concepts are contingency and congruence. Contingencies relate antecedents, transactions and outcomes, and the relationship may be logical or empirical. It is notable that intended categories are allocated a logical contingency, and Stake believes that for the practitioner, 'the contingencies, in the main, are logical, intuitive, and supported by a history of satisfactions and endorsements'. A more adequate theory of teaching would presumably lead to a more empirical base for intentional contingencies.

The data for a curriculum are congruent if what was intended actually happens. Stake's model focuses the problem of the relation of intention to realization which was located as central to curriculum study in the first chapter of this book. My own view would be that the object of curriculum study is to establish a congruence of contingencies, that is to bring anticipated and observed contingencies into agreement by achieving that blend of logical and empirical which is grounded theory.

Stake seems to me to be appealing to two reference points in broadening out the data base of evaluation. On the one hand, he argues explicitly that this breadth is needed to give decision-makers

Fig. 3 A representation of the processing of descriptive data.

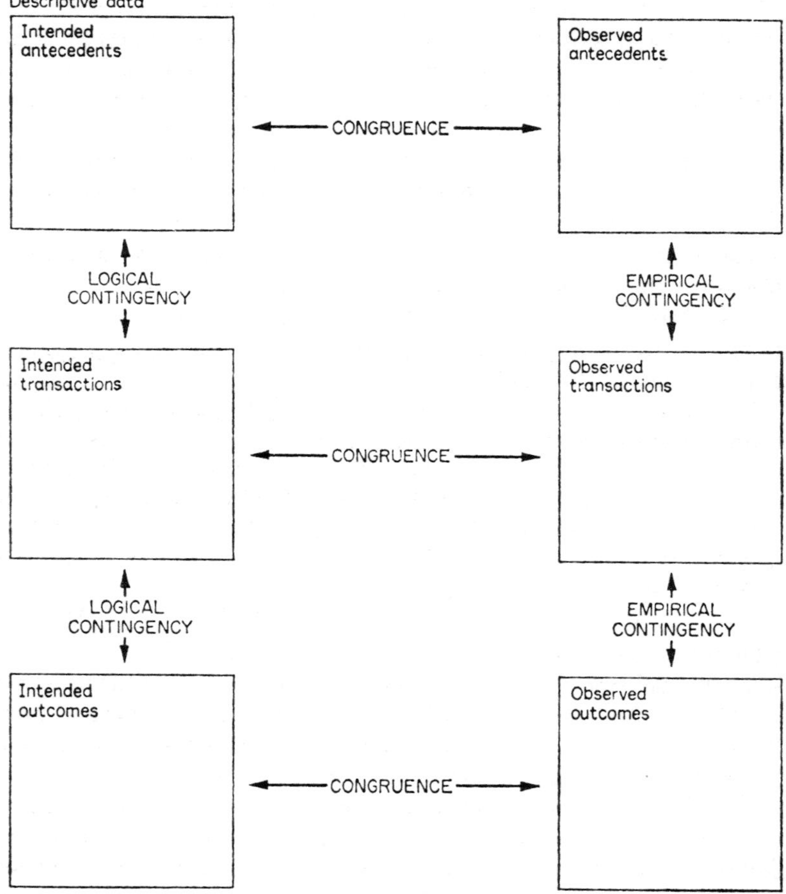

the data they need. Just as clearly but less explicitly, he is advancing the case that theoretical development of our understanding of the curriculum process also requires breadth.

The appeal to the reality of the decision-making situation has led in the United States to a convergence between some evaluators and some students of educational administration. Their critical reaction to the poverty of the traditional model of evaluation (they describe evaluation as 'ill') is well represented in a major report on *Educational Evaluation and Decision Making* produced by the Phi Delta Kappa National Study Committee on Evaluation. (Phi Delta Kappa 1971) This is an important book, though for the British reader it has limitations because of the different structure and assumptions of educational decision-making in the United States. It is also marred by a tendency to build elaborate models of decision-making processes whose congruence with reality appears doubtful. The real decision-makers, though a reference group, do not seem to be in the scholars' dialogue.

In addition to theory building of this sort, the broadening of the base of evaluation has led to a great deal of thought about the methodological problems, the craft of evaluation.

Weiss and Rein (1969), surveying the wreckage of an attempt to evaluate on the objectives model a social programme which contained educational elements, concluded that:

> . . . a far more effective methodology would be much more descriptive and inductive. It would be concerned with describing the unfolding form of the experimental intervention, the reactions of individuals and institutions subjected to its impact, and the consequences, so far as they can be learned by interview and observation, for these individuals and institutions. It would lean toward the use of field methodology, emphasizing interview and observation, though it would not be restricted to this. But it would be much more concerned with learning than with measuring.
>
> (Weiss and Rein 1969, 142)

In short, in order to evaluate one must understand. It can be argued that conventional objective-type evaluations do not address themselves to understanding the educational process. They deal in terms of success or failure. But a programme is always a mixture of both and a mixture which varies from setting to setting.

This line of thinking has established itself strongly. Hastings (1969), in a presidential address to the meeting of the National Council on Measurement in Education, suggested that such disciplines as anthropology, history, economics and sociology have much to contribute to educational evaluation.

The weakness of the objectives model from the point of view of evaluation has led to the development of what House (1973b) has called a 'counter-culture'. Simultaneously – and initially at least independently – a number of evaluators have developed alternative approaches. I shall review here a holistic approach (MacDonald), illuminative evaluation (Parlett and Hamilton), portrayal and responsive evaluation (Stake) and transactional evaluation (Rippey *et al.*).

MacDonald's holistic approach was a response to the problems he faced as evaluator of the Humanities Project. He was appointed in 1968, one year after the project started. His position was in fact that of an evaluator, but his title, Schools' Study Officer, hinted that in evaluation the study of schools was expected to be given a position of importance.

Two important conditions of his work were defined by the project, rather than by himself. First, it was held that no curriculum could be evaluated in its trial stage. The Humanities Project was under development until 1970 and MacDonald was commissioned to study it in its developmental stage in order to design an evaluation for execution after the project 'went public' in 1970. Second, the Humanities Project, as has been explained in the previous chapter, did not use objectives. In a climate in which the assumptions of the objectives model were virtually unquestioned (no one in Britiain seemed aware of the American criticisms), MacDonald was unable to use it.

His adoption of a holistic approach implied that the evaluation would not start from the assumption that certain data (such as pupil outcomes) were its area of concern, but would accept as potentially relevant all data concerning the project and its contexts. Of course, selection would be necessary, but the criteria of selection were to be regarded as problematic and would be evolved in contact with empirical reality.

Data would need to be sought and selected in order to make sense of the empirical phenomena. The evaluator found himself confronted, as he visited schools and classrooms, with phenomena not readily explicable. For example, in one school pupils responded to the discussion situation with enthusiastic participation, while in another school, indistinguishable from the first in terms of any accepted sampling typologies, pupils sat tense in agonized silence.

Case studies of eight schools were mounted during the experimental period and MacDonald (1971a) has listed some of the propositions arising from these case studies which the evaluation intended to explore:

1. Human action in educational institutions differs widely because of the number of variables that influence it. This is obvious, yet in curriculum evaluation it is sometimes assumed that what was intended to happen is what actually happens, and that what happens varies little from setting to setting.
2. The impact of an innovation is not a set of discrete effects, but an organically related pattern of acts and consequences. To understand fully a single act one must locate it functionally within that pattern. It follows from this proposition that curriculum interventions have many more unanticipated consequences than is normally assumed in development and evaluation designs.

3. No two schools are sufficiently alike in their circumstances that prescriptions of curricular action can adequately supplant the judgement of people in them. Historical/evolutionary differences alone make the innovation gap a variable which has significance for decision making.
4. The goals and purposes of the programme developers are not necessarily shared by its users. We have seen the Project used as a political resourse in an existing power struggle, as a way of increasing the effectiveness of a custodial pattern of pupil control, and as a means of enhancing the image of institutions which covet the wrappings, but not the merchandise, of innovation.*

(166)

An additional element in the design was developed from a concern for audiences.

I then explored the possibility of defining my responsibilities in relation to likely readers of my report. The idea of evaluation for consumers attracted me. In time 'consumers' became redefined as decision makers and four main groups of them emerged – the sponsors, the local education authority, the schools and the examination boards. The task of evaluation was then defined as one of answering the questions that decision makers ask.

This definition was subsequently seen as unsatisfactory because it assumed that these people knew in advance what questions were appropriate. At the present moment we see our task as that of feeding the judgement of decision makers by promoting understanding of the considerations that bear upon curricular action. Our orientation here is towards developing an empirical rather than a normative model of educational decision making and its consequences.

MacDonald had developed independently of Stuffelbeam (1971) a model of evaluation based on decision-making, but in contrast to Stuffelbeam he was not prepared to accept a rational or normative model of decision-making.

As the evaluation advanced it developed theory which worked towards 'understanding of the considerations that bear upon curricular action'. Hence its whole conception of the evaluative role broadened greatly. Thus, MacDonald can write: 'Perhaps bolder evaluation designs can give us a more adequate view of what it is we are trying to change, and of what is involved in changing it. It is this belief that lies behind a holistic approach to evaluation.' (MacDonald 1971b, 167)

* I cannot accept MacDonald's implication that the Project had intentions which precluded these uses of the Project: it was made as clear as possible that the Project intended to be docile to decisions of policy in schools.

Within the framework of these ideas MacDonald worked through a combination of measurement and case study, both of schools and of local authorities. A bulletin fed results and insights back to the participating schools. This bulletin has been edited as a single volume (Hamingson 1973). Teachers were asked to reflect about their own experience and report it. Their work has been edited, but is not yet published; and the final evaluation reports are not yet available.

Since the Humanities Project ended, MacDonald has gone on to direct the central evaluation of the National Development Programme in Computer Assisted Learning. In his proposal he describes the job of the evaluator in these terms:

> His job is to identify those who will have to make judgements and decisions about the programme, and to lay before them those facts of the case that are recognised by them as relevant to their concerns. That is the view which underlies the following definition of evaluation, which is the one adopted in this proposal.
>
> *Evaluation is the process of conceiving, obtaining and communicating information for the guidance of educational decision making with regard to a specified programme.*
>
> It is not implied that this concept of evaluation, or the activities referred to within it, are value-free. This cannot be. But what is implied is that the evaluator aspires to be a reliable and credible source, accessible to the judgement of all those who seek information about the programme.
>
> (MacDonald 1973b, 1–2)

There are distinct resemblances between MacDonald's position and that of Parlett and Hamilton, who aspire to a style of evaluation which shall illuminate the audience about a programme. They summarize their position in the following terms:

> Characteristically, conventional approaches have followed the experimental and psychometric traditions dominant in educational research. Their aim (unfulfilled) of achieving fully 'objective methods' has led to studies that are artificial and restricted in scope. We argue that such evaluations are inadequate for elucidating the complex problem areas they confront, and as a result provide little effective input to the decision-making process.
>
> Illuminative evaluation is introduced as belonging to a contrasting 'anthropological' research paradigm. Attempted measurement of 'educational products' is abandoned for intensive study of the programme as a whole: its rationale and evolution, its operations, achievements and difficulties. The innovation is not examined in isolation, but in the school context or 'learning milieu'. . . . Observation, interviews with participants (students, instructors, administrators and others), questionnaires, and analysis of documents and background information

are all combined to help 'illuminate' problems, issues, and significant programme features.

(Parlett and Hamilton 1972, 1)

In the face of the complexity of real educational settings the authors take the position that 'tidy' results can rarely be generalized to an 'untidy' reality, and they comment on the importance of studying atypical results and problems. They are concerned to give an intelligible account of a curriculum initiative rather than simply to measure it.

> The aims of illuminative evaluation are to study the innovatory programme; how it operates; how it is influenced by the various school situations in which it is applied; what those directly concerned regard as its advantages and disadvantages; and how students' intellectual tasks and academic experiences are most affected. It aims to discover and document what it is like to be participating in the scheme, whether as teacher or pupil; and, in addition, to discern and discuss the innovation's most significant features, recurring concomitants, and critical processes.
>
> (Parlett and Hamilton 1972)

In Parlett and Hamilton's model two concepts are central: the 'instructional system' and the 'learning milieu'.

An 'instructional system' corresponds pretty closely to the definition of a curriculum specification offered in the first chapter of this book. It is the blueprint. In offering that definition I tried to emphasize the difficulty of realizing the idea in practice and the way in which ideas and practice were modified in the attempt to do so. As Parlett and Hamilton comment: 'an instructional system, when adopted, undergoes modifications that are rarely trivial. The instructional system may remain as a shared idea, abstract model, slogan, or shorthand, but it assumes a different form in every situation.' They are interested in the process of implementation, which involves interpretation and re-interpretation.

In this process the instructional system interacts with the 'learning milieu', that is, 'the social-psychological and material environment in which students and teachers work together.' This interaction is crucial for the illuminative evaluator. It is his main focus of attention, because it is where the action is. 'The introduction of an innovation sets off a chain of repercussions throughout the learning milieu. In turn these unintended consequences are likely to affect the innovation itself, changing its form and moderating its impact.' Parlett and King's work on concentrated study (1971) documents an example of this process. Crucial to the approach is that the evaluator is not attempting to control the situation he is studying. He does not try to hold it still while he looks at it. In this he is like the anthropologist or the historian rather than like the laboratory psychologist.

Stake, whose conception of evaluation as portrayal (Stake 1974) anticipates Parlett and Hamilton's notion of illumination, is also reacting against the tradition of attempting to capture tight experimental control over the innovatory situation. He describes this evaluation strategy as 'preordinate' in that it relies on pre-specification and emphasizes statement of goals, use of objective tests, standards held by programme personnel and research-type reports.

He advocates 'responsive evaluation', which he defines in the following way:

> And educational evaluation is a 'responsive evaluation' if it orients more directly to programme activities than to programme intents, if it responds to audience requirements for information, and if the different value-perspectives present are referred to in reporting the success of the programme.
>
> (Stake 1972)

Particularly interesting, since it reflects an American experience likely to be replicated elsewhere, is Stake's emphasis on the presentation of results. If evaluation is addressed to decision-makers rather than research workers, the evaluator must attempt to portray the programme in a way that communicates to an audience more naturally and more effectively than does the traditional research report. He is claiming that research style information may not be the kind of information which is useful for decision-makers.

The task which Stake presents to the evaluator is not an easy one; and he is certainly no wide-eyed optimist. After contrasting responsive evaluation with preordinate evaluation, he comments:

> There are many reasons why preordinate evaluation can be ineffective. It is likely to be underfunded, understaffed, and initiated too late. But even under optimum conditions it will often fail. A collection of specific objectives will understate educational purposes. Different people will have different purposes. Side effects – good ones and bad – get ignored. Programme background, conditions, transactions are likely to be poorly described. Standardized tests seldom match objectives, criterion referenced tests oversimplify and fail to measure transfer, and custom-built tests are poorly validated. And people cannot read many of the reports or do not find them useful.
>
> Responsive evaluation is not likely to overcome all of these obstacles. But it is an approach that is attentive to them. There are problems with the responsive approach too. Not enough time or resources may be available to measure key outcomes. The results may be seen as too subjective.

The assets and liabilities of the two approaches need to be weighed before and during an evaluation study.

(Stake 1972)

In December 1972, a small invitational conference of evaluators was convened by MacDonald and Parlett. Stake and two other Americans were among the fourteen participants. Wallin attended from Sweden, and the D.E.S., the Nuffield Foundation and the Centre for Educational Research and Innovation (C.E.R.I.) of O.E.C.D. were represented. This conference led to the following statement or manifesto, which represents well enough the position of what one might call the 'new wave' evaluators.

On December 20, 1972 at Churchill College Cambridge, the following conference participants concluded a discussion of the aims and procedures of evaluating educational practices and agreed

I. That past efforts to evaluate these practices have, on the whole, not adequately served the needs of those who require evidence of the effects of such practices, because of:
   a. an under-attention to educational processes including those of the learning milieu;
   b. an over-attention to psychometrically measurable changes in student behaviour (that to an extent represent the outcomes of the practice, but which are a misleading oversimplification of the complex changes that occur in students); and
   c. the existence of an educational research climate that rewards accuracy of measurement and generality of theory but overlooks both mismatch between school problems and research issues and tolerates ineffective communication between researchers and those outside the research community.

II. They also agreed that future efforts to evaluate these practices be designed so as to be:
   a. responsive to the needs and perspectives of differing audiences;
   b. illuminative of the complex organisational, teaching and learning processes at issue;
   c. relevant to public and professional decisions forthcoming; and
   d. reported in language which is accessible to their audiences.

III. More specifically they recommended that, increasingly,
   a. observational data, carefully validated, be used (sometimes in substitute for data from questioning and testing);
   b. the evaluation be designed so as to be flexible enough to allow for response to unanticipated events (progressive focussing rather than pre-ordinate design); and that
   c. the value positions of the evaluator, whether highlighted or constrained by the design, be made evident to the sponsors and audiences of the evaluation.

IV. Though without consensus on the issues themselves, it was agreed that considered attention by those who design evaluation studies should be given to such issues as the following:

a. the sometimes conflicting roles of the same evaluator as expert, scientist, guide, and teacher of decision-makers on the one hand, and as technical specialist, employee, and servant of decision-makers on the other;
b. the degree to which the evaluator, his sponsors, and his subjects, should specify in advance the limits of enquiry, the circulation of findings, and such matters as may become controversial later;
c. the advantages and disadvantages of intervening in educational practices for the purpose of gathering data or of controlling the variability of certain features in order to increase the generalisability of the findings;
d. the complexity of educational decisions which, as a matter of rule, have political, social and economic implications; and the responsibility that the evaluator may or may not have for exploring these implications;
e. the degree to which the evaluator should interpret his observations rather than leave them for different audiences to interpret.

It was acknowledged that different evaluation designs will serve different purposes and that even for a single educational programme many different designs could be used.

(MacDonald and Parlett 1973, 79–80)

Although I am entirely sympathetic to the criticism of the old-style, product-testing evaluation from which the new-wave evaluators start, I have some reserves about their position as it emerges. I am concerned about the problem of criteria, and I feel that the general position which is apparently being assumed by evaluators is likely to block progress in research-based innovation.

The problem of criteria is a complex one. The classical model of evaluation worked on criteria of success and failure, as judged by measured student behaviours. In respect of a curriculum specification, I do not think that such criteria are appropriate. The best way to ensure 'success' is to aim low. Any ambitious curriculum will produce unique blends of success and failure in each institution which responds to it.

The new wave of evaluators still seem to me to be concerned with 'merit' or 'worth' in a curriculum or educational practice, but their criteria are not clear and their concern with audiences and presentation of results appears to me to mask their problem. They aspire to 'tell it as it is', and they often write as if that is possible if they allow for some distortion due to their own values. But there is no telling it as it is. There is only a creation of meaning through the use of criteria and conceptual frameworks. The task of briefing decision-makers in language they readily understand can too easily lead to the casual importation of unexamined assumptions and criteria. Audience response can be seductive, especially if the audience is politically powerful. And it is too easy for the evaluation which aspires to the condition of the novel to degenerate into the novelette.

I want to suggest, tentatively, five criteria which might be used in the estimate of a curriculum or an educational practice. They are derived from a consideration of the new wave of evaluation. They are: meaning, potential, interest, conditionality and elucidation.

I can best consider meaning as a criterion by referring to a paper by Mann (1969). Mann is working with the idea of 'curriculum criticism', the possibility of 'talking about curriculum as if it were a literary object'. (27) Like a literary object, a curriculum orders chaos by selection and by form. Mann speaks of a curriculum as having in one of its aspects that quality of a work of art which he describes as unconditionedness. I take him to mean that the nature of a curriculum is not entirely explained by reference to the conditions which influence its production – that is, in terms of the sociology of knowledge. It has a form and meaning which is logical and it can be considered in itself. For Mann 'the function of the curricular critique is to disclose its meanings, to illuminate its answers'. (29) 'The critic discloses meaning by explaining design.' (30)

In order to do this the critic must select those designs and meanings which he will attend to, and this implies a basis of selection. Mann sees this basis in the personal knowledge of the critic as disciplined by or grounded in a field of public knowledge. For him, this field is principally knowledge about ethical reality. This emphasis I would question, emphasizing rather epistemology.

Mann's argument is difficult and abstract. I shall draw on him to feed my own argument without fairly representing his views, for which the reader must be referred to the original.

A curriculum can be discussed critically in the light of knowledge criteria as a thing in itself. Such a discussion implies what Mann calls a 'disclosure model' (ethical in his argument) which 'is judged for its capacity to continue generating new propositions that reveal the phenomena'. (37) The data for citicism of a curriculum are not revealed by the curriculum specification or by the materials of study but only by the observation of the curriculum in action in various classroom settings.

Let me put this more concretely by taking an example familiar to me. The Humanities Curriculum Project may be viewed as an exploration of the relationship of knowledge to the authority of the teacher. An example of what is at stake is contained in the problem of whether a student accepts a proposition as knowledge because his teacher says that it is so, or whether he attempts to test it by criteria other than the teacher's authority. This problem is built into the logic of the curriculum on paper, but the extent to which it is a problem in the classroom can only be verified by empirical observation.

As a curriculum critic, I am entitled to approach the curriculum with a declared epistemological model, but I cannot apply that model without observing the curriculum in action.

In the Humanities Curriculum Project the critical dialogue about this issue has been built into the development rather than into the evaluation (though the evaluators have contributed to it), and I think that this is generally the situation. It might be argued that an evaluation team ought to contain a philosophical critic working on Mann's model.

It is interesting that the Humanities Project has had its philosophical critics, but that they have generally shot wide of the mark because they have made assumptions about the empirical reality in the classroom which are not borne out by observation. Thus, for example, there is nothing logically problematic about teachers giving their views on a controversial issue on the understanding that they are open to criticism and discussion on the same basis as any others; and critics have advocated this. The problem is that it does not seem possible to make good that understanding in practice.

I have argued that an important element in an adequate evaluation of a curriculum is a philosophical critique. The object of such a critique should be to disclose the meaning of the curriculum rather than to assess its worth, though disclosure of meaning naturally invites assessment of worth. The data for such a critique are to be found in the observation of classrooms which are responding to the curriculum. Such a critique, if attempted at all, has usually been the task of the developmental team. Often evaluators have paid insufficient attention to this aspect, and there is some danger that the growth of interest in the policy orientation of evaluation will continue this trend. Philosophers of education have not generally made the contribution they might have done because they have been reluctant to accept as their data the reality of the classroom.

The second criterion I proposed was that of 'potential'. In order to examine the potential of a curriculum or educational practice, one must answer the question: potential for what? Answers can be accumulated either by reference to theory or by reference to the interests of decision-makers, or both. Having one's questions – 'What is the potential for the improvement of reading ability?' or 'What is the potential for creating teacher stress?' for example – one focuses one's attention on data which bears on the particular variable involved. The object is not to be predictive. The evaluator is not attempting to answer the question: 'What will happen if this school responds to that curriculum?' but rather: 'What degree of X could we get out of that curriculum when the X effect is maximized, and what does that look like?' This is the study of pattern cases or ideal types within the range of implementation. And a curriculum may have potential which it is very difficult to realize in practice.

'Interest' as a criterion refers to the problems a curriculum raises in practice. The problems are interesting in so far as they recur from situation to situation in education or in so far as they have important relevance. A problem in the handling of resources of manpower or materials may be interesting because it recurs. A problem of criteria by which to judge children's work in a given curricular context may be interesting because it raises fundamental questions of quality of wide significance.

'Conditionality' as a criterion asks of the evaluator that he relate the potential and interest of the curriculum to the contextual conditions of schools and classrooms. He explores the factors which are likely to make for success or failure in realizing given potentials and in developing insights through the analytic approach to interesting problems. Given the uniqueness and particularity of educational settings, predictions as to the likely effects of responding to a curriculum or adopting an educational practice (such as unstreaming, for example) can only be made by those informed about the local variables. A study of the conditionality of a curriculum or practice helps the decision-maker to anticipate the consequences of his decision by assessing how the conditions apply in his own setting. This element of conditionality is emphasized by the new-wave evaluators.

Finally, the acceptance of 'elucidation' as a criterion poses the question: to what extent does response to this curriculum or adoption of this practice throw light upon the problems of change in education? Does it contribute to the construction of a theory of innovation at a general level or for our particular school?

These criteria are perhaps presented as too discrete, and they are not refined. My main concern here is to express the fear that too much attention to the political dimensions of evaluation and to the presentation of results in vivid and acceptable but often oblique forms, may tend to make the discussion of such criteria part of the private talk of evaluators. The issues are too important to be regarded as domestic issues in the evaluation household.

This recognition of evaluation as a household with its boundaries leads me to my concern that the position being assumed by evaluators is likely to block progress in research-based innovation.

The classical objectives model of evaluation did just this. In this model, the innovator is seen as a man with a mission or at least with a policy proposal. He offers a solution. He has a stake in having found the right answer. How are we to assess his claims? The product testing model deploys educational scholarship and research procedures to criticize his product and assess its merit.

It seems to me odd (though the observation is often borne out in practice) that innovation is seen as coming from outside educational scholarship and research.

The crucial criticism of the objectives model is that it assesses without explaining. In this respect it is unlike research. Hence the developer of curriculum cannot learn from it. His stock in trade is deemed to be the inspired guess. But the styles of evaluation developed by the new-wave evaluators are in fact the styles of curriculum research. Indeed, it is perhaps only the structure of centralized adoption of curricula – a condition which need not apply in Britain – which forces the adoption of the role of the evaluator rather than of the researcher. Certainly, new-wave evaluators can teach the developer just as researchers could.

I take the view that curriculum development should be handled as educational research. The developer should be an investigator rather than a reformer. He should start from a problem, not from a solution. And he should not aim to be right, but to be competent.

It is, of course, extremely difficult in the present climate to make this good in practice. It seems to me quite clear that the Humanities Project was primarily concerned with exploring the paradox that in controversial areas some teachers might want to be neutral, and facing the problem that we had no pedagogy to meet the needs of such teachers. Most people apparently see it as advocating that the teacher be neutral rather than as attempting to give him the choice of being so.

New-wave evaluation could help to improve this climate, to stimulate curiosity about teaching and mute over-confident advocacy. Such evaluation is research into the nature and problems of educational innovation and the betterment of schools. And it is research which is relatively non-technical and accessible. This makes the definition of the position of the developer as a research worker more accessible too.

A knowledge of evaluation research seems to me the most desirable qualification for the director of a curriculum project. Otherwise the project is likely to go for solutions rather than for problems, and the crucial problems which lie in the way of educational advance will continue to be neglected. A project director should have the same qualifications as an evaluator.

Moreover, since curriculum research of the kind I am advocating here is closely relevant to the needs of teachers and educational administrators, and is potentially their tool, they should be at home with it.

MacDonald (1975) appears to be addressing just this problem when he advocates a tradition of 'democratic' – as opposed to 'autocratic' or 'bureaucratic' – evaluation.

> Democratic evaluation is an information service to the community about the characteristics of an educational programme. It recognises value pluralism and seeks to represent a range of interests in its issue formulation. The basic value is an informed citizenry, and the evaluator acts as a broker in exchanges of information between differing groups. His techniques of data gathering and presentation must be accessible to non-specialist audiences. His main activity is the collection of definitions of, and reactions to, the programme. He offers confidentiality to informants and gives then control over his use of the information. The report is non-recommendatory, and the evaluator has no concept of information misuse. The evaluator engages in periodic negotiation of his relationships with sponsors and programme participants. The criterion of success is the range of audiences served. The report aspires to 'best-seller'status. The key concepts of democratic evaluation are 'confidentiality', 'negotiation' and 'accessibility'. The key justificatory concept is 'the right to know'.

I do not think he goes far enough. Given that there are 'professional evaluators' – and two publications by the Schools Council (1973b, 1975a) suggest that such a profession is emerging in this country – he wants them to work for an informed citizenry rather than for an informed bureaucracy or for their own position as autocratic judges. This is fair enough up to a point, and a wholly acceptable ethical position for a professional evaluator. But I would question the desirability of the emergence of the evaluator as a professional role.

The existence of the evaluator implies the existence of the developer, another role of which I am sceptical. I want to argue against the separation of developer and evaluator and in favour of integrated curriculum research.

Sparrow (1973, 1) describes the role of the developers in the following terms:

> In the early 1960s the men and women of imagination and insight who were responsible for curriculum development were determined to introduce new materials, new subject content and new methods of teaching into the schools. The first disciplines selected for change were science and mathematics; latterly the movement has spread to the humanities. The developers were certain that much irrelevant and out-of-date material was being taught in the schools, and that they could replace this outmoded curriculum with something much better – more relevant to the times and more interesting. The ideas for new content came from both outside the classroom and within it, from the universities and colleges, and from teachers who were called upon to help introduce the new materials. Indeed, the Nuffield projects were run by teachers for teachers.
>
> The first concern of the developers was the production of teaching materials, and the urgency of the task left little opportunity for them to make a cool and careful evaluation of their product, or to formulate precise hypotheses to be tested by patient educational research of the traditional kind. It can be argued that much of the strength of the curriculum development movement stemmed from the stress that was placed on immediate needs in an essentially practical situation.

Sparrow may be right – though I am doubtful of this – in his historical judgement that the stress on practical responses to immediate needs was a source of strength. However, I would argue that this phase of work in curriculum ought to be outgrown as soon as possible. The worker in curriculum ought to formulate hypotheses to be tested by patient research. But not research of the traditional kind: curriculum research gives access to problems which elude traditional methods.

We know enough now to shun the offer of ready solutions. Curriculum research must be concerned with the painstaking examination of possibilities and problems. Evaluation should, as it were, lead development and be integrated with it. Then the conceptual distinction between development and evaluation is destroyed and the two merge as research. Curriculum research must itself be illuminative rather than recommendatory as in the earlier tradition of curriculum development.

In the next chapter I look towards a research model in curriculum which is an attempt to express in practice the aspirations for the curriculum field which I have declared above.

9

TOWARDS A RESEARCH MODEL

The pure form of the objectives or engineering model is that of testing a curriculum as a product against a specification it is designed to meet. That of the process model is the evaluation of the implications of a proposal which has a high degree of flexibility within the limitations imposed by a broadly stated purpose.

The evaluative response to the process model, tending as it has done to research, and the growth of sophistication in other forms of evaluation, suggest a further possibility which I shall call here *the research model.*

As far as I know, this possibility has not been explored elsewhere; and it may well be that there is a link between this model and the British assumption that the curriculum is an area of decision to be delegated to individual schools. In a system in which curricular decisions are made centrally, the problem is seen as finding the right curriculum to prescribe. In a system where curriculum decisions are seen as resting with the individual school, the school becomes the focus of curriculum development, and a process of continuous organic development becomes possible. On this assumption every school should have a broad development plan. From year to year the curriculum will be modified as part of a continuous process of adjustment and improvement.

What kind of work in curriculum research and development is best adapted to feeding such a system? The phrase used by the Schools Council to express the aspiration behind its programme was 'to extend the range of choice open to teachers'. How do we do this?

One model is that of the supermarket. We place competing products on the shelves. The school then has a choice among these products. It may opt for curriculum A or curriculum B. Each curriculum will have its own identity, though it may offer alternatives within itself, being more of a construction kit than a finished product which must be accepted as a whole. It may be that the kit includes variations so that the ultimate outcome is a choice rather like those offered by car manufacturers – you may have various bodies, various degrees of luxury, and various powers of engine – or it may be more flexible still, more like a Meccano set from which many different things can be built. But even in this, the most flexible case, the choice offered is primarily one between products: Meccano or Lego?

Another possibility is that the principles on which a product is built are so clear that it is open to teachers both to criticize the curriculum in terms of its principles and as a result improve it in practice, or to extend the range of materials and teaching strategies by building on the curriculum offering in the light of principles. It is this kind of flexibility which Link (1972) has in mind in referring to the American social science curriculum *Man: A Course of Study* (which is an elaborate package of materials and teachers' books) as an 'unfinished curriculum'.

Yet a third possibility, fashionable in Britain, is a curriculum offering which suggests principles for the development of curricula in a particular area and provides units of material which serve as examples of these principles in action, but do not, and are not intended to, provide the raw materials of a fully structured curriculum. This is the pattern adopted by the Liverpool-based project which is developing possibilities in the integration of geography, history and social studies in the middle-school age range.

All these approaches have about them the implication that in some sense or other a curriculum is a policy recommendation expressed in a framework of action. The curriculum developer is seen as one who offers solutions rather than as one who explores problems. And his success depends upon his finding the right solution, his advocating the 'correct' course of action – or at least the best available course of action. Hence the need often seen for the separation of the function of developer and evaluator, perhaps even of a wholly independent evaluation. The developer is seen as the creative artist or the man with a mission. The evaluator is the critic or the practical man who tempers enthusiasm with judgement.

Now, it may well be that this relationship between developer and evaluator is sometimes, or even often, justified, but there must be an aspiration to grow beyond it to a more scientific procedure which builds action and criticism into an integrated whole. The dialectic between proposition and critique which is personified in the relationship of artist and critic is integrated in the scientific method. Conjectures and refutations (Poppper 1963) are woven into one logic.

In order to move from product or process models of curriculum development towards a research model, it is necessary first to cast the developer not in the role of the creator or man with a mission, but in that of the investigator. The curriculum he creates is then to be judged by whether it advances our knowledge rather than by whether it is right. It is conceived as a probe through which to explore and test hypotheses and not as a recommendation to be adopted.

Another way to look at the situation is to continue to regard the curriculum as a policy, but to take a Popperian view of policy, asserting that policies evolve and improve continuously and progressively by the study of their shortcomings and their gradual elimination. On such a view the concepts of success and failure become irrelevant. A curriculum without shortcomings has no prospect of improvement and has therefore been insufficiently ambitious. What we ask of a curriculum offering is not that it should be right or good but that it should be intelligent or penetrating. Its dilemmas should be important dilemmas. Its shortcomings should reflect real and important difficulties.

In the field of curriculum there are some who would immediately react against the idea that a project might develop a curricular line of attack which is experimental and which is expected in some sense to have shortcomings and to encounter difficulties. They would argue that this implies that we are experimenting with pupils and that we are putting their education at risk.

This view seems to me to be misjudged. In the first place, the present educational system is itself a policy, and it is clear that it is a policy with the most troubling shortcomings. Moreover, the shortcomings do not seem to have been defined and tackled in ways which lead to a continuous process of betterment. We cannot be content with our present performance in education. If we attempt to improve the situation, we cannot expect to leap for a solution to the complex of educational problems: we can only aim to embark on a line of policy development which will give promise of a fairly long process of systematic and thoughtful improvement. Such a developmental style points towards a tradition of curriculum research which focuses on the study of problems and responses to them rather on the invention of ambitious solutions before the problems have been properly studied.

I discussed in the last chapter the development of a tradition in evaluation which is research oriented in that it aims at understanding rather than merely judgement of merit. It seems possible to build on the experience gained in this tradition by letting the evaluation, as it were, lead the curriculum rather than follow it. The curriculum would be designed with its potential contribution to research strongly in mind. Of course it would have to be justifiable on educational grounds as well as on research grounds, but it would have the function of a research probe.

This may well mean that schools taking part in a curriculum project would do more self-consciously and systematically what they would have done anyway. For example, an integrated studies project might work with schools introducing integration on various different logics and with various different organizational principles.

The full implications of the shift of emphasis involved are not easy to see at this point in time. I can best put flesh on the bones of a difficult argument by describing a project which has reached towards a research model. This is a project on the problems and effects of teaching about race relations, which is supported by the Social Science Research Council and the Calouste Gulbenkian Foundation.

It starts from two premises:

1. that nobody knows how to teach about race relations;
2. that it is unlikely that there is *one* way of teaching about race relations which can be recommended.

A number of approaches to teaching about race relations (taken in the broadest sense) have been attempted in the United States. These range from black studies – often taught through the medium of formal academic curricula and in clear intention taught from a black point of view – through controversial issues programmes (Oliver and Shaver 1966, Epstein 1972), to encounter groups in racially mixed situations. None of these approaches has been established by evaluation as having a potential which clearly marks it out from the others. Moreover, the racial scene is so different in Britain that it is doubtful if results would transfer.

One of the more widely reported experiments in Britain is that of Miller (1967, 1969), who worked with day-release students in further education using a wide range of teaching methods intended to attack racial prejudice. He found that prejudice was high in his group and that it increased during the experiment. Miller is the first to admit the limitations of his findings, which cannot be reliably generalized. Nevertheless, they do suggest the existence of considerable problems in handling race relations through education. Moreover, the results have had some influence in making teachers doubtful of the wisdom of teaching about race relations at all.

On the basis of personal experience – which should not be underestimated – there appear to be a fair number of people both in the field of race relations and in education who have strong views about how teaching about race relations should or should not be conducted. There appears however to be little consensus of view among them. This probably indicates more clearly than the limited research that there is no basis for any claim that we know how teaching about race relations should be conducted. Such a situation points clearly towards a research approach.

So too does the observation that no suggestion for teaching is likely to hold for the full range of circumstances which obtain in schools. It is clearly highly unlikely that the same materials and the same teaching strategy would be desirable in a multi-racial inner urban school in which two racial groups are strongly represented, a multi-racial school in which three racial groups are strongly represented, and a rural school in which pupils have little contact with any cultures other than that of their own locality. Moreover, if a school has a multi-racial neighbourhood to serve, it probably matters for the design of curriculum and teaching whether there is in that neighbourhood relative harmony, an uneasy truce or acute tension. In education we are dealing with situations which contain many variables, and over a wide range of subjects it holds true that the curriculum is not the most important variable to be taken into account in attempting to understand the results of curriculum development. Failure to recognize this is the greatest weakness in curriculum research. All suggestions about curriculum are conditional suggestions and the conditions need to be spelt out.

It is against this background that the project on the problems and effects of teaching about race relations should be viewed. And it had an antecedent in the work on race relations done in the context of the Humanities Curriculum Project.

When that project was asked by the Schools Council to take race relations as one of its themes, there was some hesitation on the part of the team. The problem was that the project had given its attenion to controversial issues which were considered open issues. Race relations, though certainly controversial in our society, was sharply distinguished from our other themes in that the project team themselves were firmly committed to the promotion of inter-racial respect and that there existed in legislation an apparent warrant for a programme of teaching towards that end.

The aim of the Humanities Curriculum Project was 'to develop an understanding of social situations and human acts and of the controversial value issues which they raise'. (Humanities Curriculum

Project 1970, 1) In teaching about race relations should one aim more directly at influencing attitudes in the direction of greater inter-racial tolerance and respect?

Two considerations tipped the balance in favour of tackling race relations within the project. It seemed arguable that in the context of education any attempt to foster inter-racial respect should be founded on understanding. Respect, it might be claimed, should be reasonable and intelligent. It was recognized that this position implied a respect for the pupil's autonomy and hence his freedom to develop his own view, but it was felt that this dilemma could not in reality be avoided.

The second point was a matter of classroom practice. If the teacher, when confronted with racial prejudice, sought by the use of his authority to lay down the law to a pupil, would he in fact change attitudes? It seemed likely that prejudice would take shelter in a psychological underground bunker. Perhaps an attempt should be made to face it, rather than to drive it under cover.

We were not aware at the time of closely parallel approaches being made in the United States, and reported later. (Epstein 1972) The project decided to proceed cautiously with a limited experiment conducted by a task force in which J. Hipkin headed the development and B. MacDonald and G. K. Verma undertook the evaluation. They worked with a mini-pack of teaching materials (the contents of which are listed in Parkinson and MacDonald 1972) in six schools, three of which were new to the project style of teaching. It seemed necessary to look at the situation of schools which embarked on the theme of race without much experience in the project.

The experiment was monitored both by case-study and by a small measurement programme. Those involved in the exercise would be the first to acknowledge that it had the limitations of an *ad hoc* response to a problem which had arisen within the context of a large project. The instruments to hand were used.

The case-study work was briefly reported by Parkinson and MacDonald (1972). Some of the problems in the classroom obviously required sensitive handling by the teachers, and it was clear that in some circumstances implicit conflicts were made explicit. Pupils appeared to be prepared to defend this. In general they

> maintained that their attitudes had not been modified as a result of the study, although many added that their understanding had been enhanced . . . What seems clear is that there were no marked differences in terms of personal relationships between the pupils involved . . . several boys said that they did not feel that their relationships with

their peers were in any way threatened . . . One of the English boys in the group expressed the view that the study had helped 'the welding of the school community'.

(Parkinson and MacDonald 1972, 306)

A fuller report of the case-study work is in preparation and a preliminary version of this has been made available to teachers taking part in the present project.

Reports on the measurement results (Verma and MacDonald 1971, Bagley and Verma 1972, and Verma and Bagley 1973) are summed up as follows:

> We conclude that the present results do not contradict those of Miller (1969) since the subjects in our present study were younger, generally better educated, and held less highly prejudiced attitudes than Miller's day-release apprentices. In addition, teaching was longer, more concentrated and more carefully prepared and standardized than teaching in Miller's study, and occurred in the context of full-time rather than part-time education. This experimental study has shown that teaching designed to enhance inter-ethnic attitudes in the school setting* can, at least, be moderately successful.
>
> (Verma and Bagley 1973, 58)

Verma and MacDonald were cautious in their conclusions:

> The combined picture of the results seems to indicate that there was no general tendency towards intolerance after a seven- to eight-week teaching programme. There is no evidence to suggest that the students generally became less sensitive to or tolerant of members of other racial groups. These results cannot be considered as constituting proof. Analysis of the pilot study along other lines is incomplete, but a decision has already been made to proceed with the editing of a full collection of materials on race, on the grounds that none of the problems encountered in the course of the study would justify the abandonment of further research. No teacher involved in the programme abandoned the course, or found it necessary to reject any of the premises described earlier. In February 1971, each of the schools which participated sent team members to an evaluation conference at which they expressed willingness to undertake the teaching of race with other students in the future.†
>
> (Verma and MacDonald 1971, 199–200)

The project prepared for publication a collection of teaching materials on race relations similar to those on its other themes.

* This is not strictly accurate since the aim of teaching within the H.C.P framework is not as direct as this suggested.

† In the event this statement has not been justified. One of the six schools now seems hesitant in continuing the teaching.

As it turned out, the programme committee of the Schools' Council, after considerable deliberation and for complex reasons, vetoed the publication of these materials.

Further research was not abandoned, however. Support was attracted from the Social Science Research Council and the Gulbenkian Foundation for a project on 'The Problems and Effects of Teaching about Race Relations'. One of the Humanities Project team (L. Stenhouse) and one of the Evaluation team (G. K. Verma) passed on to this project.

It is probably necessary at this point to make clear the position taken up as a result of the experience of the Humanities Project and its evaluation.

First, there seemed reason to believe that some positive effects, modest though they might be, might accrue from teaching to adolescents in the area of race relations for from six weeks to one term, and further that much might be learned about the problems of teaching about race relations in the context of such teaching. This is not to deny that there is a need for a much more thorough-going programme of education for a multi-racial society. However, we believe that an experimental approach to the problem with adolescents is not only justified in itself, but is also likely to stimulate reflection about needs farther down the school.

Second, the Humanities Project strategy does not stand or fall on the case of race relations. We feel that we have no vested interest in that strategy in this context. Moreover, our hypothesis is that a variety of different strategies will be found useful in a variety of different contexts, though in view of the research evidence we do feel some reserve about authoritarian approaches to teaching in this area.

Third, experience in the field of curriculum suggests to us that the contextual variables in the school and its environment are so important that there can be no basis for general recommendations. Each school will have to assess its own problems and evolve its own policy. A research on problems and effects of teaching about race relations should concentrate on collecting the data which schools will need to support them in exercising their own judgement.

Fourth, in the field and style in which we are working, materials are needed in many cases to support teachers, but they are not the major variable.

Any research would necessarily be tentative and exploratory. Research design may be subtle to a degree, but it should be robust rather than elegant.

Three groups of schools are taking part in the present project.

Fourteen schools are following Strategy A, sixteen are following Strategy B, and ten are following Strategy C (Drama). Teachers from each strategy came together for a strategy-based conference before embarking on the teaching.

The first group to meet were the Strategy B schools. Their problem was to find some consensus within which they could work together. In the end the consensus was embodied in a conference paper. It is not possible to quote this in full here, and the result may be to make the statement appear more abstract than it is. Here are the aim, some agreed principles of procedure, and a definition of the role of the teacher:

Aim

to educate for the elimination of racial tensions and ill-feeling within our society – which is and will be multi-racial – by undermining prejudice, by developing respect for varied traditions, and by encouraging mutual understanding, reasonableness, and justice.

Principles of Procedure

1. We should help pupils become aware of their own attitudes.
2. We should assist pupils to detect bias and the motives behind this.
3. We should help pupils become aware of the emotional content in racial tension or conflict.
4. We should make clear the historical and social factors which help explain the presence of racial/ethnic groups in society.
5. We should help pupils to see that many problems which appear to stem from racial causes may be predominantly social.
6. We need to help pupils to see the possibility of organizing for change.

Role of the Teacher

The teacher should be an example of a person critical of prejudiced attitudes and opinions held by himself and by society at large and trying to achieve some degree of mutual understanding and respect between identifiably different human groups.

Two points of importance need to be made about this position.

First, the teachers we recruited on to Strategy B were not prepared to take an authoritarian line or even to assume that they were not prejudiced while their pupils were. They saw prejudice as a social problem in which everyone is involved. Whether this rather open posture of the teachers who joined the project is typical of committed teachers we have no means of knowing. It is possible that the project was generally associated with non-authoritarian views and attracted teachers who were inclined in that direction, but it should be noted that in most cases schools were selected by local authorities. If the project were a laboratory experiment it might be argued that it would have been more fruitful to have an authoritarian Strategy B, but curriculum experiment does not allow us to override teacher judgement for the sake of experimental neatness or to pursue policies which do not appear to offer promise (in the view of the research workers and teachers involved).

Second, the specification of aim, principles, and role reached by the Strategy B teachers is complex and subtle. We do not know exactly how to play consistently in the classroom the role they have defined. The Humanities Project took two years, working with 150 teachers, to begin to define the criteria which applied to a role of similar complexity. Within the present project there is no opportunity for intensive developmental work of this kind. The Strategy B specification has an ethical base. It represents an ambitious aspiration whose pedagogical implications would take time to work out. It must be regarded more as an expression of intention than as an empirical specification. Accordingly, we must expect a good deal of diversity in Strategy B schools. This means that the process and the results in each school must be studied separately. Strategy B probably represents teachers using and building out from existent skills, having had one conference opportunity to think out their position.

I would conclude that within the experiment, comparisons of the effectiveness of Strategy B with other strategies are invalid. This is an important point. The natural but naïve assumption might be that an experiment of this sort is directed to testing the strategies against one another. As I shall explain more fully below, it is not.

Strategy A is relatively straightforward since it derives from the Humanities Project. The aim is 'to develop in the area of race relations an understanding of social situations and human acts and of the controversial value issues which they raise'. The hope is that this will in general conduce to better race relations. The teacher submits his teaching to the criterion of neutrality, and can draw on the techniques and insights provided by the work of the Humanities Project.

Strategy C is concerned with teaching about race relations through drama. The potential of such an approach is obvious. The schools will be working mainly through situational improvised drama. The main divergence within the group concerns the issue of whether to approach racial situations directly or within the context of a study of human relations.

In each of the schools, teaching about race relations will be part of a more general course – in social studies, humanities, or drama – and the emphasis on race relations will fall in the spring term of 1974 (January to March).

So much for the action. What of the research?

Leaving research design on one side for the moment, there is a logistic problem for the central team. How is one to study the work of forty schools and about a hundred and twenty teachers with the limited resources available? The task may appear to verge on the impossible. And yet, given the fact that our previous research was criticized for including only six schools and one teaching strategy, it can perhaps be taken that this is the typical problem of curriculum research. I do not think that it has been solved yet, nor that we shall solve it within the project. The most we can hope for is progress in the development of better ways of coping with it.

Teacher participation in research is a key factor. Our starting point for this position is twofold: the logistic problem of covering the large number of schools and our working within a tradition (in the Centre) which is concerned for teacher participation in research as a basis for the betterment of teaching.

However, Wild, who carries within the present project the main responsibility for the development of field study strategies, is now adumbrating an approach in which teacher participation is more intrinsic to the study.

Originally he suggested, in a paper addressed to the project conference of teachers, the following conditions for teacher participation in research:

1. Research should be located in the reality of the particular school and the particular classroom.
2. The research roles of the teacher and of the project team member should complement one another.
3. The development and maintenance of a common language is a prerequisite.
4. The role of the teacher as a researcher must relate closely to the role of the teacher as teacher.

Questions raised and tentatively discussed by Wild are:

1. Can the teacher sustain the dual role of teacher and researcher?
2. What is the availability of time for research work?
3. What form should the research take?
4. How wide should the span of research be?
5. How far can research be open in its findings?

The model of research adopted by the project is based on the following assumptions:

1. The responsibility for research work within the classroom rests largely upon the teachers concerned.

2. It is not possible to prejudge which classroom dimensions will be most useful for an understanding of the process taking place.
3. The teacher's commitment to teaching limits time available for research.
4. Simplicity of design would seem to be an advantage.
5. There should be some attempt to link case-study work with measurement.

On this basis Wild is now reaching towards a methodology which places central emphasis on the teachers' own perception of their work and their situation. This is a matter of building up a map of the conditions, problems and effects of teaching about race relations as seen through teachers' eyes. The perceptions of individual teachers serve as triangulation points for such a map. It is at this stage too early to define the elements of continuity and reappraisal relating his work to other case-study approaches.

In addition teachers are accumulating data about the actual process of teaching. Here the basic desideratum is that the teacher should tape-record his teaching and a reasonable proportion of the teachers taking part in the project have agreed to tape all their teaching in the area of race relations for the entire team. These tapes are valuable to the teachers themselves. They provide a means of monitoring and reflecting on their own work. It is, of course, clear that the central team cannot listen to all the tapes and process all the data. Nevertheless, they can sample adequately and they can study particular groups of pupils longitudinally.

In addition to taping, some teachers are undertaking research tasks in studying their schools and their catchment areas. In at least one instance a second teacher is observing the work of the experimental teacher and keeping running notes.

The functions of the central team in relation to the study of schools is twofold. First, Wild will undertake detailed study of a limited number of schools in collaboration with the teachers. Second, the team will act as research consultants in other schools and interview teachers and pupils. At this stage the team has dropped the term 'case-study' in order to leave open certain methodological questions and questions of presentation which the use of the term may seem to pre-empt.

In order to set the measurement programme in its context it is necessary to consider problems of experimental design.

In the Humanities Project Evaluation, MacDonald (1971) spoke of 'briefing decision makers'. A report on a curriculum project should offer decision-makers data on which to make decisions. The array of decision-makers was a broad one and included sponsors, L.E.A.s, heads, and teachers. Teachers were cetainly not neglected in the work of the evaluation project or as an audience for its reports but two circumstances led to their being given a rather less central place in the design rationale than in the present project on the problems and effects of teaching about race relations. First, the Humanities Project offered, however tentatively, a proposed curriculum which could be adopted. This led to an emphasis on the adoption as a decision and a need to brief L.E.A.s and heads. The second circumstance was that the Humanities Project was so structured and so developed that the task of briefing teachers as decision-makers was a responsibility shared between the project team and the evaluation team.

The present project aspires to integrate some of the roles of the project team and some of the roles of the evaluation team in the Humanities Project in an attempt to evolve a research model in curriculum. This appears to be possible only when, as in the present case, the project has no curricular recommendation. Three strategies are being explored in the expectation that eclectic responses will emerge. The aim of the project is to develop an understanding of the problems and effects of teaching about race relations in all the participants and to transmit that understanding to others.

What others?

Primarily to teachers. This is not to say that L.E.A.s, for example, may not have to make crucial decisions about the teaching of race relations. Some of these decisions will have to be made taking into account the growing body of data and theory about problems of change in educational settings. Contributions such as those of Shipman (1968) and Richardson (1973) will have to be weighed alongside those of MacDonald (1971) and MacDonald and Rudduck (1971) and of MacDonald's current project studying success and failure in recent innovation. The present project may make some contribution to a theory of innovation but its over-riding concern will be to address itself to teachers as decision-makers who will design a curriculum in race relations and control its implementation from moment to moment in the sequence of classroom decisions which constitute the fabric of teaching.

The project will study the classroom experience of teachers working in the area of race relations against contextual data about schools and environments. This is not an attempt to define the limits of what is useful, but a judgement about the contribution which can best be made within the resources available and taking into account the contributions of complementary research.

MacDonald (1971) has emphasized that 'no two schools (or classrooms) are so alike in their circumstances that prescriptions of curricular action can adequately supplant the judgement of the people in them'. This implies considerable restrictions on generalization. We can perhaps generalize about variables likely to be important and needing therefore to be monitored. Certain concepts may prove of general value. But when it comes to causal links we are likely to have to say simply that X or Y or Z appear to have effects A or B or C, the intervening variables controlling the links between X, Y, Z and A, B, C being insufficiently understood for us to narrow and define the prediction. The research produces alternative hypotheses between which it is not possible to discriminate because of the variability of cases.

Curriculum research is not fully replicable at project level. The field situation in which the action takes place is unique. No attempt to replicate it can succeed. And the uniqueness of the situation is not nominal, but significant.

Nor does curriculum research generalize readily from school to school. The present project is concerned with the problems and effects of teaching about race relations. Neither problems nor effects are likely to be similar in a rural school in Lincolnshire and a multi-racial school in Derby. What is needed is a grasp of the range of problems and effects with enough contextual data to allow schools embarking on teaching about race relations to anticipate what sorts of things are likely to happen and to know how other teachers have handled the potential and problems of these situations.

Accordingly the research must aspire to situational verifiability. That is, the findings must be so presented that a teacher is invited not to accept them but to test them by mounting a verification procedure in his own situation.

The project is concerned with the problems and effects of teaching about race relations. The primary data for the study of problems are derived from the study of classrooms and schools. So too is much of the information about effects. Data drawn from such studies in schools and classrooms are in a useful sense hard data. They are rooted in real situations and have a high degree of verisimilitude. Above all, conclusions drawn from them and interpretations of them are verifiable by teachers in a way that data from testing are not. Moreoever, in so far as generalizations about problems and effects drawn from them define only the range of problems and effects to be expected and not their distribution, they are well founded. The accumulated experience of curriculum research casts doubt on whether a higher degree of predictive generalization can penetrate the specificity of teaching situations.

If such a position is assumed, what is the place of a testing programme?

Again let us look at the classical model of curriculum development and evaluation. The curriculum represents a proposal whose intention is expressed by the proposer in terms of behavioural objectives or intended learning outcomes. The curriculum is then treated as an experimental procedure and a pre-test/post-test design is employed to assess the effectiveness of the curriculum as compared with the performance of control groups. The specification of objectives provides a basis for the design of criterion-referenced tests or the selection of norm-referenced tests which are judged to be relevant. The emphasis is on measurement of the effects of the programme or curriculum.

For the purpose of the measurement exercise the teacher and context are not taken into account as variables but are regarded as constants. In the Humanities Project Evaluation it was recognized that the variability ignored by this conventional assumption would have to be examined in the light of case-study. No objectives were offered by the project, but an attempt was made to focus on the effects of the curriculum by asking those who had experience of it to offer hypotheses about the effects it was having or by generating such hypotheses through case-study. The emphasis was still on the measurement of the effects of the programme.

The measurement results of the Humanities Evaluation have not been fully reported, though a preliminary report is available. (Hamingson 1973, 406–453) A large battery was used and unexpectedly marked trends were thrown up. Among the most robust results were correlated shifts on the Manchester Reading Test, the Mill Hill Vocabulary Test and measures of pupil self-esteem. Although these shifts were significant only in Humanities Project schools which had access to training, it could be argued that the hypothesis that the three variables correlate in a wider range of settings is worth exploring. That is to say, patterns among observed effects are not necessarily linked to the setting of a particular curriculum.

The place of the testing programme in the design of the project on teaching about race relations is a first attempt to respond to this observation.

The project has no objectives in the strict sense. The aims and intentions of the teachers in the teaching situation are not influenced by a detailed consensus on intended learning outcomes. Within a very general aim there will be divergence of teacher intention and teacher set. Hence there is no rigorous way of assignng to any effect a logical relationship to the teaching. And since tests have to be selected within the project before the teaching has been studied empirically, the link would have to be a logical link. We cannot assert *prima facie* that the tests will measure the effects of the experiment. They will measure changes in pupil performance on those tests.

What might cause such changes? Since schools are engaged in the promotion of a wide range of cognitive, affective and attitudinal changes in pupils, it is not unreasonable to expect that during the course of the experiment (which represents only a small proportion of the teaching the pupils receive) changes will take place as a function both of the experimental treatment and of the contextual treatment which the school is offering at the same time. If this is so, there is likely to be interaction between experimental and contextual effects. It is therefore worth attempting to design a battery which will monitor both the experiment and the context.

This position has been reached during the design of the test battery, and its implications for the design of testing programmes in curriculum research and development will take time to work out. It might well be possible in the future to design and justify a battery which monitored a range of changes likely to result from schooling. If for example there were a significant correlation in the context of a mathematics project between increments in mathematics scores and increments in reading scores, it would tend to indicate that the project produced its strongest effects when placed in a school where the teaching of reading was relatively effective.

We might look towards a battery which, placed alongside tests oriented on a particular programme, gave an indication of the contextual variables in any one setting. Well-standardized tests exist which would be strong candidates for inclusion in such a battery.

This is not the place to pursue these methodological considerations further. It is sufficient to say that they have influenced the design of the test battery in the present project.

The data from the measurement programme are soft data in two senses. First, the tested variables are no more than indicators and approximations. The tests are not criterion-referenced in terms of the project, but derive their validity from other contexts. Second, the testing programme is not replicable in terms of the experiment, since the experimental situation cannot be replicated. Thus the measurement programme must be opened to verification by two strategies: its translation into hypotheses which teachers can verify in the classroom and its expression as theory about schools as educational contexts which can be verified in settings other than this experiment.

The great advantage of measurement data is that they are quantified and can therefore be processed in ways that field study data cannot. Field study data are data 'strong in reality' which are difficult to organize. Test data are data 'weak in reality' which are susceptible to organization.

Against the background assumptions which have been prevalent in educational research, this position may seem paradoxical. It is in many ways liberating. Its recognition invites one to use testing in a speculative and suggestive style. If it is the case-study data rather than the test data which consolidates, then the tests can be instruments of exploration. If results prove to be statistically significant – and there is no doubt that the enterprise, though worthwhile, is risky in that respect – then data from the testing programme will be operating on the boundaries of our knowledge of the relation of teaching in attitudinal areas to its contexts.

The battery contains four tests of inter-racial attitudes. One of these is a standardized test, the adolescent version of the Bagley-Verma Test. The others are more risky measures: a comprehension-type test (E. Peel), an opinion questionnaire (L. Stenhouse) and a perception test with ambiguous pictures (G. Verma). Between them these tests should give some indication of shifts of inter-racial attitude.

However, since the teachers are not teaching to prescribed objectives which tally with the instruments used, even where the tests have content validity (face, logical and factorial), they have low empirical validity in terms of *fit* with the teaching. The extent to which the movements of attitude recorded on these tests correspond to or act as indicators of what is desirable must to a large extent lie within the judgement of the reader of the research. They do not adequately represent what the teaching is about, but concessions are made in this respect for the sake of data which can be processed. I would myself believe that significant movements on these tests are indicators of, but not descriptors of, movements in attitude likely to be of general significance.

The tests of inter-ethnic attitude draw their main significance, however, from their relation to the other tests in the battery. These are:

1. Catell's JR–SR High School Personality Questionnaire, which claims to measure fourteen dimensions and two second-order factors.

2. Coopersmith's questionnaire designed to measure the self-esteem of adolescents.
3. A test intended to measure various aspects of pupils' attitudes to school life (Sumner, N.F.E.R.).
4. The Verma-Sumner questionnaire designed to measure pupils' attitudes to school authority.
5. The Himmelweit-Swift version of the authoritarianism scale.
6. The Brimer Wide-Span Reading Test.

It is quite clear that none of these tests is related to the aims or objectives of the project. Rather their inclusion is, as has been explained, an attempt to grasp after contextual and related variables. Do pupils with certain personality profiles change attitude more readily than others? Is a shift of racial attitude associated with shift on the authoritarianism scale? Are schools which are succeeding in improving reading more likely to be able to foster inter-ethnic tolerance?

These questions become accessible because of the pattern of control groups in experimental schools. Where we have shifts in both experimental and control groups in the same school – for example in reading achievement – we have data about the school context rather than about the experimental procedure.

We hope that both at pupil level and at school level the tests will throw up important hypotheses and spotlight issues which can be explored through field study and in other research.

One problem of this approach is of course the size of the battery required. There are also problems with reading levels in the tests, though in this case the reading test can be used as a screen.

From the above account it will be clear that we have attempted to integrate action and evaluation into a unified research model. The aim is knowledge about the problems and effects of teaching about race relations. That knowledge is intended to form a basis for the local development of curricula relevant to those problems.

The project does not aspire to recommend a particular programme or approach. The teaching strategies within the project are lines of action adopted by the teachers in order to gain greater knowledge and understanding.

The measurement programme is directed towards understanding the complex relationships between inter-racial attitudes, school variables and personality variables. It is not intended to compare the effectiveness of strategies. Any such comparison would be possible only if the relationship between the strategy and its contextual variables were not complex.

The key to the whole approach is the role of the teacher as a researcher. Not only is the project a study of teachers who are studying themselves: the application of its results depends on teachers' testing its tentative hypotheses through research in their own situations.

A particular kind of professionalism is implied: research-based teaching.

IO

THE TEACHER AS RESEARCHER

For me this chapter is of central importance. In it I shall try to outline what I believe to be the major implication for the betterment of schools emerging from curriculum research and development. Stated briefly, this is that curriculum research and development ought to belong to the teacher and that there are prospects of making this good in practice. I concede that it will require a generation of work, and if the majority of teachers – rather than only the enthusistic few – are to possess this field of research, that the teacher's professional self-image and conditions of work will have to change.

Let me review some strands in the argument.

First, I have argued that educational ideas expressed in books are not easily taken into possession by teachers, whereas the expression of ideas as curricular specifications exposes them to testing by teachers and hence establishes an equality of discourse between the proposer and those who assess his proposal. The idea is that of an educational science in which each classroom is a laboratory, each teacher a member of the scientific community. There is, of course, no implication as to the origins of the proposal or hypothesis being tested. The originator may be a classroom teacher, a policy-maker or an educational research worker. The crucial point is that the proposal is not to be regarded as an unqualified recommendation but rather as a provisional specification claiming no more than to be worth putting to the test of practice. Such proposals claim to be intelligent rather than correct.

Second, in my definition of the curricular problem in Chapter I, I have identified a curriculum as a particular form of specification about the practice of teaching and not as a package of materials or a syllabus of ground to be covered. It is a way of translating any educational idea into a hypothesis testable in practice. It invites critical testing rather than acceptance.

Finally, in the previous chapter I have reached towards a research design based upon these ideas, implying that a curriculum is a means of studying the problems and effects of implementing any defined line of teaching. And although, because of my own location in the education industry, I have drawn my example from a national project co-ordinating and studying the work of many teachers, I believe that a similar design could be adopted by an individual school as part of its development plan. I have argued, however, that the uniqueness of each classroom setting implies that any proposal – even at school level – needs to be tested and verified and adapted by each teacher in his own classroom. The ideal is that the curricular specification should feed a teacher's personal research and development programme through which he is progressively increasing his understanding of his own work and hence bettering his teaching.

To summarize the implications of this position, all well-founded curriculum research and development, whether the work of an individual teacher, of a school, of a group working in a teachers' centre or of a group working within the co-ordinating framework of a national project, is based on the study of classrooms. It thus rests on the work of teachers.

It is not enough that teachers' work should be studied: they need to study it themselves. My theme in this chapter is the role of the teacher as a researcher in his own teaching situation. What does this conception of curriculum development imply for him?

Hoyle has attempted to catch the implications of curriculum development for teachers in the concept of extended professionalism as opposed to restricted professionalism.

> The *restricted professional* can be hypothesized as having these characteristics amongst others:
>
> A high level of classroom competence;
> Child-centredness (or sometimes subject-centredness);
> A high degree of skill in understanding and handling children;
> Derives high satisfaction from personal relationships with pupils;
> Evaluates performance in terms of his own perceptions of changes in pupil behaviour and achievement;
> Attends short courses of a practical nature.
>
> The *extended professional* has the qualities attributed to the restricted professional but has certain skills, perspectives and involvements in addition. His characteristics include the following:
>
> Views work in the wider context of school, community and society;
> Participates in a wide range of professional activities, e.g. subject panels, teachers' centres, conferences;

Has a concern to link theory and practice;
Has a commitment to some form of curriculum theory and mode of evaluation.

(Hoyle 1972a)

I am sceptical about some of this. Why child-centredness, for example? And surely theories should be the objects of experimental testing, not of commitment. The extended professional appears to fall short of autonomy and this is confirmed elsewhere in Hoyle's writing:

> This does not mean that we are underestimating the significance of the teacher in the innovation process. The teacher is important in three respects:
> (a) He can be independently innovative at the classroom level;
> (b) He can act as a 'champion' of an innovation among his colleagues;
> (c) Ultimately, it is the teacher who has to operationalize on innovation at the classroom level.
>
> (Hoyle 1972c, 24)

I don't think this limited role and limited autonomy is a satisfactory basis for educational advance. The critical characteristics of that extended professionalism which is essential for well-founded curriculum research and development seem to me to be:

> The commitment to systematic questioning of one's own teaching as a basis for development;
> The commitment and the skills to study one's own teaching;
> The concern to question and to test theory in practice by the use of those skills.

To these may be added as highly desirable, though perhaps not essential, a readiness to allow other teachers to observe one's work – directly or through recordings – and to discuss it with them on an open and honest basis.

In short, the outstanding characteristics of the extended professional is a capacity for autonomous professional self-development through systematic self-study, through the study of the work of other teachers and through the testing of ideas by classroom research procedures.

What techniques of classroom study are available to the teacher who takes this position?

Probably the best-known technique is that of interaction analysis, which has in one form or another a long history, though modern developments are often seen as descendents from Bales' work in studying small groups (Bales 1950). Flanders is the best-known figure in this field, having been the centre of a group in the United States which has developed interaction analysis methods for the study of teaching and for teacher training. (See for example, Amidon and Hunter 1966; Amidon and Hough 1967; Flanders 1970)

Flanders has defined classroom interaction analysis in the following terms:

> Classroom interaction analysis refers not to one system, but to many systems for coding spontaneous verbal communication, arranging the data into a useful display, and then analysing the results in order to study patterns of teaching and learning.
>
> (Flanders 1970, 28–29)

It is in fact a method of organizing data from the observation of classrooms. The problem, as Flanders sees it, is

> . . . to decide how teachers and college students can explore various patterns of interaction and discover for themselves which patterns they can use in order to improve instruction.
>
> (Flanders 1970, 17)

> An observer sits in the classroom or views a video-sound playback, or just listens to a voice recording and keeps a record of the flow of events on an observation form. . . . He is trained to use a set of categories. He decides which category best represents each event and then writes down the code symbol of that category.
>
> (Flanders 1970, 5)

Flanders' own category system, F.I.A.C. (Flanders Interaction Analysis Categories), which is shown in Figure 4 on the following page (Flanders 1970, 34) can serve as an example.

Interaction analysis of this kind is a useful but an extremely limited instrument.

Hamilton and Delamont (1974, 3) suggest that

> interaction analysis techniques are an efficient way of discovering the norms of teacher and pupil behaviour. Thus, a particular teacher's 'score' from an interaction analysis study will 'place' her in relation to her colleagues; but it will supply very little other information about her as an individual.

The authors suggest (3–5) a number of factors which impose restrictions upon the use of interaction analysis:

> 1) Most interaction analysis systems ignore the context in which the data are collected. They make no provision for data concerning, for example, the lay-out of the classroom or the equipment being used.

Fig. 4 Flanders' Interaction Analysis Categories* (F.I.A.C.)

Teacher Talk	Response	1. *Accepts feeling.* Accepts and clarifies an attitude or the feeling tone of a pupil in a non-threatening manner. Feelings may be positive or negative. Predicting and recalling feelings are included. 2. *Praises or encourages.* Praises or encourages pupil action or behaviour. Jokes that release tension, but not at the expense of another individual; nodding head, or saying 'Um hm?' or 'go on' are included. 3. *Accepts or uses ideas of pupils.* Clarifying, building, or developing ideas suggested by a pupil. Teacher extensions of pupil ideas are included but as the teacher brings more of his own ideas into play, shift to category five.
		4. *Asks questions.* Asking a question about content or procedure, based on teacher ideas, with the intent that a pupil will answer.
	Initiation	5. *Lecturing.* Giving facts or opinions about content or procedures; expressing *his own* ideas, giving *his own* explanation, or citing an authority other than a pupil. 6. *Giving directions.* Directions, commands, or orders to which a pupil is expected to comply. 7. *Criticizing or justifying authority.* Statements intended to change pupil behaviour from non-acceptable pattern; bawling someone out; stating why the teacher is doing what he is doing; extreme self-reference.
Pupil Talk	Response	8. *Pupil-talk – response.* Talk by pupils in response to teacher. Teacher initiates the contact or solicits pupil statement or structures the situation. Freedom to express own ideas is limited.
	Initiation	9. *Pupil-Talk–initiation.* Talk by pupils which they initiate. Expressing own ideas; initiating a new topic; freedom to develop opinions and a line of thought, like asking thoughtful questions; going beyond the existing structure.
Silence		10. *Silence or confusion.* Pauses, short periods of silence and periods of confusion in which communication cannot be understood by the observer.

*There is *no* scale implied by these numbers. Each number is classificatory; it designates a particular kind of communication event. To write these numbers down during observation is to enumerate, not to judge a position on a scale.

2) Interaction analysis systems are usually concerned only with overt, observable behaviour. They take no account of the intentions which lie behind such behaviour.
3) Interaction analysis systems are expressly concerned with 'what can be categorized and measured'. (Simon and Boyer 1970, 1) But, by using crude measurement techniques, or ill-defined category boundaries, the systems may well obscure, distort or ignore the qualitative features they claim to be investigating.
4) Interaction analysis systems focus on 'small bits of action or behaviour rather than global concepts' (Simon and Boyer 1970, 1). Inevitably, therefore, they generate a super-abundance of data. Yet, to interpret such data it has to be linked to a set of descriptive concepts – typically the categories themselves – or to a small number of global concepts built up from the categories.
5) By definition, the systems utilize pre-specified categories. If the systems are intended to assist explanations, then the explanations may be tautologous.
6) Finally, by placing firm boundaries on continuous phenomena, the systems create a bias from which it is hard to escape. Reality – frozen in this way – is often difficult to liberate from its static representation.

The authors note that some of these limitations have been acknowledged by the originators of the systems. In particular, the first three have been clearly defined by Flanders (1970, Chapter 2).

Adelman and Walker (1973) in a critical comment on the F.I.A.C. system suggest that 'the most significant weakness in the theoretical basis of the technique is in its naïve conception of "talk" as a means of human communication'. In their own study of classrooms they found that the talk did not fit the categories available for coding it. The suggestion is that Flanders' analytic categories are based on classrooms which are instructional and where talk is in a public dialogue form. It 'makes little sense when applied to some of those intimate conversations between teachers and children where both are talking but where the only questions that are being asked are those asked by the children'. In short, F.I.A.C. – and for that matter other available interaction systems – does not fit open classrooms in which talk is not as stereotyped and limited in range and tone as it tends to be in the teacher-dominated instructional classroom. Adelman and Walker make this observation in their summary.

> Flanders' system for the analysis of classroom interaction is limited by its inherent conception of talk. This limits it to seeing teacher-student interaction in terms of the *transmission* of information – sometimes one-way, sometimes two-way. It does not concern itself with talk as the expression and negotiation of meanings; as the medium through which

people see themselves as others see them. The underlying concept is simply one of information-exchange, it does not touch on the relationships between talk and knowledge, between talk and identity, both for oneself and for others. In short, it sees talk as transmission, not as communication.

This finding confirms the experience of Elliott and MacDonald who attempted to produce an interaction analysis system on classic lines to monitor discussion in the classroom and found themselves unable to devise a limited category system which caught the important distinctions they were able to draw in qualitative analysis.

My conclusion is that interaction analysis is a technique of very limited use to the teacher in researching his own classroom. It can be used if he is engaged in basically instructional class teaching, to obtain a crude descriptive impression of some aspects of his verbal behaviour in classroom situations; and it provides a basis for quantitative comparison of his behaviour with that of other teachers. In research terms, however, I believe it is a cul-de-sac. And many of its weaknesses come from the attempt to provide quantitative data which will support generalizations, an attempt not of central importance to the teacher seeking an understanding of the unique as well as the generalizable elements in his own work. Interaction analysis systems provide *Mirrors of Behaviour* (Simon and Boyer 1967, 1970), but they are distorting mirrors.

An alternative approach to the study of classrooms which is available in the research literature pays much more attention to the content of teaching than does interaction analysis. This approach is concerned with the logic of teaching.

The lead in this type of work was given by B. O. Smith and his colleagues at the University of Illinois. They worked from the transcripts of eighty-five tape recordings made in five high schools, and successively adopted two different category systems for their analysis.

In their later work they distinguished logical sequences of teaching which they called *ventures*, and classified according to their objectives. Thus, for example, *causal ventures* had as their content objective 'a cause-effect relationship between particular events or between classes of events', while *conceptual ventures* had as their objective learning 'a set of conditions either governing, or implied by, the use of a term'. (25) They distinguished and exemplified eight types of ventures.

Within the logical structure of the venture, they distinguished strategies.

> Pedagogically, strategy refers to a set of verbal actions that serves to attain certain results and to guard against others. From a general stand point, strategies may serve to induce students to engage in verbal exchange, to ensure that certain points in the discourse will be made clear, and to reduce the number of irrelevant or wrong responses as the students participate in discussion, and so on.
>
> (Smith, Meux *et al.* 1967, 49)

One dimension of strategy is identified in the various kinds of verbal manipulation of the content of teaching. These Smith and his colleagues call 'moves'. And a consecutive sequence of moves of the same type is called a play.

It will be clear that Smith's categories rest more on logic than do those of the interaction analysts, but the 'strategy', as defined above, distinguishes teacher control moves in interaction with the pupils. Even more than the interaction analysts Smith is teacher-centred – he sees the crucial element in the classroom as teacher utterances – and the eighty-five classroom sequences he and others have studied and analysed over ten years are examples of extremely formal teaching.

As Walker (1971) comments:

> What is significant about Smith's work is that he is able to use this highly restricted approach to classroom activity and to realize a meaningful picture of life in at least some classrooms. Obviously, the fact that he is able to do this means that in the sample of classrooms he studied the semantic aspects of the public verbal behaviour of the teacher constitute the major communication system, and the social structure of the class is geared to this restricted channel of communication.
>
> (60)

And after surveying the work not only of Smith but also of Nuthall and Laurence (1965) and of Bellack (1966), and Kliebard (1966), the same author concludes:

> Perhaps the most valuable thing to be learned from all these studies is that among the many possible ways that a teacher might function if his sole concern was the presentation of knowledge, only a narrow range of options is taken up in practice by the teacher. The main reason for this seems to be that the teacher operates primarily in terms of roles other than his concern with the presentation of knowledge. He acts as if his main task was that of establishing and maintaining a certain social structure within the classroom group. The main feature of this social structure is the thing that Bellack and Smith both assume – formality in verbal communication, and given this overriding concern of maintaining formality it is not surprising that teachers tend to dominate verbal output, to give a large part of lesson content over to such arbitrary things

> as routine and management, and to rely heavily on description rather than on higher cognitive operations. It is simply easier to manage a formal context in this way.
>
> The question that needs to be kept in mind through all this research is, How does the teacher manage knowledge in other contexts? In other words, What happens in the 'open' classroom? and just what is the role of private verbal communication in the classroom?

These are crucial questions in the present context for curriculum innovation often involves changing conceptions of the relationships between knowledge and teachers and learners and these changes are of critical significance for the social structure of the classroom. New curricula often involve the teacher in abandoning the role which is studied in most interactional and logical analyses of the classroom. We must neither minimize the usefulness, limited though it be, of interactional and logical analysis nor assume that further development of these approaches will not capture a wider applicability. It remains true that we must look towards other approaches more able to face the complexity of the classroom.

The alternative approach which has been most attractive to research workers may be called 'social anthropological'. It 'has used direct observation of classroom events as a starting point in the development of theory [and] . . . it rather shies away from quantification and uses only detailed field notes as a means of recording'. (Walker 1971, 83). In this it resembles the approach of the anthropologist who studies a community or of the student of animal behaviour. Theory is gradually built up from the examination of accumulated observations. It is partial and fragmentary. Above all it attempts not merely generalization but also the characterization of the uniqueness of particular situations.

> For the observer who chooses to use an anthropological style of observation there can be no clear cut results. The aim here is to uncover concepts that classify different classroom situations in a meaningful way, and so the observer is programmed, not with explicit, unambiguous and closely defined categories, but with broad, general theories and expectations. If the observer is to look for the unexpected and the unusual event in the classroom then he must have some idea, some prediction of what might happen, or what should happen. Most classroom events are relatively trivial and untraumatic and to raise them to the level of interest and observation the observer must have some fundamental theory at the back of his mind. The secret of good observation is to create the unusual from out of the commonplace.
>
> (Walker 1971, 87)

This may sound elusive. At the theoretical level the approach is a complex one, methodology is subtle and debatable, generalization and summary are difficult. But the product, the study which emerges and is presented to the reader is vivid and generally speaks very directly to teachers.

This makes the problem of characterizing the approach adequately in a brief summary of the kind appropriate here an intractable one.

Walker (1971) offers an excellent critical survey of the studies of Henry (1955a; 1955b; 1957; 1959; 1960; 1966); Smith and Geoffrey (1968); Jackson (1964; 1965; 1966; 1968); Kounin and his associates (Kounin 1970; Kounin, Friesen and Norton 1966; Kounin and Gump 1958; Kounin, Gump and Ryan 1961).

Walker himself built his own study on this review of the work in the field which he concludes with the following judgement:

> My overall impression of this literature is that where it is precise and reliable, that is to say where it attempts to measure; it is generally narrow and limited. The definitions of 'teaching' that it imposes on the realities of the classroom are narrower than the varieties of experience that are actually found there. . . . The choice that the available research methods provide is between being precise and simple-minded, or being vague and inaccurate.
>
> (Walker 1971, 142–143)

Accordingly, Walker sets about developing 'a descriptive language within which to frame some of the variables involved in educational innovation'. (144) He worked by observing two classrooms closely, strengthening his observation by tape recordings. He sought a kind of observation and descriptive language which should have the quality of 'variable sensitivity'; 'in other words it must be capable of looking simultaneously at what happens in the classroom both in terms of great detail, and in considerable generality – it requires the conceptual equivalent of a zoom lens'. (143)

In the nature of the case, the language he evolved is too extensive to report here in a way that would be meaningful for the reader.

He distinguishes the 'context' and 'content' of classroom activities, assimilating to context those concepts which provide a means

> of describing classroom activity in a way that is content-free, and it is done by looking at the way in which verbal messages are communicated. [And he stresses that] the categories are used primarily to show how changes are made between different states of activity, rather than as essential descriptions of individual forms. In this way they are rather

> different from the terms 'authoritarian', 'teacher-centred', 'direct', etc. that are traditionally used in this kind of research.
>
> (180)

He is concerned to catch the dynamics of the classroom process rather than to harden off into a necessarily static categorization of styles in terms of role analysis. And he takes account of pupil interaction, not merely teacher-pupil interaction.

In his analysis of content, Walker's work complements that of Bernstein, Young and Esland (Young 1971a). His terms are often clearer and they generally have better empirical anchorage.

He uses the term *definition* to refer to 'the level of generality of the teacher's control on content' (185), and distinguishes three other dimensions:

> The Particular-General Dimension: "The observation of this dimension simply involves scanning content for moves from statements about general objects or events to particular examples, or vice versa'.
>
> (190)

> The Personal-Objective Dimension: 'Here content has to be watched for moves by either the pupils or the teacher to personalize public information. One of the commonest ways of doing this is in the telling of an anecdote'.
>
> (191)

> Content Open – Content Closed: 'A sequence may start from a single statement, from which successive statements are generated by either logical or associational processes, to form a kind of branching pattern. This pattern indicates that there has been some divergence in content and so content is described as "open". . . . Alternatively, a sequence of statements may be directed towards the construction of some overarching theme or explanation, so that there is an overall narrowing in the range of content. When content is closed the sequence of statements invariably converges on a target statement to complete the sequence.'
>
> (193)

These four dimensions are interrelated through the diagnosis of observed classroom transactions and reveal 'certain patterns in the sequences by which knowledge is organized and transmitted'. (195) At this stage Walker claimed no more than to have found a way of presenting an understanding of his own limited observations.

This work seems to me to catch some important aspects of the reality of classrooms. It requires sensitivity and judgement on the part of the observer, but it is capable of contributing to a public tradition supportive of such sensitivity and judgement.

Subsequently Walker and Adelman undertook a study of a wider range of classrooms and faced more squarely the problems of observing and describing open and flexible styles of teaching. In this later work they adopted Bernstein's concepts, 'classification' and 'framing', though they found the nature of teachers' 'codes' more difficult to diagnose than might at first be expected. For example, they found a case where teaching with strong classification and framing was so overlaid with the humour and intimacy of a likeable teacher that the underlying code was in effect camouflaged. (Walker and Adelman 1972)

They paid particular attention to 'transitions' which 'occur in the process when the teacher (usually) has to change or progress to a fresh aspect of the task'. They distinguish six interrelated transitional aspects of classroom action, which are carefully defined and studied. This concentration on the point of change from sequence to sequence in the classroom process is profitable because the intentions, control strategies and background assumptions of the teacher are thrown into relief at such points.

I find their work at this stage (Walker and Adelman 1972) conceptually dense at times and also think that in some of their theoretical wrestling they are struggling with problems most readers will feel less keenly than they do. Nevertheless, they are able to throw into vivid relief many aspects of the classroom which are recognized as soon as they are noticed; and they pick up the role of jokes and allusions of a kind that have escaped most observers.

Another aspect of their work is the use of stop-frame film with synchronized sound recording in order to supplement their own field notes and highlight elements of classroom activity which they were missing in direct observation. (Adelman and Walker 1974) This provides the zoom lens effect which Walker earlier asked of his concepts (see page 151), and they make strong claims for the technique:

> Having incorporated the technique into our repertoire of skills, we find that what we are doing is no longer strictly 'participant observation'. At the time of observation what we do is not too dissimilar from regular participant observation, but outside the immediate situation we have available material which is qualitatively quite different to the usual observational record. It is not only more reliable, but also more flexible and more vivid, and this opens up opportunities for research that have been little explored in the past.
>
> (Walker and Adelman 1972, 21)

Hamilton (1973) used more conventional techniques of classroom observation supplemented by questionnaires, but like Walker and

Adelman associated his work closely with innovations in teaching. Whereas they studied teachers whose innovative style derived from an interest in 'open education' of one sort or another, Hamilton's teachers were working within a 'public innovation' – Scottish Integrated Science. In this context his work is more assimilable to curriculum evaluation than is theirs, and indeed he suggests that classroom analysis of the kind he is undertaking is necessary for an understanding both of curricular reforms and of secondary school reorganization.

In the most substantial part of his empirical work Hamilton is studying a team of four teachers – a physicist, a chemist and two biologists – who are engaged in teaching integrated science. The teacher's subject ideologies are in tension with the demand for integration and the observation 'shows the Scottish scheme fulfilling objectives directly opposed to those originally intended by the curriculum planners'. (Hamilton 1973, vi)

Hamilton offers eight propositions which are of interest to all who are concerned to observe teaching, and are therefore worth presenting here:

> I. Within the classroom context students and teachers never learn nothing. (Equally nothing never happens.)
> II. Students (or for that matter teachers) are never ignorant or know nothing.
> III. Taken all together the occupants of a classroon comprise an interactive social nexus.
> IV. As knowledge is unevenly distributed (and redistributed) in the classroom, classroom life is inherently unstable.
> V. Within the classroom context, the relationship between teacher and taught is best understood as a refracting rather than a transmitting medium. (Thus, for example, different individuals learn different things from the same event.)
> VI The learning milieu is not a pre-ordained setting, but, instead, is socially constructed.
> VII. Within the classroom context time is a potent influence suffusing all that takes place.
> VIII. Within the classroom context communication is not merely verbal. Both participants and objects are transmitters of a range of additional 'messages'.
>
> (Hamilton 1973, 177 *et seq.*)

Of particular interest here is Hamilton's discussion of his role as an observer. He observed in two sessions and towards the end of the first also taught for a short time in the classes he had been observing.

In one case in particular he experienced some problems in shifting role from observer to teacher. On the other hand he felt that his teaching validated him with the teachers he was observing. Hargreaves (1966) and Lacey (1970) also report tensions between the role of teacher and that of participant observer.

This issue is clearly of crucial importance if we are to consider the teacher as researcher into his own work. Hamilton makes an important point which I think has a bearing on this.

> At a more general level, I would argue that in a school situation where (as Hargreaves puts it) 'any adult not dressed as a workman usually has some strong connection with the teaching profession' (1966; p. 201) a researcher is unable to define himself in the eyes of the children *except* in relationship to the teaching figures they are accustomed to. (In short, there is no such thing as an 'objective' observer role.) The observer's relationship with children is strongly influenced by his relationship with the teacher. Before he can effectively establish his own role, an adult observer must first recognize and understand the teacher's role. Thus, while it is possible and relatively easy for an observer to have an 'open' relationship with children in an 'open' classroom, it is not so easy, as Hargreaves found in a problem secondary modern school, to establish a similar research relationship in a 'closed' setting.
>
> (Hamilton 1973, 190–191)

Considered in this light, it seems probable that a teacher can assume the role of a researcher, but that this will be possible only in an 'open' classroom. The particular characteristic of the 'open' classroom (the term is not a precise one) which is relevant here is that of open negotiation and hence definition of the teacher's role. Such a definition is of course a gradual and progressive definition because it is learned by the participants in the classroom situation. Now, in order to be an observer/researcher, the teacher needs to teach that definition of himself to the pupils. In my experience, this is quite possible provided he makes it clear that the reason he is playing the role of researcher is to improve his teaching and make things better for them. I shall look at this situation more closely later. For the moment it is enough to state it clearly.

A teacher who wishes to take a research and development stance to his own teaching may profit at certain stages in the development of his research by the presence of an observer in his classroom. In the project on teaching about race relations reported in the last chapter, there have been several instances of teachers working in pairs teaching and observing by turns. In one school, members of the social studies department have acted as observers for a drama teacher. These arrangements have been fruitful, but they imply staffing deployment likely to be secured in present circumstances only in the validating context of a national project.

Another possibility is that a research-oriented teacher may train a student in a tradition of observation by observing the student and inviting the student to observe him. At the moment, where this occurs, it is something of a breakthrough. And it demands unusual sensitivity and good personal relationships on both sides. If we could get general acceptance of the proposition that all teachers should be learners and create a public research methodology and accepted professional ethic covering this situation, we would have a basis for observing the teaching of colleagues which greatly reduced the element of threat in the situation.

Most of the work done in this area has relied on observers who are research workers rather than teachers. And, generally speaking, these workers have been more interested in building a theory of teaching and reporting observations in a form addressed mainly to the research community, than in improving the classrooms they have studied. This is not true of all the work reported, but there are almost always traces of the separation of the research worker from the teacher.

Hamilton (1973) advises participant observers: 'Recognize that research relations are facilitated if the observer can find some way to "give" as well as to "take". Just taking an interest in a school and being a sympathetic listener may well be enough.' (203)

The strength of assumptions in the research tradition, and the limited openness he negotiated with the teachers he was observing, conspired to hide from him the obvious point that his observations might have been used to develop and improve the teaching in a very direct way. In fact the observer/teacher duo can define the situation to the pupils in these terms just as the teacher/researcher can. Classroom research is about bettering classroom experience. The main barrier to pupils' understanding this is our having taught them that the teacher is always right. This elevates personal wisdom at the expense of professional skill.

Let us now take stock.

I began this chapter by arguing that effective curriculum development of the highest quality depends upon the capacity of teachers to take a research stance to their own teaching. By a research stance I mean a disposition to examine one's own practice critically and systematically. I have reviewed the tradition of classroom research which professional research workers have built and tried to explore the possibility and the problems of teachers casting themselves in the role of researchers. Given that they can define themselves in this way, what theoretical and methodological problems do they face?

It is important to make the point that the teacher in this situation is concerned to understand better his own classroom. Consequently, he is not faced with the problems of generalizing beyond his experience. In his context, theory is simply a systematic structuring of his understanding of his work.

Concepts which are carefully related to one another are needed both to capture and to express that understanding. The adequacy of such concepts should be treated as provisional. The utility and appropriateness of the theoretical framework of concepts should be testable; and the theory should be rich enough to throw up new and profitable questions.

Each classroom should not be an island. Teachers working in such a tradition need to communicate with one another. They should report their work. Thus a common vocabulary of concepts and a syntax of theory need to be developed. Where that language proves inadequate, teachers would need to propose new concepts and new theory.

The first level of generalization is thus the development of a general theoretical language. In this, professional research workers should be able to help.

If teachers report their own work in such a tradition, case studies will accumulate, just as they do in medicine. Professional research workers will have to master this material and scrutinize it for general trends. It is out of this synthetic task that general propositional theory can be developed.

But what of the methodological problems? If I leave aside problems in the economy of time which probably exclude all but the most energetic teachers from such work, given present staffing and organization in schools, there are two main areas in which methodological problems occur. First, there is the problem of objectivity. Second, there is the problem of securing data.

The problem of objectivity seems to me a false one. Any research into classrooms must aim to improve teaching. Thus any research must be applied by teachers, so that the most clinically objective research can only feed into practice through an interested actor in the situation. There is no escaping the fact that it is the teacher's subjective perception which is crucial for practice since he is in a position to control the classroom.

Accordingly we are concerned with the development of a sensitive and self-critical subjective perspective and not with an aspiration towards an unattainable objectivity. This is difficult enough. Illusion, assumption and habit must be continually tested. Illusion may be destroyed when disclosed. Assumptions and habits will be changed.

The problem is one of awareness. Walker (1971), writing from the point of view of a classroom observer, says: 'You also need to think at a level of detail that is below the threshold of awareness of the teacher, *and* at a level roughly approximate to the level of conscious teacher strategies'. Conscious study can lower the threshold of awareness and help the teacher to be more perceptive. But he can never escape from the process within which he must respond as he does his work. I believe that much teaching must be habitual in the way that playing tennis is: it is a question of cultivating habits I can defend and justify. And note that the good player often improves his performance by becoming self-conscious. At practice he is converting deliberate awareness into reliable habit.

How do we get the data on which to do this?

A games player often uses a coach, who is in effect a consultant observer. Similarly, a teacher may, as I have suggested, invite an observer into his classroom. In this case, the data may be gathered in the light of the participant observer research tradition I have reported in this chapter. Some adjustment is necessary because within the tradition the teacher is usually seen as the object of the observation, and not as a co-worker with the researcher. Thus Louis Smith 'explained his presence in the school . . . by saying, "In a way it's kind of like Margaret Mead, the anthropologist, who went to the South Seas to observe the natives." To which the teachers invariably responded, "And we are the natives." ' (Walker 1971, 83)

In Smith and Geoffrey's work, however, there was a research partnership between observer and teacher.

> . . . they worked out a research design which involved Louis Smith spending as much time as possible sitting in the back of Geoffrey's seventh grade classroom as an observer, while Geoffrey himself made notes when he could. The two observers, one 'inside' and the other 'outside' the system, then compared notes at various times, and in the final analysis of the material used each other as checks and sources.
>
> (Walker 1971, 99)

Walker and Adelman also worked collaboratively with teachers, but it is noteworthy that they wrote the reports whereas Smith and Geoffrey published their work as co-authors.

Where it is not possible for a teacher to have the services of an observer, an obvious recourse is to some form of recording. Videotape is costly and as a rule requires assistance. The stop-frame photography technique employed by Walker and Adelman involves expensive equipment, though there are ways of photographing one's own classroom with an ordinary camera. On the whole, however, the most accessible means of gathering data is audio-tape. This too is limited by acoustic problems, but within these limitations it is of great value. Walker and others have criticized its use on its own on the grounds that the incomplete record it gives is difficult to interpret reliably; but they write from the point of view of outside observers, and I do not think that the objection applies nearly so much to the situation of the teacher studying his own classroom. The teacher is more able to interpret a tape than a stranger is, given an adequate degree of self-critical awareness.

A further possibility is to gather perceptions of the classroom situation from the pupils. This strategy has exciting possibilities and progress in it has been made by Elliott and Adelman whose work is reported at the end of this chapter.

I conclude that the main barriers to teachers' assuming the role of researchers studying their own teaching in order to improve it, are psychological and social. The close examination of one's professional performance is personally threatening; and the social climate in which teachers work generally offers little support to those who might be disposed to face that threat. Hence for the moment the best way forward is probably through a mutually supportive co-operative research in which teachers and full-time research teams work together. The situations in which this becomes possible are most likely to be created within research and development projects in curriculum and teaching, and in the remainder of this chapter I want to review some work of this sort.

First, a very simple and elementary example, In the classic curriculum project the impulse towards monitoring one's own performance in the classroom arises from the need to verify whether one is in fact succeeding in implementing the pedagogy of the curriculum. Thus in *Man: A Course of Study*, in which pedagogic or process aims (see page 92) are important, the teacher is offered a very simple observation schedule structured on continua between poles (Fig. 5). This schedule is a crude device, but within limits it is an effective one, though it can scarcely be regarded as a research instrument as it stands.

The Humanities Curriculum Project went farther than this. First, it defined its pedagogy in terms of principles – the aim and the concept of neutral chairman. Then it suggested variables likely to be of importance in relation to that aim and concept and invited teachers

Fig. 5 Classroom Observation Checklist

Evaluation of the lesson		
Factual questions	——:——:——:——	Opinion questions
Short answer	——:——:——:——	Lengthy response
Questions mostly from teacher	——:——:——:——	Questions mostly from students
Exchanges largely student to teacher	——:——:——:——	Exchanges largely student to student
Teacher sets and controls agenda	——:——:——:——	Students initiate topics of discussion
Teacher's role: authority	——:——:——:——	Teacher's role: non-participant
Students have no clear sense of purpose	——:——:——:——	Students have clear sense of purpose
Less than 1/3 student participation	——:——:——:——	Almost all students participate
Student interest low	——:——:——:——	Student interest high
Class is quiet	——:——:——:——	Class is noisy
General teacher style		
Teacher's stance: apart from students	——:——:——:——	Physically close to students
Practically no teacher movement	——:——:——:——	Much teacher movement
Teacher doesn't draw out students	——:——:——:——	Teacher makes efforts to draw out students
Teacher is strict with regard to student behavior	——:——:——:——	Teacher is permissive
Teacher 'talks down' to students – much	——:——:——:——	Teacher 'talks down' to students – none
Teacher dominates the class	——:——:——:——	Teacher and students work together co-operatively

to evolve their own 'neutral chairman role' by testing the operation of these variables, and of course any others whose influence they detected. There was a considerable problem in communicating this research stance. Curriculum projects were expected by teachers to tell them what to do rather than to invite them to undertake research. Dale (1973) has described this communication problem at the first experimental stage of the project.

> I do not think that at any stage during the first months with the project did we feel that we had either the authority or any of the basic skills to research into our own teaching effectiveness. Research into teaching involves special techniques and an expertise that is normally found only in university departments. . . . It was therefore not surprising that we left all comment about our classroom performaces to the central team, and were somewhat frustrated when little in the way of such comment was forthcoming. But it established the pattern of dependence on the central team as the experts, the authority on whether we in the schools were 'doing the Project' correctly. No matter how often they attempted

> to reject this dependence and to reiterate the statement about being partners in the development of the Project, and how often they assured us that they needed to learn from the trial schools, we in those schools did not accept this. We could not believe that the central team were really in this position, and that they really did not have answers to our never-ending classroom problems. As teachers we expected to come to the fountain head, and to receive reassurance. And I do not yet see how the fallibility of the project director or the central team can be appreciated by the trial schools. All the traditions of teacher training militate against it, all teachers' expectations militate against it, and the position of the central team as the focal point of the development militates against it. . . . It is all too easy for exploratory ideas and suggestions from the central team to become authoritative statements in the eyes of the trial schools. When we were presented with what the central team saw as a series of hypotheses to be explored in the classroom, they became in our hands no longer hypotheses but matters of H.C.P. policy or a series of rules to be obeyed at all costs. Failure to adhere to them implied a failure to operate the project. We had neither the confidence to challenge these hypotheses nor the belief that we were able, as part of our brief, to explore and investigate them in the classroom situation and so test their validity.

The problems of research co-operation between teachers and research teams could not be put more clearly. In the present climate it is extremely difficult to overcome them. Nevertheless, in spite of Dale's pessimism, I believe progress has been made. There is certainly evidence that some groups of teachers have taken the research role in the dissemination stage of the Humanities Project. Consider the following report of a course for Humanities Project teachers organized by the I.L.E.A. (I.L.E.A. 1973):

> To begin with we tried to decide what criteria we considered when we talked about improvement and progress within discussion. We decided on the following:
>
> Interchange between group members: this includes such thing as the students taking the initiative instead of the chairman (as in the Bishop Thomas Grant tape – after the second reading on the second tape there is no lead-in by the chairman, the boys start straight away). We agreed that this interchange is the responsibility of the chairman. In the Further Education tape, for example, the chairman (a student) is totally recessive – this has resulted in lack of direction and the result is a poor level of discussion, lacking depth, from a group of students who appeared very articulate. In the school tapes the chairman often used short questions to clarify and reinforce answers, to guide discussion and to maintain relevance. The discussion, we felt, was very much the same at the beginning and at the end – it had neither progressed nor developed. We saw on all three school tapes at some time or another certain points of interaction between

teacher and one pupil – we would consider progress in discussion had taken place if there was direct interaction, i.e. pupils questioning each other and not looking at the chairman but to the group when talking. Pupil questioning did not really occur significantly on any of the video-tapes. However, talking to the group as a whole, instead of the chairman, was achieved by most groups by the end of the taped sessions. This links up with group sensitivity and understanding of each other – for instance in the Bishop Thomas Grant tape: support for Maureen when she cannot express what she wants to say is shown when the group wait for her and let her finish. We also looked under the heading of group interchange at the tolerance or discipline of discussion and opinions, leading not to blind acceptance but greater understanding, while still having a divergent point of view. All tapes had examples of slight points of agreement and disagreement but nothing truly extreme. The Bishop Thomas Grant tape probably revealed most divergence and we felt that the discussion was growing towards being 'disciplined' and points of view were respected.

The second heading really considers the content and development of discussion. Most of the discussion at the beginning of the tapes was personal, relating to direct experiences, and throughout the discussion language remained expressive whatever the content. What is talked about tends to be known and concrete. We considered a marked development had taken place when students started dealing with and considering hypothetical (and therefore to them abstract) situations. We felt that this had developed in the discussion on Peckham's first tape with Ron: for example his insight into children who say 'yes sir, no sir', for the sake of peace and quiet, and his later comment on the situation of teachers – if there were no case 'he'd be in a box by himself'. In the second Peckham tape the lads were trying to make positive suggestions and criticising each other while considering the problem of the disruptive boy. They were putting themselves in the position of thinking about problems of the teacher. Flashes of insight were apparent – for instance, 'By walking out on a teacher you're not really getting to know him.' The students in all school tapes followed the discussion well, and we felt there was little that was irrelevant.

I believe that fruitful development in the field of curriculum and teaching depends upon evolving styles of co-operative research by teachers and using full-time researchers to support the teachers' work. This probably means that research reports and hypotheses must be addressed to teachers, that is, they must invite classroom research responses rather than laboratory research responses. It may also involve research-trained personnel in taking consultancy roles in teacher groups, and support roles in schools and classrooms.

These are the premises on which the project on the problems and effects of teaching about race relations is founded, and there is evidence that it has come much nearer to communicating the research position than, on Dale's witness, the Humanities Project did. For example, most schools are writing their own reports on the work; and conference dialogue has been across schools rather than between schools and the central team.

What the 'race project' is attempting at one level and in one context, the Ford Teaching Project, directed by John Elliott, is attempting at another. It is working at a greater level of detail and depth of penetration into classrooms.

In the Ford Teaching Project, Elliott and Adelman have been working closely with teachers and advisers with the following aims:

> 1. To help teachers already attempting to implement Inquiry/Discovery methods, but aware of a gap between attempt and achievement, to narrow this gap in their situation.
> 2. To help teachers by fostering an action-research orientation towards classroom problems.
>
> (Elliott and Adelman 1973a, 10)

They took the position that 'action, and reflection on action, are the joint responsibilities of the teachers' (12). They thus combined in a team teachers from different schools, primary and secondary, and from a range of subjects.

One of the their important roles as outside researchers was to interview pupils in order to compare the teachers' and the pupils' perceptions of particular sequences of teaching. With the pupils' permission, tapes of interviews were played back to their teachers. Substantial perceptual disparities emerged. Teachers and pupils were then able to discuss these and attempt to resolve them, and in many cases the outside researchers were able to withdraw from the task of pupil interviewing having helped teachers to establish an open dialogue with their pupils about their teaching.

In *New Era* (Elliott and Adelman 1973b; Rowe 1973; Thurlow 1973) the researchers and two teachers on the project reported on the progress of the research, one teacher writing on 'The cyclical structure of evaluatory schemes' (Rowe) and one on 'Eliciting pupils' interpretations in the primary school' (Thurlow), this latter reporting the development from the pupil interviews described above.

The project is an excellent example of teachers' adopting a research and development stance to their work and of the development of a researcher role which supports such a stance. Moreover, in investigating inquiry- and discovery-based teaching it chose a line of study which caught the pedagogical implications of a variety of new curricular developments, and documented the difficulty of implementing these in practice.

Cooper and Ebbutt (1974), two of the teachers involved, have published a paper on 'Participation in Action-Research as an In-Service Experience' in which they summarize their conclusions as follows:

> 1. We have found that it is possible to participate in action-research, although the constraints of the day-to-day secondary school situation tend to reduce its effectiveness.
> 2. So far the Project has made teachers here think deeply about their methods and techniques. We feel that this and the discussions which have followed such thoughts have been very valuable.
> 3. The research has shown to us that the interpretation of interviews with groups of pupils, with or without the teacher, must be treated with great care.
> 4. There is some evidence to suggest that a teacher's intentions may not be achieved because:
>   (a) for some reason the class misinterpret his aims
>   (b) he chooses the wrong method to implement his aims
>   (c) his seemingly chance remarks counteract some of his aims.
> 5. We believe that the Project is going to prove extremely valuable for in-service training, especially as it allows teachers to evaluate their own performances, and to see and judge other teachers at work.
> 6. We feel that teachers of a sensitive nature might not be suitable for this type of research, or indeed for the subsequent in-service training where similar techniques are to be used.
> 7. We believe that teachers taking part in a project of this nature need careful and sympathetic help as well as understanding, especially when they are exposed for the first time to feedback on their own lessons. This care and help have been much in evidence in this research, but we feel that others trying to emulate the techniques used may need to be reminded that there are dangers. This is especially true when outside agencies come into the classroom situation.
> 8. Some of the teachers on the Project seem to have found it difficult to stand back from the classroom situation and identify certain important problems connected with their teaching. This research has helped them to become more aware that such problems exist.
> 9. We are pleased that this project has brought research workers into the school – it seems to have helped them to understand our problems, and helped us to understand theirs.
>
> (Cooper and Ebbutt 1974, 70–71)

This estimate of the problems of research-based teaching is perhaps a little optimistic, and there are some signs of tension between the roles of teacher and researcher. I believe, however, that it is worth facing these tensions and attempting to resolve them. For in the end it is difficult to see how teaching can be improved or how curricular proposals can be evaluated without self-monitoring on the part of teachers. A research tradition which is accessible to teachers and which feeds teaching must be created if education is to be significantly improved.

II

THE SCHOOL AND INNOVATION

The power of the individual teacher is limited. Without his strengths the betterment of schools can never be achieved; but the strengths of individuals are not effective unless they are co-ordinated and supported. The primary unit of co-ordination and support is the school.

The school is the basic organized community in education, and it is at school level that the problems and possibilities of curriculum innovation have to be negotiated. In this chapter I shall consider some of the constraints and problems schools face in improving themselves and some of the patterns of leadership and management in schools. Finally, I shall look at possible developments which can help the school to organize for improvement.

It is pertinent to ask how far a school is free to change, given the context in which it is set. I am thinking at the moment of the pressures exerted on it from the outside and not of its internal resistances. And there seem to me two major restrictions on the school's capacity to change.

The first constraint upon the school's capacity to change is restriction of resources. Schools are underfinanced. Buildings often set intractable problems, staffing is difficult, there is a shortage of books and materials. In particular, teachers are hard-pressed. A good adult education tutor or university teacher will spend half an hour in preparation immediately before teaching. The school teacher is in virtually continuous contact with his pupils.

These are serious limitations on change. However, it is possible that if change is radical enough conditions can be ameliorated. For example, the shift to flexible grouping and team teaching helps towards flexibility of staffing. One possible response to pressure is to innovate.

This is more easily written than done. And it requires strong local authority support.

As I write, local authorities are faced with agonizing cuts in expenditure which threaten to eliminate initiative resources.

A second limitation on the school is parental and social opinion. Traditionally, British schools are rather independent of parental opinion. Musgrove and Taylor (1969) have argued that they are too independent. Nevertheless, middle-class parents in particular do exert a pressure on schools. Examination results, sports programmes and uniform are valued and schools are pushed towards them.

At present morale in British schools is often low. This is by no means general. Visiting schools all over the country, I find amazing variation. But many of the schools most needing betterment are those where morale is lowest. It is difficult to see how they can gather their energies to change without strong initiative and support from outside.

All this points to the difficulty of change; but it also points to the need for change. I think it further suggests that it is not a simple change of heart that is needed in schools. It is a change of organization and pedagogy which is founded on a development of the professional skills and knowledge of teachers. Morale is founded on professionalism.

Given a commitment to such a view as the basis of betterment, and given reasonable conditions, what barriers to change exist in the schools themselves?

I believe that the most important barrier is that of control.

Schools are – with the possible exception of the armed forces in war-time – the only institutions taking in a conscript population covering the whole of society. It follows that the school has a considerable problem of morale and control. In an earlier chapter I reviewed work which suggested that the knowledge taught by the school is distorted by control problems. If this is so, curricular changes, in so far as they imply changes in the nature of educational knowledge, threaten the teacher's control habits and thus threaten control.

More important still, curricular changes of real significance almost always involve changes in method and ways of working. To a considerable extent the control element in the relation of teachers and pupils rests on the teachers' fulfilling the expectations the pupils have about how they will behave; and change also threatens this.

Accordingly, any innovation at classroom level must face the problem of control, and too many innovative proposals have given insufficient attention to this.

But the problem does not stop there, for radical curriculum changes involve changes in the entire tone, code or ethos of the teacher-pupil relationship. As Schools Council *Working Paper No. 2* has it: 'If the teacher emphasizes, in the classroom, his common humanity with the pupils, and his common uncertainty in the face of many problems, the pupils will not take kindly to being demoted to the status of children in other relationships within the same institution.' (Schools Council 1965, 22)

I believe that change does threaten control and order and that it is perfectly reasonable that teachers should be concerned about this. Most teachers would assent to the proposition that 'coercion . . . is preferable to disorder'. (Shipman 1968, 109) The professional satisfaction and even the personality of the teacher can be destroyed by 'disciplinary problems'. And there is more fear of disorder than is commonly admitted.

> Disorder itself is epidemic in a school. Teachers know well that certain behaviour, once started, tends to go through the entire school, passing from one room to another with little loss of time and none of intensity . . . Such behaviour is that of pitching pennies, dropping shot on the floor, throwing stink bombs, etc. When the school is located in a ramshackle building, it is possible for students to shake it by small and almost undetectable movements if these movements are properly synchronized; when behaviour of this sort is once started it is very difficult to stop . . .
> (Waller 1932, 173)

The response to this ever-present threat runs through the school and shows itself both in staff sanctions against teachers who are seen as putting order at risk – through incompetence or through innovation which tests their competence – and in institutional arrangements.

> . . . life is organized to contain the children within a system or order. Staff learn where and at what times disorder is likely to break out. They see the juniors into school, making sure they are seen in the corridors and never leave the class alone in the room for any length of time. They anticipate trouble at certain times of the day and year, and organize to avoid it. They know who are the potential trouble-makers and ringleaders, and are quick to check or isolate trouble from these.
> (Shipman 1968, 84)

In short, order in schools is partly achieved by institutional arrangements and institutional norms. Any far-reaching innovation which is likely to affect attainment or attitude is likely to need to be faced by the school as a whole and to be implemented by policy. This has often not been sufficiently recognized in secondary schools where departmental autonomy is a strong tradition.

These observations do not imply that effective change is necessarily based on consensus. Change most often comes through conflict within a staff; but it is important for the leadership of the school to recognize squarely what is happening and to manage conflict within the school rather than to pretend that it does not exist.

Another barrier to change in the school is closely related to that of order. I shall call it the problem of justification. The school exercises great power over its pupil population and through these hostages power over parents. There is thus an acute need to justify the way that power is used. As a consequence schools often assume a position of rectitude.

Miles (1967) has called this 'moralism', and he comments: 'Outside observers often comment that people working in schools tend to invoke ideological, judgemental, or moralistic bases for making decisions. "Should" and "ought" seem to outweigh "is" and "can".' (16) The same observation holds for much writing about education.

Moreover, society has commonly endorsed this stance historically by demanding particular moral standards of teachers. Waller (1932) documents this amusingly. Teachers are supposed to be better than others.

Given this, the moral authority of the school may appear to be threatened if doubts are cast on its present practice and change is advocated. It is not easy for the shool or the teacher to concede 'common uncertainty in the face of many problems'. (Schools' Council 1965, 22)

The result of this moralism is that it is difficult for the school to question its moral claims and if it does so, it often grasps for a new moral certainty. Innovation of quality needs to be experimental, provisional and tentative. The need for certainty causes many schools to assert in moral terms the rightness of the innovation they are about to embark on. This leads to cults and band-wagonning, neither favourable to the spirit of critical experiment which would seem the appropriate temper for innovation.

A further barrier to innovation in schools is the threat innovation poses to the identity of the teacher and the burdens it imposes on him. I wrote earlier of the teacher as a man of learning skilled in teaching. He identifies strongly with his subject knowledge and his professional skills and often it is upon these that his professional self-respect is based. Most innovation changes both subject content and method. As innovators teachers are asked to take on, initially at least, the burdens of incompetence.

One teacher, who was thinking of joining the HCP team in his school, made the following remark after a spell of classroom observation:

> 'It seemed to be stretching the staff in all sorts of ways. Had they gone into a class to teach their ordinary subject and been so put about one would say they were incompetent or they've only done three months on the job. But in fact —— is an experienced teacher as well as a competent teacher, as are the others. None of these people have the signs of being green or incompetent yet this was suddenly standing them on their ears. They had problems which I could not understand.'

> Incompetent pupils, incompetent teachers. Incompetent Project? Not necessarily. Genuine innovation begets incompetence. It deskills teacher and pupil alike, suppressing acquired competences and demanding the development of new ones. . . . In the end the discomfort will be resolved one way or the other, by reversion to previous practice or by achieving new skills, and new frameworks. But the discomfort and dismay are built in; they are defining characteristics of innovation. . . . Perhaps if the relationship between innovation and incompetence were better understood, teachers would be less anxious about their performance, observers would employ more appropriate response criteria, and fewer people would be surprised when a process that looks and feels like failure yields evidence of significant achievement.
>
> (MacDonald 1973a, 91–92)

Dale (1973) has described how teachers often enter upon innovation, especially within the framework of a curriculum development project, with quite unrealistic expectations. 'We expected to take back an educational package that we would introduce into our respective classrooms, which with the pack of materials available, would mean successful lessons and involved and committed students.' The disparity between these expectations and the reality – particularly when the expectations are held by heads and advisory staffs – constitutes a major barrier to innovation.

The control problem of the school, its moralism and need for rectitude, and the strain which genuine innovation places on the identity and competence of teachers seem to me to be major barriers to be faced by any school attempting innovation. There are also problems in the organization of schools.

In most schools which are going concerns (as opposed to new schools) there are complex organizational arrangements which hold the educational pattern in place. It seems doubtful if it is advisable to attempt to revolutionize a large school which is in operation. Too great a load of innovation may be taken on. If this view is correct, then gradual adaptation is required. Unstreaming works upwards from the first year. Pupil options are gradually extended in the fourth and fifth.

In this process the timetable is crucial, and it is the modification of the timetable year by year which dictates the rhythm of change. It also represents the bargain struck in negotiation over the resources of staff, of time and of rooms. It is a major focus of the battle for innovation.

In viewing this battle it is important to bear in mind that most innovations have strong implications for the internal politics of the school. The school has a hierarchy of status and power. Curriculum and organizational change disturbs that allocation of status. Integration threatens the power base of subject departments. The introduction of new subjects increases the competition for resources and may create new opportunities for promoted posts. Pastoral emphasis also creates new power structures. There is strong evidence of tension in many schools between staff with pastoral and staff with curricular responsibilities.

In the face of these political conflicts most schools develop a 'party system' as well as pressure groups and lobbies.

> Innovators and rebels become leaders of groups pressing for change, opposing authority and resisting official influences. Ritualists and retreatists form withdrawn minorities. In both cases, whether active or passive, groups form and develop their own subculture, frequently clashing among themselves and with the dominant group.
>
> (Shipman 1968, 79)

The management of innovation in a school is a matter of orchestrating these different voices and negotiating the right to experiment. In most British schools the head assumes the responsibility for the general direction of policy and for such management. More and more commonly he consults and takes advice, often from staff assemblies and committees, but in the last resort he is responsible to the local authority and few are prepared to take responsibility for decisions which go against their better judgement. The government of most British schools is consultative rather than democratic.

The head of a school commonly has great power in making appointments and he can use this to endorse conservatism or innovation. Particularly important are posts of deputy-headship, in which the pattern appears to be changing. Musgrove has this to say of deputy headship:

> The deputy headmaster specializes in internal communication. In particular, he is the link between the headmaster and the assistant staff: 'he is classically poised between the head's study and the classroom'.

(Burnham 1968) He is the communications expert, although the head may see him as primarily concerned with routine organization – timetables, room allocation and examination schedules. A study of 277 deputy heads in secondary modern and grammar schools showed that they conceive their duties differently. They see their job as requiring first and foremost skills in dealing with school staff, listening to their problems, suggesting solutions, and interceding with the head on their behalf. They do not see themselves primarily as organizers; they consider that 'concern for teachers' is the most important part of their job.

(Musgrove 1971, 119)

Another commentator sees the head as stressing his instrumental role with the deputy head's role taking a more expressive cast; and he comments of the deputy's position:

In a grammar school this role is a terminal one since further promotion is not common. One of the main criteria for appointment is long service. When a vacancy occurs, usually through death or retirement, external recruitment is rare. Thus, deputy heads tend to be older graduates who have been in the service of their school for some time and who have thoroughly learnt the norms of their school. As a consequence, they will tend to have a conservative influence.

(Musgrove 1968, 48)

As we shall see later, in large comprehensive schools with multiple deputy headships the role of the deputy head is changing. Innovative heads are deploying deputies as 'change agents' with responsibilities for curriculum development or staff development. We know too little of changing patterns in school organization. The whole question of new management styles is raised.

These styles generally tend towards the establishment of an 'innovative' or 'creative' school. They face the dilemma pointed up by Hoyle (1972a): 'Curriculum innovation requires change in the internal organization of the school. Change in the internal organization of the school is a major innovation.'

The tendency is to seek a change of organization which institutionalizes innovation in the school and opens the way to a continuous programme of betterment rather than the attempt to leap at a sudden and radical solution of problems.

The question as to what organization and climate is implied by the notion of a creative school is a difficult one. Miles (1965) has proposed the concept of 'organizational health' which he defines as 'the school system's ability not only to function effectively, but to develop and grow into a more fully functioning system'. His criteria of organizational health are:

clear goals;
adequate communications;
optimum equalization of power between leadership and teachers;
optimum use of resources;
cohesiveness;
high morale;
innovativeness;
autonomy;
adaptiveness to change;
adequate procedures for resolving internal problems.

This strikes me as an analysis relatively uncontaminated by contact with empirical reality. In particular I am doubtful if innovative schools do tend to have clear goals and cohesiveness, and whether equalization of power does not lead to a stalemate. It is by no means apparent what styles are most favourable to the betterment of a school.

It is clear that in Britain the ultimate decisions about decision-making lie with the head, who is legally responsible to his governors and the local education authority. Four styles of decisions have been distinguished:

- 'tell decisions' which are either trivial or so vital to the accountable person that he had to make the final decision himself;
- 'sell decisions' are such that the accountable person can contemplate only one possible course of action but clearly realizes that its success depends upon its acceptance by others;
- 'consult decisions' for which the accountable person before choosing an alternative seeks to get maximum input from everyone concerned or with special knowledge, but is not prepared to share the ultimate responsibility for deciding; and
- 'share decisions' where the accountable person is willing to let someone else share in the decision, accepts the joint decision and shares accountability with others.

(Loubser, Spiers and Moody 1971, 239)

The 'tell' style is not infrequently encountered in the adoption of curriculum projects by schools. It appears to lead frequently either to apparent, but not real, compliance or to compliance with a degree of determination to prove the decision wrong.

The 'sell' style is not uncommon. Although it can possibly be brought off by some personalities, it tends to produce a situation in which an innovation has been so distorted by the sales talk that those involved in it can neither sustain difficulties nor achieve depth and quality. In many cases the innovation is assimilated to the existing assumptions to produce 'innovation without change'. (MacDonald and Rudduck 1971, 151)

The 'consult' style may well be the emergent one in England today. Given the right decision-maker and given that the consultation is one from which he learns rather than merely camouflage for a 'sell', this seems a strong model in the British situation. Accountability is clear and decisions may be much more open to critical review than when they are the result of hard-won democratic majorities. A good consultative leader can often look after the rights of a minority and preserve their commitment whereas they may be alienated when they have been outvoted.

The 'share' style is probably in fact rare, though Countesthorpe is a good example. In England such a style can only be initiated by the head.

> The initial paradox at Countesthorpe, therefore, is that McMullen has employed the traditional authority of his status to divest himself of his authority within the bureaucratic organization of the school, and though, at this early stage, pupil participation in school government is limited, there is a very strong framework of staff democracy.
>
> (Bernbaum 1973, 51)

Countesthorpe will probably tend to develop both because the staff were appointed for their innovativeness and because the school is subject to a good deal of debate and public discussion to which it tends to need to respond. One might predict that in the end a democratic regime is almost certain to become conservative of what it has established, but there is rather slender evidence for this.

One of the problems is that both consultative and sharing styles involve much more responsibility and work for the staff as a whole. This may be the cost of thoughtful innovation, but there is some evidence that it is not always welcome and that staff are prepared to let the head take a good many decisions. (Musgrove 1971, 73–74) This is borne out by personal observation.

It is difficult to deny the centrality of the head in innovation. Hoyle points to:

> (a) his traditional authority;
> (b) the opportunity which he has to view the school as a whole and hence to perceive the need for innovation;
> (c) his contact with the 'messengers' of innovation, e.g. inspectors, lecturers in education, etc.;
> (d) the expectation that he will be an innovator held by L.E.A. officers and others.
>
> (1972, 26)

It is equally difficult to offer prescriptions about how he should play his role.

On the one hand, perhaps because the values pressing towards democracy in schools appeal to those interested in curriculum innovation, there is a tendency to associate innovation with 'a collegial pattern of authority whereby professional equals govern their affairs by internal democratic procedures'. (Hoyle 1972a) On the other,

> There is little doubt that innovation owes much to the most progressive of British headteachers. The question must be asked whether the same initiative can be given by the collective leadership of teachers or whether self-cancelling 'veto-groups' might not inhibit innovation.
>
> (Hoyle 1972a)

There is little empirical study which helps to settle the question of leadership styles. Indeed, although there is an increasing number of studies of schools' responses to particular innovations, and some studies of problem schools, I know of only two studies of schools that might be reckoned innovative.

One is a rather sketchy account by Bernbaum (1973) of Countesthorpe College. Countesthorpe was started from scratch as an innovative enterprise. The planning was based on the idea that 'the opportunity is being offered by the foundation of the new school to rethink the total process of learning within the school . . . "it should mean that we do not automatically repeat an established practice without considering why" '. (34) The building is radical, the school 'attracts teachers who are especially committed to change and innovation' (36), the head was specially chosen with this in mind. Bernbaum comments: 'a variety of new ideas has been put into practice at Countesthorpe. Each on its own is probably not totally novel, though the accumulation of innovation in one school most certainly is.' (45)

In short, Countesthorpe is in a sense an experimental school and perhaps the first radically experimental school in the state system. Bernbaum's account was written too early in the life of the school to be more than a sketch and a speculative prediction. Perhaps the crucial question if Countesthorpe achieves marked successes is: how can these experiences be made relevant to other schools in more typical situations?

The other British study is that of Nailsea by Elizabeth Richardson (1973). This study is executed in great detail, but it is restricted in its purpose since it is concerned not to study the school as such, but its management. Richardson reveals clearly the complexity of the management process in a large comprehensive school in the process of change. She raises issues, but she does not draw prescriptive conclusions, and her work casts doubt on the models for innovative leadership which are sometimes offered. So much inevitably depends upon the combination of keeping purposes and goals under review and negotiating with staff with responsive sensitivity.

I am inclined to believe that the key quality needed in a school, if development is to take place, is reflexiveness: a capacity to review critically and reflectively its own processes and practices. This seems to imply review structures, and a language and style of review. In Nailsea this language and style was developed by the use of Elizabeth Richardson as an interpretative consultant. It should be possible to achieve a parallel basis for reflexiveness through school-based research and development founded on a school's own programme of in-service training.

School-based in-service training is, however, in its infancy and there is little experience to guide us.

In an all-too-brief account of in-service training at the Thomas Calton School, Peckham, the head of the school, Ron Pepper (1972), gives some information about a programme which began by establishing 'areas of need'. These were:

1. Use of audio-visual equipment.
2. Development of team-teaching and integrated studies.
3. Visits to other schools.
4. Co-ordination and communication.

(15)

Audio-visual equipment training sessions were staffed by visiting teachers and took place after school.

The development of team-teaching and integrated studies was a co-operative task undertaken by interested staff.

> What emerged from the weekly meetings of the teams was that they were learning as they went along. For the first time some of us were having to justify to our colleagues our teaching approach and methods. The mere act of working together has itself been a training process, one which promises invaluable returns as our work and experience develop. One other aspect of this 'self-training' programme has been the way in which individuals have become aware of the gaps in their own past training and experience; . . .

(16)

Out of a feeling of need to extend experience came visits to other schools. And the gathering of ideas and experience threw up the need for communication and co-ordination.

In all that we are doing and intend to do communication and co-ordination of effort are essential. Gaining information and experience on a personal basis is valuable: its value is multiplied if this information and experience can be shared. We have a fortnightly Staff Bulletin which not only carries reports of meetings and group activities but also articles from members of staff who have attended particular courses or lectures which are thought to be of interest to the rest of the staff. Likewise, we include press cuttings and comments on developments. We are also building up a comprehensive library of relevant books and publications. The Staff Association invites visiting speakers to lead discussions on educational topics.

(16–17)

The account from the Thomas Calton School gives neither information about the administrative arrangements for staff training nor much detail about the activities. In Ashmead School, Reading, the head, Peter Judge, has built school-based in-service training into the formal structure of the school by appointing a Training Deputy Head. The situation which has been created is sufficiently interesting to justify extensive quotation from primary sources – the school's internal papers.

The job specification for the Training Deputy Head was as follows:

1. The organizing of teaching practice for student teachers and the setting up of any necessary counselling of such students.
2. The forging of close links with Berkshire College of Education and the University of Reading School of Education both for assisting their students at Ashmead and gaining help in training Ashmead staff.
3. The supervision of probationary teachers during their first year, including the setting up of induction courses and the briefing and training of senior experienced teachers as individual supervisors to new staff.
4. The arranging of courses for existing Ashmead staff. These will need to be of a wide variety of subject matter, approach and duration. Some may be residential and it is expected both the school's own cottage and the local authority's centre could be used for this purpose.
5. The counselling of all staff with problems (e.g. housing, health, discipline, etc.) and the setting up where appropriate of support groups.
6. The arranging of all interviews for new appointments, in consultation with the Head and heads of department where appropriate.
7. The induction of all new arrivals (e.g. advice on housing, timetable details, etc.).

8. The introduction of regular job appraisal sessions and the training of senior staff in their use.
9. The regular appraisal of inter-staff communication and suggestions for improvement (i.e. supervision of staff bulletin, close consultation with Staffroom Committee etc.)
10. Liaison with the Curriculum Development Centre.

The incumbent of this post, John Bull, works through an in-service training committee on which the following serve under his chairmanship: a Year Head with counselling skills; a young teacher with links to staff discussion groups; a probationer designated annually; an experienced teacher; a mid-career teacher with specialized careers knowledge; and a head of department involved in curriculum training problems.

The committee's functions were defined in the following terms:

1. Proposing and designing Staff Support. With the co-operation of Heads of Departments and Year Heads, arranging ongoing support for members of Staff in several ways.

(a) In defining their roles and, thereafter in helping Staff members to receive the kind of help they may need in carrying out these roles. This function may in some cases arise as the result of specific requests from individuals, or from those involved with them in their work. In its enactment, it might – if a generalized need is indicated (e.g. Role of the Form Teacher) – entail the setting up of a study group to look at the problems and offer practical advice. If a more specific need, then less formal remedial help would depend very much on that need but would aim essentially at helping people to cope rather than making critical judgements against preconceived standards. This cannot be a remote function and in many cases may prove to be best enacted by close colleagues rather than by members of the committee itself, whose role in this would be facilitatory to that end.

(b) In setting up relevant courses in school, and in advising the local A.T.O. (through the school's contact with it), Berkshire College of Education (very interested in the problems of school-based training), the Curriculum Development Centre and our H.M.I. on the perceived needs for more formal courses outside school. In school-based courses, it may become desirable for the committee to co-opt other staff members for working out course strategies and content, or in some cases to act as separate working parties for this purpose. Such courses might materialize as Workshops, or as series of sessions aimed at producing a particular organizational programme (e.g. to inform next year's timetable structuring).

2. Informing School Organization. Because of its proposed contact with Staff, and the hope that such a contact might evoke a confidence in its work, the committee might well see itself as concerned to look at

organizational factors in the school and recommend appropriate changes (e.g. the means by which policy decisions are made and thereafter conveyed meaningfully through the Staff). Again, this particular advisory function, led by the Deputy Head (Training) might prove of value in pursuing organizational changes with the L.E.A. in matters of financial support and employment information. Within the school, there may be organizational needs to be channelled to Heads of Departments and other senior managers on things like resource production facilities, better support for particular curriculum development plans and so on. And, of course, for acquiring time for In-Service activities.

3. Staff Welfare. Subsuming the kind of welfare areas that the role of the Deputy Head (Training) has already encountered -- from staff salary problems to housing: matters which in industry might fall largely within the personnel welfare system – this function to some extent cuts across that currently seen as operated by the elected Staff Room Committee, and far from taking over any work currently assumed to be that body's, the Committee on In-Service Training might instead see itself as supportive of the former's work. There are numerous gaps at present in that area concerned with what happens to Staff who are ill, short on salary, baffled by the travel-claim system or simply and miserably out of social contacts in a large and not-too-well-endowed town.

4. Curriculum Development. The Deputy Head (Training) is formally closely-linked, role-wise, with the Deputy Head (Academic) in this area. With strong, and often seemingly conflicting, pressures for curriculum reform in the school, curriculum development becomes not simply a matter of timetable and financial provision, but also one involving training problems and the dissemination of information amongst those groups of teachers involved in what may otherwise become discrete and quite isolated pockets of teaching. It may be a legitimate function of the Committee to take upon itself, with the co-operation of Heads of Departments and the Deputy Head (Training), a review of Curriculum Development in the school from the standpoint of disseminating information about it in the hope that this may provide a better framework than they have at the moment for their own thoughts and plans on their teaching.

In his Annual Report to the school governors on in-service training in the year 1972–3, Bull makes this comment:

The basic In-Service Training problem at Ashmead is that of reconciling the processes of fundamental organizational changes with the more complex difficulties of human adjustment that inevitably follow. We tend to think pessimistically about the human costs of change, but in fact it is generally only when we are unable to *understand* the nature of a change process that we find its implications deeply disturbing. At Ashmead, the scale of change has been such as to produce a range of

> adjustment problems. The task of I.S.T. is seen to be that of two remedial activities: first to provide a pastoral-support function for Staff who are necessarily in an intermediate stage of adjusting their perspectives from the old to the new regimes in the school; and, second, to try to identify specific retraining needs and to provide the right styles of training to facilitate sensitive and effective teacher-development. Both are complex processes, rendered perhaps more so by the traditional assumption that subject-knowledge is the teacher's stock-in-trade, and that bringing any demands for refusing this assumption into the teacher's workplace is both a professional insult and a threat.
>
> One essential feature of I.S.T. at Ashmead is its implied formal status. Instead of opting for the James' Report proposition of the Professional Tutor, which in theory seems an attractive idea, the Ashmead principle of appointing the Trainer to a nominal Deputy Headship gives the incumbent some responsibility in policy-making and – more important perhaps – an access to both the Head and the three other Deputies that is probably vital if he is to effectively perceive the full cause-and-effect syndrome of training problems in the school. (Interviews with Professional Tutors confirm the view that their relatively low formal status in their schools seriously inhibits any attempts to consider the retraining of experienced high-status staff. At Ashmead, we feel more free to include such teachers in our purview.)

One of the problems thrown up is the financial provision for an ambitious scheme of school-based in-service training of this sort, though its advantages and strengths may well make it more cost-effective than cheaper programmes of centralized in-service work which do not face the realities of particular school situations.

In any event it is clear that the reflexive school with its own programme of research, development and training needs to be supported and fed by agencies outside itself.

12

SUPPORT FOR SCHOOLS

The critical problems in evolving an effective system of support for schools are those of power and authority.

Power is at stake because support implies the allocation of resources. On the one hand, an innovative school may require material resources and financial support. On the other, it may want to use the time of advisers or consultants and this too is a scarce commodity. Accordingly, support is necessarily selective support. Some ideas and some schools are likely to get more support than others. The right to make decisions about the allocation of resources constitutes power and implies a degree of control.

Authority is involved because schools derive support from access to ideas and expertise. To an extent ideas and expertise are available from books. But they also depend on experience, and given the fact that teachers have limited time for study, it is often economical for schools to gain access to ideas through persons who act as consultants or advisers rather than through books. Such people readily acquire the authority of experts. And as power may imply control, so authority may imply dependency.

Issues of power and authority have a particular nuance in this country. In England and Wales teacher autonomy is seen as the ethical basis of professionalism and a cornerstone of the educational tradition. The extent to which such autonomy exists in practice is a matter for discussion, but the tradition is certainly strong enough for any teacher to appeal to it.

The origins of this autonomy have been analysed by Owen (1973). The transition from the Revised Code system of payment by results, which was administered by Her Majesty's Inspectorate as an arm of government, to the organization and financial supervision of education by local education authorities led to a conflict between the central and the local power. It was out of this conflict that the teacher won his autonomy. Owen describes the situation very neatly.

> In 1905 the original edition of *A Handbook of Suggestions for Teachers in Public Elementary Schools* told schools that the only uniformity of

practice that the Board of Education wished to see was that every teacher should think for himself and should work out for himself such methods of teaching as would use his powers to the best advantage. It was also added that in this way it was hoped that the capacity of teachers would be best suited to the particular needs and conditions of individual schools. It was denied that uniformity in detail of practice – apart from the mere routine of school management – was in any way desirable; it was even denied that such uniformity might be attainable. Nevertheless, the moral was driven home quite hard – any freedom which the teacher might acquire from this line of reasoning would imply a corresponding responsibility in the use of that freedom.

Although, then, the teacher was taking part in a conflict which he did not fully understand, there were two influences at work: the one was influence which we could describe as political. The battle between the Board of Education and the new local education authorities could be claimed to have led the Board to the point of doing one of two things. It could lay down a form of government which would ensure the type of uniformity which would secure comparability of standard, of method, and of the content of curriculum throughout England and Wales, or, alternatively, it could deny a comparable power of influence to the local education authorities. It could do this by insisting that true professionalism for the teacher meant that he should make up his own mind. The second major influence which was at work on curriculum was not a personal one; it was connected wholly with professionalism in itself – and not simply with professionalism as a catchword. . . .

Essentially the professionalism of the teacher in deciding upon the appropriate curriculum for his pupils is concerned not with subjects but with what were then known – and remained with the same title for many years – as activities.

(19)

The intention was less that the teacher should decide which subjects to teach than that he should have a freedom and a responsibility to interpret the subjects as classroom activities. In doing so he would take account of the individual needs and experiences of the children, and of the problems and opportunities which presented themselves in the classroom. In short, teaching is an art, and as such, highly individual. It can be sustained only in individual freedom.

There are a number of factors which make this highly individualistic conception of teacher autonomy difficult to maintain in present circumstances.

At the time when this autonomy was forged, there was a considerable consensus within the teaching tradition. For example, the method of teaching reading by phonics was virtually universal. Accordingly, individuality did not express itself in gross disjunctions of practice in a single school. Now there exist reading schemes radically divergent in assumptions and structure. We cannot have three teachers successively facing children with *Words in Colour*, *I.T.A.* and *Breakthrough to Literacy*. On these grounds it would appear that a school needs a policy, and this is a constraint on the autonomy of its teachers. Some have argued that given population mobility with consequent school transfers, we need a national policy at some points. I am uncertain of this, feeling that we might well lose more than we gain.

The line between subjects and activities has also become blurred. You change the nature of content when you change the approach to teaching. We have seen that instructional teaching tends to transmit a rhetoric of conclusions while enquiry-based teaching inculcates a speculative approach to knowledge and ways of knowing. Teacher individuality no longer rests upon and is integrated by a common view of knowledge. Again we need either a policy within the school or at least a negotiated integration of teachers' contributions.

Third, the privacy of the classroom has been broken down by the development of styles of co-operative and team teaching. It is quite clear that teachers adopting such approaches are aware of the sacrifice of autonomy in the interests of co-operation within a teacher group.

Finally, many innovations now being adopted have implications for both the ethos and the organization of schools. They affect what Hoyle has called (by analogy with the sociologists' use of the term 'deep structures of knowledge') the 'deep structure' of the school, that is, the assumptions which support its surface practices and organization. He argues that 'changes in this "deep structure" are being stimulated by the curriculum innovations themselves', suggests that 'attention should be given to the supports which the school may need to effect this more fundamental shift without undue strain and anxiety for the staff', and concludes that 'professional development of the individual and the improvement of the creativity of the school proceed simultaneously'. (Hoyle 1972a) This position is consonant with my own in the previous chapter.

The conclusion seems inescapable. I value highly the tradition of professional autonomy as the basis of educational quality but it seems that this must now be negotiated at school level. Concessions must be made in individual autonomy in order to provide a basis for collaborative working, for the school staff can no longer be seen as a federal association of teachers and departments: it must be a professional community. And it is with that community that professional autonomy must lie.

From this position two consequences seem to follow.

First, teachers must be given and must accept a much higher degree of participation in the shaping of the policy of their school. Such participation may be through a consultative system or through a democratic system. In either case it involves heads and senior staff in accepting accountability to their colleagues for their use of power. This seems the only acceptable basis for a moderation of the claim to individual autonomy.

Second, such a structure involves negotiation and negotiation implies the existence of a public tradition which supports discussion and a common approach to planning. It is a central argument of this book that such a tradition should be one of research and development. The appeal in negotiation should be to procedures for increasing understanding and for evaluating and developing proposals. A major instrument of arbitration should be inquiry.

But of course policy issues cannot be settled simply by research. Value issues are involved. The criteria of evaluation are at stake. Let me say two things about this problem. First, I believe there is a great deal of divergence within schools which masquerades as value divergence though it is in fact disagreement about issues susceptible to empirical elucidation. Second, where the value divergence is about man, knowledge or society, I know of no way to resolve it in practice. It is for this reason that I incline to consultative rather than democratic modes of school government. I can see no alternative to the assertion of certain basic values on which the school is based.

White (1973) has not only argued a value position but has suggested that the policy it implies should be centrally enforced on schools. And this of course is the assumption in such a country as Sweden. Moreover, many of the arguments I have used to suggest that professional autonomy should rest with the school rather than with the individual could be used to support a plea for centralization.

My belief in decentralization at school level rests on the proposition that a rich and complex cultural tradition of co-operation through research and development can only thrive in a group which functions as a fully interacting community. The quality of schools depends on the quality of involvement of the individuals in them. 'Efficiency' can be pursued in large bureaucratic organizations only when quality of involvement is not an important factor. And industrial relations in large industries tend to suggest that the pursuit of efficiency without involvement may turn out to be an illusion.

This position is of the greatest significance for the problem of support for schools.

If we back the individual professional autonomy of teachers, support is a matter of supporting individuals. This has been the practice in our tradition. For example, teachers have attended in-service courses and conferences or have been released to take higher qualifications. They have seldom been asked to report back to their colleagues; and this is still true.

If we take the systematic efficiency model, then accountability is substituted for responsibility. In this sense accountability is responsibility without freedom. Teachers and schools have little control of the criteria of accountability. They are tested, usually in terms of their 'product', as in payment by results. Support for teachers then rests on a deficit model. Those who fail to meet the criteria are given access to training to improve their performance. I do not think that this model exists in pure form, but there is a strong flavour of it in the courses offered to teachers in some centralized systems to enable them to meet the demands laid upon them by curricular legislation.

The acceptance of the position argued here, that the school is the unit for development and also the unit of professional autonomy, has strong implications for support. It means that supporting agencies should aim to help schools to build traditions of autonomous, self-critical improvement. And this means that supporting agencies cannot simply take people out of school for in-service training: they must go into schools and work with problems where they are and in their context.

We have in Britain a wide range of supporting agencies: Her Majesty's Inspectorate, local advisory services, teachers' centres, research and development units, in-service training agencies and initial training institutions. It is my thesis that they and the schools should be united in a common research and development tradition.

Let us consider each of these support resources in turn.

The role of H.M.I. seems to be ambiguous and changing:

> Certainly H.M.I. have throughout the greater part of the present century remained steadfast to their first duty of being independent arbiters of the quality of schools, of teaching and of teachers. They have admittedly lost their role of inspecting the attainment of children. Both teachers and L.E.A.s are, however, still comparatively unclear as to whether H.M.I. have, in fact, dropped their function of inspecting. It is insisted by the Department of Education and Science that H.M.I. do not inspect L.E.A.s; by implication this means that they inspect schools. However, since the mid-1960s it has been accepted that schools are no longer to be regularly *inspected* by H.M.I. and there is even doubt whether any schools would within the next half decade be inspected at any time by those who work nationally.

> This raises the question of whether H.M.I. are employed in order to help schools or to help L.E.As, or simply to act as informants of the Secretary of State for Education and Science about the quality of the system over which he or she presides at any one time. And even this definition of the function is one which would be difficult for either the department or for the Inspectorate as an independent or quasi-independent *corps d'élite* to accept.

There are strong indications that the Inspectorate is reviewing its role and position and it is not easy to see what will emerge. But there are certainly a number of points at which they have great strength.

The Inspectorate is the only body with an opportunity to view the whole system. Hence it is able to make judgements of trends and tendencies which are frequently of considerable use to both local education authorities and schools and to help school or locality to a clearer self-appreciation. Moreover, as in a recent survey of guidance services in schools, the Inspectorate is able both to highlight weaknesses in the system and to report good practices.

Another function of the Inspectorate concerns in-service training, where again they are able to interpret trends and needs and respond to them. Their effectiveness here has recently been increased by regulations supporting joint courses arranged by the D.E.S. and Area Training Organizations.

It seems to me apparent that H.M.I. could be crucial for a tradition of research-based schools. Its capacity to work at a national level in surveying problems, in communicating information and insights across local authorities, and in bringing together for in-service conferences and workshops teachers from all over the country, is an invaluable element in the creation of a public tradition. Moreover, the breadth of experience of H.M.I.s should enable them to see possibilities of development which elude those with a more intensive view. They would, however, have to cultivate a more consistent research stance. There are the roots of this in some of the work undertaken in support of government committees.

The local inspectorates and advisory services are quite distinct from H.M.I. 'There is very little connection between the work of the two kinds of inspector; there has been practically no consultation until very recently about the ways in which national and local inspectors might work together or supplement one another's efforts.' (Owen 1973, 102)

The local advisory services vary enormously in resources and structure. Often they are overweighted in physical education, music, art and home economics, areas in which primary school teachers have traditionally required a good deal of help and support. Reorganization and regrouping of local advisory services might be expected to follow on the recent local authority reorganization but at present financial constraints impose narrow limitations on the possibilities. This is a pity. Local advisory staffs are probably critical for the improvement of schools (whether the view about the way of advance taken here be accepted or not).

Local advisory staffs have the advantages and disadvantages of being seen by teachers as having real power in the system, through their influence in appointments and promotions, through their control of such rewards as release and financial support to attend courses and conferences, and in many cases through their access to funds which can be used to support particular innovations by supplementing the resources of individual schools. Moreover, they often share with teachers' centre wardens the role of gate-keepers in the flow of information mediating research and curriculum projects to teachers in the area. They are clearly key figures in innovation.

This key position involves the problems of power and authority which are inseparable from responsibility.

So far as power is concerned, there appears to be every advantage in openness in its use so far as this can be achieved. It is not always possible politically to state criteria for the allocation of resources, but it seems important to avoid the situation where advisory staffs allocate their time and resources to schools on a courtier system. It does sometimes happen that access to such resources is felt to depend on grace and favour and this sets the context for personal intrigue on the part of heads and teachers. The situation is not helped by the persistence of the fiction that L.E.A.s have no curriculum policy. Rudduck (1974) has shown the importance of local authority action for a particular line of curriculum development. *Geography for the Young School Leaver* has gone straight for L.E.A.s almost as an American curriculum project seeks school board adoptions; and it seems to have worked!

The use of authority is perhaps more delicate than the use of power. Owen says of advisers that they have been most useful when

> . . . They have not assumed that teachers could venture on comparatively new ground without *any* assistance; nor have they truly accepted any sense of *right* in their own participation in local work. It is not by stealth that the local adviser or inspector reaches the point where he or she is trusted by the teacher. Rather, it is on the exercise of sensitivity, on a realistic sense of practical needs and practicable methods by which

teachers may learn to meet their own needs that the good adviser can best base his efforts.

(Owen 1973, 104)

Rudduck (1974, 30), reporting the experience of a particular curriculum project, comments that advisory staffs do not easily succeed in casting themselves in the role recommended by Owen. 'There are, almost inevitably, problems of authority. What aspires to be a balanced presentation of a curriculum possibility to teacher judgement, is construed as an L.E.A. recommendation or mandate.' However, given the importance of local advisory staffs for local development, there is no alternative but for them to work through these problems.

All in all there is considerable evidence that it is through the local authority and its advisory services that the opportunities open to schools and teachers are created, defined and negotiated. Cave (1974, 57), himself an L.E.A. Chief Inspector, refers to 'the pinching, scraping, committee persuasion and sheer hard slog necessary for example in getting Curriculum Development Centres and Schools Council Projects off the ground', and this picture rings true with my own experience of the conscientious local adviser.

In addition to local advisory services, L.E.A.s now have teachers' centres. Their foundation was stimulated by the Schools Council Working Paper No. 10, *Curriculum Development: Teachers' Groups and Centres* (1967), which declared:

The Council's hope is that teachers will, more and more, meet in groups to discuss curriculum problems and that local education authorities will do all that is practicable to encourage such groups, and in particular help them with the use of accommodation, apparatus and secretarial assistance as may be necessary.

(3)

Owen (1973) comments on the unconventional origin of teachers' centres and the problems this can cause:

The Schools' Council, after all, was acting independently of the Department of Education and Science. It was also acting independently of the Inspectors. This is in contrast to the way in which local advisers and inspectors had, from the beginning, been involved in the growth of local systems of curriculum development.

(104)

There is great variety in the sources available to teachers' centres and also in their staffing:

> The Centre may have a full-time warden, a part-time warden or no warden at all. The warden may be a part-time adviser; he may have the title of Curriculum Development Officer. He may have been a teacher or headmaster in a school in the locality and he may still be teaching part-time. He may be young and ambitious and see the post as a short-term stepping stone to higher responsibilities, or he may be playing out his last years before retirement. The leader may see himself as a Jack-of-all-trades, a well-informed entrepreneur or he may act as a specialist, shaping his programme according to his interests and expertise. He may be a supporter or a leader of teachers.
>
> (Rudduck 1975, 96–97)

Thus with teachers' centres there came teachers' centre wardens or leaders, new personnel seeking new roles in the system. Sometimes advisers and teachers' centre wardens co-operated wholeheartedly. Sometimes there was tension.

Collins (1971) has distinguished four roles of the adviser in curriculum development:

that of 'change agent', the stimulator and supporter of change in the curriculum in schools.
that of a depository of knowledge about the curriculum.
that of director and organizer of in-service work.
that of assisting schools to *evaluate* new curricular ideas.

And he declares: 'I consider that the Adviser and the Teachers' Centre Warden do exactly the same job' in relation to curriculum development. In so far as this is true, it can clearly be a basis for co-operation or competition. When tensions occur, advisers will often capitalize on their closeness to decision-making and real power: wardens will respond by playing their closeness to teachers. Collins hints at this division. 'Obviously they do not do the same job when it comes to inspectorial and administrative tasks and I venture to think not many Wardens would wish to be involved in such work because of the threat this could pose to their special relationship with teachers.'

There are many problems in designing an integrated support system for schools at local authority level. In prosperous American school districts, each of which enjoys a high degree of autonomy, there often exists a fairly large team of supervisors and curriculum specialists. Their role is twofold. They are concerned with the support of schools and also with the control of schools. In the United States the practical and ethical problems of this link between support and control are often debated through an exploration of the concept of 'educational leadership'. This concept figures in the proceedings and publications of the national professional organization which caters for educationally oriented school-district personnel, the Association for Supervision and Curriculum Development. There is a marked tendency to stress the need for styles of leadership which minimize the formal authority of the supervisor, but maintain it in informal guise. And on the whole there appear to be traces of a manipulative attitude towards teachers.

Perhaps what is needed is a consideration of the idea of 'educational leadership' in an English context. It may be that our style is less leadership in action than leadership in creating a climate in which action takes place. I have already made it clear that I believe this climate should be one favourable to inquiry and research.

One possibility is that the new local authorities should have teams capable of giving research and development support. Such teams would then be the natural links between research conducted nationally and local programmes. There are many important theses about education being argued at present and many problems are being thrown up. The optimum conditions for innovative development will occur when any school wishing to explore the possibilities opened up by these theses, or to attack systematically one of its problems, can turn to the local authority for the same support, research-backing and research consultancy as experimental schools now draw from a national research and development project. It would then be an important part of a national projects' job to make that response possible for L.E.A. research and development units by evolving methodologies of school study, of evaluation and of in-service training.

An excellent account of work based on teachers' centres of a type which throws up the need and the possibility of developments of the kind suggested above is given by Cave (1971, Chapter 3). What is quite striking is the tendency of teachers to evolve agenda for their groups which raise quite explicitly research questions, and which do not anticipate easy answers. Cave instances the agenda developed in a group of teachers concerned with language development:

1. Is language development the result of faulty education?
2. Should the emphasis be on conversation or enrichment by stories?
3. Does 'family grouping' allow a greater opportunity for language development?
4. Does television act as a stimulating and enriching influence on language development?
5. How far can adults (parents, students, etc.) be brought into the classroom to help the teacher by listening and talking to children?

6. Do our schools provide a suitable environment for speech development? are there enough tactile materials? does the child hear enough adult conversations?

(32)

These are not basically how-to-do-it questions. They demand explanations towards understanding, not prescriptive answers. And indeed no firm answer can be given to them.

The approach of the teachers in this situation was experimental. The movement was towards the design of inquiry and research.

> Arising from the point regarding the use of parents in schools, three members of the group took positive steps to contact a number of parents and invite them into the schools to talk with the children. One headmaster, Mr. J. Golightly of Swaffham Bulbeck C.E. Primary School, subsequently reported that by using one parent per group of three children the results had been quite significant. Children who had previously not been very forthcoming in a free classroom situation responded well to this small family set-up. Other members reported great interest shown by the parents in the work and it was felt that by using adults, students and older schoolchildren, some headway into problems of language development could be made. We then began tape recordings of young children talking with and without their teachers and studying transcripts of their conversations. Without any additional information it was often clear which children had come from disadvantaged backgrounds. An interesting point arising from this investigation was that in free association, children of similar linguistic ability tended to collect in their own peer groups.
>
> (Cave 1971, 32–33)

One could hardly find a clearer example of the kind of study and experiment, characteristic of the best teachers' centre work, or indeed of leadership, creating a climate in which genuinely teacher-based inquiry can be naturally pursued.

It is interesting that part of the impulse with which this language development group started is attributed by Cave to a lecture by Bernstein, and that the group later called in as a consultant a specialist in language development from Cambridge University Department of Education. Those who work in college departments and schools of education are also a potential source of support for schools and teachers.

Here again there are problems in realizing the potential that is there, and they are partly problems of authority and status. Those involved in teacher training and the teaching of education are in a vulnerable position. On the one hand, since they are not teaching in schools they can be seen by teachers as removed from reality, the occupants of ivory towers. On the other hand, their reference point in the context of their own institutions is the academic establishment of the University.

I must concede that many 'educationists' succeed in overcoming the problems set them by this situation, but many do not. The educationist is inclined to validate himself to the academic establishment through research which attempts to prove itself by their canons, and through either talk of education as a discipline (currently unfashionable) or identification with the constituent disciplines (currently fashionable) He is also inclined to validate himself to teachers by appealing to experience, often through anecdote. His research aspires to be pure while his anecdotes aspire to be applied.

But of course the opposite should be the case. The contribution he can make to the improvement of teaching is through the close application of his research skills, and this is also the basis for organizing an experience in classrooms which is extensive where the teacher's is intensive. He has little to offer by recalling his experience as a teacher or by reducing his experience as a worker in many classrooms to the level of anecdote.

This is an argument for research in curriculum and teaching. But such research is threatening in another way. While many kinds of academic work are readily reported and contained in academic books, which are relatively self-contained and insulated from the day-to-day realities of the school, research in curriculum and teaching is best expressed through curricular proposals and research techniques which can be operationalized only by the teacher. This means that the teacher gains authority in the field where the 'educationist' is working.

Accordingly, in order to offer support for schools, the 'educationist' needs to assume a consultancy role in the fullest sense. He needs to see himself as notionally employed by the teacher, and as accountable to him. This is not an easy position for many 'educationists' to take up. I believe, however, that the extent to which they can do so governs the extent to which they can work in a genuinely supportive role.

In the support of schools, H.M.I., L.E.A. advisers, teachers' centre personnel and 'academic educationists' need to avoid building their own status and personal security on a conviction that they are superior to teachers. I return to where I started this chapter: the problems of power and authority.

Competent curiosity is a better basis for working with schools than the wisdom of experience and the tone of goodwill. In this field it's heads, not hearts, in the school.

13

MOVEMENTS AND INSTITUTIONS IN CURRICULUM DEVELOPMENT

In this chapter I want to consider some changes, still under way, in the perception of the nature of curriculum innovation. I see a move from the idea of a curriculum reform movement to that of institutionalized curriculum research and development. Towards the end of the chapter I shall consider briefly the principal institution which has emerged in England and Wales, the Schools' Council, and some of the problems it faces. One is a problem in perception.

It seems to me that the problem in perception can best be thrown into relief by considering educational innovation first as a function of social movements based on beliefs, and then contrasting this style of innovation with that based on research and development. For it is my thesis that many of the misperceptions of research and development arise because of a disposition to see educational change in terms of movements. This even afflicts people engaged in research and development.

Heberle (1951) defines social movements in these terms.

> Social movements are a specific kind of concerted-action group; they last longer and are more integrated than mobs, masses and crowds, and yet are not organized like political clubs and other associations. . . . Group consciousness, that is, a sense of belonging and of solidarity among members of a group, is essential for a social movement, although empirically it occurs in various degrees. . . . By this criterion social movements are distinguished from 'social trends' *which are often referred to as movements* and are the result of similar but unco-ordinated actions of many individuals.
>
> (439)

Gusfield distinguishes the directed segment of a movement which embraces members and the undirected segment which embraces partisans:

> . . . there is a mixture of formal association and informal, diffuse behaviour encompassed in the concept of a movement. A significant distinction can be made between 'directed' and 'undirected' movements or segments of movements. The *directed* segment of a movement is characterized by organized and structural groups with specific programmes, a formal leadership and stated objectives. Its followers are *members* of an organization as well as partisans to a belief. The *undirected* phase of a movement is characterized by the reshaping of perspectives, norms, and values which occur in the interaction of persons apart from a specific vocational context.* The followers are *partisans* but need not be members of any association which advocates the change being studied.
>
> (Gusfield 1968, 445)

In the present context I take a movement to describe a collection of people distinguished by certain convictions or beliefs. A movement has a doctrine. An educational movement has convictions or beliefs about an educational doctrine. An excellent example of such a movement is 'Progressivism'. And it is worth looking at progressivism in some detail since it is the movement to which curriculum research and development is often assimilated by its opponents.

Cremin (1961) characterizes American progressivism as follows:

> First, it meant broadening the programme and function of the school to include direct concern for health, vocation, and the quality of family and community life.
>
> Second, it meant applying in the classroom the pedagogical principles derived from new scientific research in psychology and the social sciences.
>
> Third, it meant tailoring instruction more and more to the different kinds and classes of children who were being brought within the purview of the school . . .
>
> Finally, Progressivism implied the radical faith that culture could be democratized without being vulgarized, the faith that everyone could share not only in the benefits of the new sciences but in the pursuit of the arts as well.
>
> (viii–ix)

There is, of course, much more to it than that. In England child-centredness, of a kind not adequately covered by Cremin's third

* Educational movements are in a sense vocational movements; but partisans (as opposed to members) do not have membership of associations for which the movement is a 'vocation', e.g. the New Education Fellowship.

point, has been important as has, recently, the notion of 'openness'. The Plowden Report is often taken as an up-to-date statement of progressive education as it is interpreted by British primary schools.

I am not concerned here to estimate progressive education, but to consider its nature *as a movement*, something which it shares with the Black Paper 'traditionalists'. Crucial to both is a strong conviction or belief about what educators ought to do; and second, the idea that the main problem in improving schools is that of converting people to that belief. Typically, evidence is not taken account of to modify that belief, but *used* to support it.

Later, I am going to contrast with this posture of conviction and belief that of curiosity and doubt, which I see as the desirable attitudes in research and development. But it is instructive, before moving on, to consider Cremin's diagnosis of the failure of progressivism in America (a post-mortem which may have been premature if current American interest in British progressive primary schools is anything to go by).

'Why', asks Cremin, 'this abrupt and rather dismal end of a movement that had for more than a half-century commanded the loyalty of influential segments of the American public?' (348)

He offers seven reasons.

First, distortion. He attributes this to internal dissension within the movement. 'The strife made the headlines, and within these headlines lay the seeds of many a cartoon version of progressive education.' (348) Death by slogans!

Second, he cites negativism, and comments:

> Like many protesters against injustice, the early progressives knew better what they were against than what they were for. And when one gets a true picture of the inequities of American schools during the half-century before World War I, he realizes they had much to be against; the physical and pedagogical conditions in many schools were indescribably bad, an effrontery to the mildest humanitarian sentiments. Yet, granted this, a protest is not a programme. Shibboleths like 'the whole child' or 'creative self-expression' stirred the faithful to action and served as powerful battering rams against the old order, but in classroom practice they were not very good guides to positive action. At least the generation that invented them had an idea of what they meant. The generation that followed adopted them as a collection of ready-made cliches – cliches which were not very helpful when the public began to raise searching questions about the schools.
>
> (348)

Theory is to unite the movement: it is not closely related to practice.

Cremin's third point is closely relevant to British curriculum reform:

> ... what the progressives did prescribe made inordinate demands on the teacher's time and ability. 'Integrated studies' required familiarity with a fantastic range of knowledge and teaching materials; while the commitment to build on student needs and interests demanded extraordinary feats of pedagogical ingenuity.
>
> (348)

Fourth, Cremin claims, apparently contradicting his previous point, that the progressive movement, 'incorporated into schools at large', was a victim of its own success. I think it was vocabularies which were incorporated into discourse rather than practices adopted in schools.

Fifth, Cremin cites a general swing to conservatism in post-war political and social thought.

Sixth, the professionalization of the movement, that is, its loss of lay support and adoption as a teachers' creed.

Seventh, and perhaps rather tritely, progressive education 'failed to keep pace with the continuing transformation of American society'. (35)

At the root of the failures of a movement there seem to me to be two linked weaknesses: an insistence on 'hearts, not heads', and the lack of a public tradition of improvement by systematic self-criticism. Unfortunately, good-will and the 'right' aspirations are not enough in education, yet when ideas – perhaps sound enough in themselves – are spread through a movement it is the aspiring good-will which seems to be catching. The ideas often seem more important for the personal and professional identity of the teacher than for his practice. And, partly because of a widespread and persistent lack of honesty about the difficult realities of teaching, success is reported publicly but problems, difficulties and failures are features of private rather than public experience. Apart from Dewey, very few progressives learned from failure. And in the improvement of practice there are narrow limits to what we can learn from success.

It is one of the problems of research and development in curriculum that it is continually threatening to turn into the Curriculum Reform Movement. If those of us who are interested in the improvement of schools by research – that is, by reflective questioning and constructive criticism – are to avoid this fate, we must address ourselves to heads as well as hearts, we must deal in hypotheses rather than slogans, we must ensure that theory is about practice and we must ensure that techniques are developed to match aspirations.

What is at stake is the close association of research with practice. I do not intend by 'research' a body of techniques, though technique is important. I mean 'Investigation, inquiry into things . . . habitude of carrying out such investigation.' (*O.E.D.*) The methods must be those appropriate and practical in the case.

The application of research to education should be seen as the investigation of our experience as educators and the attempt to verify hypotheses drawn from work in the 'constituent disciplines' of philosophy, history, psychology and sociology. When it is regarded as a matter of applying the findings of these disciplines, the result is generally disastrous. Let me give two examples.

Government reports have frequently attempted to apply research *findings* in this way. The Spens Report is the classic example:

> The Spens Report is dominated by psychological ideas, or probably misconceptions of these psychological ideas, and divided the pupils into three imagined categories of academic, technical and 'practical'. Curriculum from that time onwards has been distorted by the notion of separate kinds of curriculum for separate kinds of children.
>
> (Lawton 1973, 91)

Lawton's survey highlights the continuity of this with the Taunton Report (1864–8): 'First Grade Secondary Schools were suitable for the upper middle class children; Second Grade Secondary Schools were a proportion of the respectable upper working classes seen as possible pupils and allowed to mix with the children of the lower middle classes for the kind of education which they themselves described as "a clerk's education".' (87) The pattern is still there in the Crowther and Newsom Reports.

It is not only policy which is afflicted by this kind of application of research. So is teacher education. Over the past years I must have read as external examiner hundreds of student essays which, drawing mainly on the work of Bernstein (who denies the implication) and other sociologists, paint a picture of working-class educational disadvantage based on bad home background and linguistic deprivation. In only one case has a student argued that her careful study of six working-class children and their homes flatly contradicted what she was being taught in college.

I draw two conclusions. Findings from research are not to be accepted but to be tested, and to be tested by attempting to overthrow them. And whenever findings rather than investigation are taken to be the basis of practice they will be selected and interpreted to fit our prejudices; for without a 'habitude of carrying out investigation' research findings can never be called to account.

Curriculum research will be useful to the extent that it is able by testing theory against practice to avoid the excesses of the movement and the complacencies of rationalizing practice by reference to 'findings'. How does 'the state of the art' measure up to that demand? It will help us to look at the recent history of curriculum development in order to take stock. Two themes are interwoven. One is caught in the words research, development, renewal, innovation: the other in the words diffusion, dissemination, utilization, implementation.

No adequate history of curriculum development has been attempted, and it would be a major research enterprise to provide one. I shall have to content myself with snapshots.

Modern curriculum development can be taken to be characterized by the setting up of 'projects'. And this trend started in the United States. Thus I open up my album at an American snapshot dating from 1966, when the initial American effort was at its flood.

Curriculum Improvement and Innovation: a Partnership of Students, School Teachers and Research Scholars is a well-bound volume edited by W. T. Martin, the Head of the Department of Mathematics, Massachusetts Institute of Technology, and Dan C. Pinck, Deputy Director, Educational Services Incorporated, an organization which later became the Educational Development Centre. The format speaks of confidence and established status; and big names are involved.

I want to quote extensively from the preface, as a primary source, to document the spirit and strategy of the time.

> From 1956 to 1958, Professor Zacharias and his colleagues on the Physical Science Study Committee, most notably the late Professor Francis L. Friedman, worked to develop a new high school physics course which through its integrity, style, and precision of content created a pattern of educational development subsequently followed by curriculum reform groups throughout the world. One of its essential characteristics is the partnership of university research scholars, teachers, and students – enough of them working for long enough periods of time to attain the precision and style that they wanted.
>
> It was intended that the new course would include an original text, teachers' guides, motion picture films, laboratory experiments with specially designed inexpensive equipment with appropriate guides, tests and examinations, and institutes for high school physics teachers. A set of paperback books for collateral reading was begun as a hedge against success and independent adoption. In 1958, after two years of intensive work by more than fifty professional physicists and more than one hundred high school physics teachers, the PSSC course was ready, in its preliminary form, for trial use and evaluation in the schools. It

was not until 1960 that the course was ready for extensive trial use in the schools.

As the work advanced, it became evident that a new organization should be established to handle arrangements for publication and distribution. Consequently a private, non-profit corporation was formed, called Educational Services Incorporated, with a membership drawn partly from MIT but including representatives from other institutions of learning throughout the nation.

As soon as ESI was formed, requests began to come from scholars and teachers for ESI's assistance in attempting to improve curricula in other disciplines, in both schools and universities. ESI now has responsibilities for nine school curriculum projects, in the sciences, mathematics and social sciences; five university curriculum projects, in the physical and life sciences and in several branches of engineering; and two university research and development projects (in India and Afghanistan); and the ESI Film Studio is now making films for ten separate curriculum projects. ESI's course materials are being used in schools and universities throughout the United States and in many nations overseas. About 450 faculty members from 228 colleges and universities and 400 school teachers have worked either full or part-time on ESI's programmes in curriculum development and teacher education. They have come from over twenty-five countries. Eighty-four faculty members from MIT have worked on ESI's programmes.

Let me interpret the evidence.

1. Curriculum development began in science. (Mathematics also came into the picture early.)
2. The centre of concern was the renewal of content.
3. There was a considerable involvement of content experts in the shape of university personnel, who worked outside education faculties.
4. Teaching materials were produced, they were elaborate, and there was some emphasis on audio-visual presentation.
5. Materials were subjected to field trials before final publication.
6. Special institutions or groups were set up for dissemination, that is, publication and distribution.
7. Success was attested by the number and range of schools adopting the curriculum.

There is another, more muted strand represented later in the Preface:

8. 'Education is an experiment and by its nature an incomplete one; the course materials themselves are for the most part in

transition; on the basis of further teaching in the classroom many of them will be modified or changed.' (vi)

In Martin and Pinck (1966) we catch curriculum development moving out from science and mathematics into other areas. There are articles on history curricula, 'Men and Ideas', 'From Subject to Citizen' and 'The Death of the Roman Republic'. There is the 'Newton Social Science Sequence' (Newton, Massachusetts, is a wealthy and progressive suburban Boston school district). Basically the model here is similar to that in the hard sciences.

In addition to these subject developments, some specific attention is given to innovation in methods, but this is concentrated on 'Learning by Teaching', the involvement of students in the education of other students. There is, however, notice of problems of teaching the new curricula. Frank, in an article on 'The Co-operative Programme in Teacher Education', has this to say:

> We now find ourselves in the situation where there is real danger that the very large investment, both in money and in talent, in generating first-class course-content improvement projects will be largely wasted unless adequate numbers of teachers are educated to teach effectively both the currently developed new materials and those that will emerge in the future. . . .
>
> One approach to the solution to the problem of finding capable teachers is to retrain teachers in service to handle adequately the new curriculum materials. This has been and is being done with the help of special summer institutes, in-service institutes and the exhibition of teacher-training films. . . .
>
> It is clear . . . that the crux of the problem of providing large numbers of competent teachers lies in the adequate education of these teachers while they are still in college. . . .
>
> There must emerge first-rate courses that prepare the student adequately, not only to teach the new educational material effectively but also to exercise critical judgement of such material and to contribute to its future growth.
>
> (179–180)

Already, in the United States in 1966 much of the experience we have subsequently gathered in Britain is foreshadowed, and this is not surprising.

Curriculum development in England was influenced by the movement in the United States, though it differed from it in spirit. It laid less emphasis on bringing 'scholars' to the assistance of the teachers. Maclure and Becher (1974) offer a diagnosis of the American situation which has been an important strand in British curriculum work.

One of the reasons why some of the early science curriculum programmes in the USA attracted a disappointingly small following, despite the large resources which supported them, was that the main work was done by university specialists with whose approach the average high school teachers found it difficult to identify, and who were in any case totally unfamiliar with the problems of teaching science to pupils of secondary age.

In England systematic curriculum development began, as it did in the United States, with subject renewal, but the source of the initiative was different. The School Mathematics Project was 'initiated co-operatively by a group of university and school mathematicians'. (Halsey 1973, 65) This may sound exactly like the American situation, but it is subtly different. For in fact the initiative and leadership came as much from the teachers as from the universities; and note the difference between the U.S. formulation, 'university mathematicians and school mathematics teachers', and the British formulation, 'university and school mathematicians'. In America, the expertise of scholar and teacher is carefully distinguished. In England, university teachers and school teachers are seen as having a common field of scholarship.

Thus the Association for Science Education – a school teachers' association – played a key role in the science projects. In most subject-based projects the natural starting-point is the teachers' subject association. And in some cases – for example, the National Association of Teachers of English – curriculum development of radical significance has been based on a subject association without the formal structure or the financial support of a project. In English, projects have followed on N.A.T.E., consolidating and giving precision, rather than leading the way.

The first programme of projects in England and Wales was initiated by the Nuffield Foundation. Nuffield Science, Nuffield Maths and Nuffield Modern Languages are the classic programmes in English curriculum development. In all cases there was close co-operation between project team and serving teachers and the project teams themselves were staffed largely by seconded teachers. From these Nuffield projects and the early Schools Council projects there emerged a tradition of practice which has been characterized as follows:

1. First came a study of the chosen curriculum area, leading to the identification of new curriculum aims in relation to current practice and methods of work, and perhaps types of new teaching materials which might be developed. This stage could lead to the publication of a report

which would help towards the development of an appropriate climate of opinion.

2. The second stage was the establishment of a small team of teachers and others to devise and develop new teaching materials of the kind which appeared to be needed. As soon as drafts were ready trials of the new materials in schools were organized; these resulted in improvements to the materials and enabled the project team to identify the kind of help or training teachers needed before they could successfully adopt the new materials. Arrangements were also made at much the same time for the publication of the materials by one of the educational publishers.

3. In some cases it was necessary to develop new experimental examinations to be used in conjunction with the new materials. This involved co-operation with the examining boards. It was also necessary sometimes to negotiate acceptability of the new examinations with universities for entry to higher education and degree courses. Again this was part of the work towards creating a favourable climate of opinion.

4. Once the publication stage was reached then it was necessary to encourage the teacher training agencies, including local education authorities, universities, colleges of education, and the Inspectorate to co-operate in providing those teachers who wanted to use the new materials with appropriate training courses. The projects generally were able both to advise on the kind of training teachers would need (based on their experiments in schools) and also to provide individuals from their own strength or from schools which had taken part in the testing procedure able to play leading parts in the in-service work.

(Halsey 1971, 66–67)

An interesting feature of this description of project practice is the central emphasis placed on materials. Halsey does not take account of the fact that some projects have started from the end of teaching methods and approaches. This is an important difference in logic, since then the materials are *not* the message. Some projects – the prime example is Project Technology – have been much more concerned with influencing the educational climate than with producing materials or developing methods, and they have, I think, felt some pressure from the Schools' Council towards materials production. Materials are important, but they are not all.

Banks (1969), another member of the Council staff, writing two years earlier than Halsey and preserving for us an earlier Council view, places some emphasis on the preparation for a project through a feasibility study which is conceived as based on discussions and consultations with teachers and others. This concept has tended to drop out of the Council's thinking. One reason is probably the difficulty noticed by Banks.

> The feasibility study is, ideally, entrusted to the person who, if feasibility is established, will be responsible for the ensuing development project. One could go further and say that it is unlikely that a feasibility study will be of great value in the development stage to a director who did not himself carry out the study.
>
> (248)

This condition of continuity was often not met. What *was* a feasibility study seems to have turned into a planning phase which is more a test of viability of an idea and the capacity of a potential director than a testing of climate and a review of existing practice.

Banks also makes more of evaluation than Halsey, a surprising fact given that he is earlier and that evaluation developed comparatively late. Ideas of evaluation have tended to shift from evaluation of materials to evaluation of the project as an action programme in all its aspects. This shift is documented in Chapter 8.

Between them Banks (1969), Halsey (1971) and Nisbet (1973) document the tradition of assumptions in the Schools' Council within which a project will have to negotiate.

Projects themselves may be set up as a result of a Schools' Council initiative or as a result of a bid for funding from an individual or a consortium. The Humanities Project was a case where the title, duration and budget of the project were conceived by the Council and a director was invited in without making a proposal. The Careers Project was largely a result of Council initiative. Many projects are put forward by potential directors or by institutions which nominate a director. Most often, perhaps, proposals are evoked by the knowledge that the Council intends to take a research and development initiative in a certain direction and the Council quite freqently makes statements about its developing policy, presumably to encourage and inform initiatives.

The 'project' itself is an interesting form of organized activity. It is, in Miles's terms, a 'temporary system'. 'The basic or applied research project is also an undertaking sharply limited at the outset in terms of its effective life. Like the task force, it is a system set up to discover or apply a certain brand of knowledge, and will die, like all temporary systems, at some more or less clearly defined date.' (Miles 1964, 439)

In my experience this raises a series of interesting and insufficiently studied problems:

1. A project must build rapidly and run down rapidly a relatively complex administrative system with contacts and records at a national level.

2. It must select staff rapidly, and on the time scale on which it works, errors of selection are crippling.
3. It offers fixed-term appointments and there is a consequent difficulty in holding a team together until the completion of the task.
4. As a temporary system it has a highly ambiguous relationship to professional career structures.
5. In moving from birth to death the project changes its tasks: planning; materials' conception; methods' conception; editing; teacher induction; study of schools; research reporting; communication; dissemination; teacher training, etc. A wide range of capacities is needed, and it must battle with other people's conception of it as static.
6. If it is to succeed, it must ask for exceptional effort both from the central staff and from the participant teachers.
7. It is, in education, entrepreneurial in a system which lacks entrepreneurial styles.
8. At the conclusion of a project, if it has held its staff together, there may be difficulties and crises of confidence about securing posts.
9. It must fight constantly against what has been called 'the yearning toward perpetuity'.

I believe that a good deal of the investment of funding agencies of all types is lost because of difficulties in resolving the administrative, morale and ethical problems of the project as a temporary system.

The funding agency itself is an interesting phenomenon. Its own permanent staff are in an unusual position, having the job of dispensing money wisely. In the case of the Schools' Council, the joint secretaries are, like project directors, in their posts for a limited time. In that time they must learn their trade, make their contribution and pass on. And the Council is 'not just a piece of machinery for spending research funds, or administering examinations. It is a witness to a certain style of running an educational system.' (Caston 1971, 52)

One of the problems of maintaining this style is the changing membership of Council committees. A project lasting five years can towards the end of its life find itself negotiating with a committee, few or none of whose members remember its origins. A great problem for the Council is institutionalizing a corporate memory.

The most stable of the committees is Programme Committee, which acquires its stability from the fact that organizations are represented on it *ex officio*. As the main committee of a very large enterprise, it is bound to suffer from pressure of business and a large amount of paper has to be read for each meeting by members who are not in full-time service with the Council. It has taken the wise step of convening week-end meetings when it can consider policy rather than simply business.

Programme Committee represents and must represent some kind of political reality. If it did not, the link of the Council to the educational system would be merely notional. Because it represents these realities, it must struggle with the difficulties they create for it.

> Three member interests hold a controlling power. The first two, the Department of Education and Science and the local education authorities, provide it with its finance. The third, the teachers, constitute a majority on its committees. To whom are the teacher representatives accountable? Their immediate responsibility is to the union or association which nominates them. The teachers' associations, therefore – and in particular, the National Union of Teachers, which has the largest number of members – have a special responsibility, in that they could exert a powerful influence on the Council. To this extent, the health of the Schools' Council is linked to the vitality of democracy in the teachers' associations.
>
> (Nisbet 1973, 72)

Caston (1971) summarizes the ideal values of the Council in two concepts, pluralism and professionalism.

> *First:* pluralism. Philosophically, this means a system which acknowledges that there are many good ends, that these ends conflict, and no one of them is necessarily over-riding. Translated into social and political institutions, it means that there are – and indeed ought to be – many centres of influence, and that we should not worry when these conflict.
>
> Briefly, then, I use 'pluralism' in this paper to mean 'the dispersal of power in education'.
>
> (50)

> The second value is professionalism; and here too I must make clear my definition. For educators, the essence of professionalism lies in the exercise by individuals of choice and judgment in the interests, not of ourselves or our employers, but of our clients: in this case our pupils.
>
> (51)

The dispersal of power and the responsible professional response to it is the central problem for the Council, and needs continuous efforts within its own political structure.

Caston had this comment to make:

> All of us that have watched Council committees and working parties in discussion have been greatly heartened by the visible process of mutual

education between individuals starting from quite different viewpoints. I remember with some satisfaction a moment after a recent committee meeting when a newcomer had expressed very vigorously views with which I happened to disagree strongly. Someone came to me afterwards and said 'he must be a National Union of Teachers man'. In fact he was a chief education officer. People's roles get submerged in a new co-operative Council role, and this is very encouraging. I remember also people saying when the Council was set up that nothing could be achieved by a collection of 'interests', teachers' associations, local education authorities and others, all striking required attitudes. In fact, it has not been like that – individuals once appointed have modified their sets of prejudices and opened their minds.

(59)

I want to conclude this chapter with a consideration of two elements in the shaping of the present situation which are not generally noticed: the academic reflex to the Schools' Council projects, and the growth, within the Nuffield and Schools' Council programme, of a second tradition. Both appear to me important in the development from reform to research.

The setting up of a large programme of heavily financed curriculum research and development, based on seconded subject teachers, introduced a major new feature in the educational landscape. Those who worked on the projects were generally innocent as regards experimental design and proceeded pragmatically in the light of common sense.

In the universities and colleges of education there existed an establishment of educationists. Their field was the subject of a major curriculum reform. The undifferentiated study of education was giving ground and in a search for greater rigour educationists were identifying themselves with the 'constituent disciplines' of philosophy, history, psychology, sociology and comparative education. The implication was that methodologies and findings in these disciplines could be applied to educational practice, even though the work in the disciplines might not be founded on the close study of educational practice.

And here in the curriculum development programme was a major field of research growth, closely knit with practice, from which the discipline-based educationists were excluded. They were theoretically less innocent than most of those working on the projects, but they were cut off from practical experience. Confidence in their new rigour disposed them to offer advice to the projects, even to bring pressure to bear on them, but as a rule their knowledge of curriculum research was restricted to a cursory reading of out-of-date American literature. Hence they tended to urge on the curriculum developers the classic objectives model; and often the developers, feeling vulnerable to the academic educational establishment, yielded to their advice. After all, there was no British tradition of curriculum theory and research design on which they could fall back. They needed a more rigorous and defensible model which fitted teacher participation, but it was not there.

Within the Nuffield and Schools' Council work, however, a significant mutation was taking place. Some projects – for example, Nuffield Resources for Learning, the North-West Curriculum Project, the Keele Integrated Studies Project, the Humanities Curriculum Project, the York General Studies Project, the Middle School Years Project and the Liverpool Project – were not subject-based. And as a result, instead of recruiting subject specialists, they often attracted staff who might be either 'educationists' from universities and colleges or teachers. In either case they tended to identify themselves with curriculum problems rather than with subject problems. They were more interested in curriculum theory and design than in the reform of a teaching subject which commanded their first loyalty.

Parallel to this development came the inclusion in projects of 'evaluators'. They too had an interest in curriculum which over-rode their subject affiliation.

The common ground of these two groups was the cross-fertilization of theory and practice. It is out of this emerging tradition that this book is written, and it is an attempt – all too personal and fragmentary – to reach for a growing point in curriculum as a field of research and study. In my view one of the significant contributions of the Schools' Council is the contribution it has made to the founding of a coherent tradition in this field.

The crucial problem for curriculum research and study is the development of theory and methodology which is subservient to the needs of teachers and schools. This means that the theory has to be accessible. And it means that the personnel who identify themselves with this field should not allow themselves – or be allowed – to use their knowledge and expertise to divide themselves from teachers. This is an ever-present danger. When it comes to proving oneself as a researcher, the school is often a less attractive setting than the international conference. There is a place for the latter, but not as a substitute for the former.

If my diagnosis is correct, then the emergence of a healthy tradition of curriculum research and development depends upon a partnership of teachers and curriculum research workers. And such a partnership depends on the sharing of this tradition. The development must be through co-operation and towards a more solid basis for that co-operation.

The key factor would seem to be the induction of teachers into such a tradition in the course of initial training and the accessibility of the tradition to experienced teachers through in-service education. Research workers have a contribution to make; but it is the teachers who in the end will change the world of the school by understanding it. (Halsey 1972, 165)

14
PROBLEMS IN THE UTILIZATION OF CURRICULUM RESEARCH AND DEVELOPMENT

Curriculum development started in a spirit of great optimism. Both Martin and Pinck (1966) and the Schools' Council's *Working Paper No. 2* (1965) show this. Bliss was it in that dawn to be alive!

This unrealistic optimism soon encountered the disappointments of stubborn reality. Kerr (1968b) is in two minds. 'At the practical and organizational levels, the new curricula promise to revolutionize English education. Better decisions should be made by teams about the selection and organization of the content of courses, and about the relative merits of different teaching methods.' (15) 'Although some effective courses and materials are certainly being produced, the movement is not realizing its full potentiality.' (11)

Rudduck (1973) records the way in which experience in other countries flashed a warning to British curriculum workers.

> The message of the reports from abroad, mainly from the USA, can best be summed up in two quotations:
>
> > For nearly two decades now, we have seen large amounts of capital invested in the production of a variety of new curricula. Unfortunately, evidence is beginning to accumulate that much of this effort has had relatively little impact on the daily routine of the average classroom teacher. Why?
> >
> > (Herron 1971, 47)
>
> The writer goes on to identify the critical event in the process of extinction: it is when 'A grant expires and an outside consultant or team leaves the scene'. The other comment is from a Norwegian writer:
>
> > Even in those schools where primary experiments have been carried out in selected classes, the experience has not been spread to the rest of the classes! Schools in the same neighbourhood have for a number

> of years been unaffected by these experiments, and schools in surrounding communities have shown very little interest in them.
>
> (Dalin 1969)

[And Rudduck comments:]

> We were warned! Curriculum innovations that are left to make their own way may for some time travel comfortably on the passport of their sponsors' prestige . . . but without adequate structures for communication and support, innovation is unlikely to survive.
>
> (Rudduck 1973, 145–146)

Shipman (1973) studying the response of schools to a small-scale local project, found that it was often not implemented in practice, even when the head of the school concerned claimed that it was in action. Wastnedge (1972) asks the question: 'Whatever became of Nuffield Junior Science?' and finds that it has virtually faded away in Britain, though oddly 'It is alive and well and living in Canada'. Gross, Giacquinta and Bernstein (1971) in an extended study of an American innovation (which seems to have been particularly hamfisted) found that 'the educational innovation, the catalytic role model, announced in November was not being implemented in May despite a set of apparently positive antecedent and prevailing conditions in the school system, community, and school'. (121)

One way of thinking about these difficulties is to conceive them in terms of resistance to change, and some writers have used this idea. But such an approach appears to be unacceptable in the context of curriculum for two reasons. It may be possible in some fields to prove an innovation, but in education – at any rate in the British view – it is not. The teachers' judgement is crucial, and adverse judgement by the teacher can too easily and misleadingly be assimilated to such a concept as resistance. Moreover, many, if not most, of the failures in implementation occur, as Gross notes, where conditions are apparently favourable and where the participants do have a desire to implement the curriculum. Hence, the concept of 'barriers to innovation'.

Gross, Giacquinta and Bernstein comment: 'One of our basic reservations about the "resistance to change" explanation was that it ignores the whole question of barriers that may be encountered by members of organizations in their efforts to carry out innovations.' (1971, 196) They list some of the barriers they diagnosed:

> One barrier that blocked the teachers' efforts to implement the innovation throughout the six-month period was their lack of clarity about the new role model. . . . These findings suggest that the *clarity of an innova-*

> *tion to organizational members* needs to be taken into account in conceptual schemes designed to explain the success or failure of implementation efforts.
>
> A second barrier to the implementation of the innovation uncovered by our inquiry was the teachers' lack of the skills and knowledge to carry it out. . . .
>
> A third barrier to which teachers' were exposed was the unavailability of required materials and equipment. . . .
>
> A fourth obstacle that blocked teachers in their efforts to implement the innovation was a set of organizational arrangements existing prior to and during the innovation's introduction that were incompatible with the innovation, for example, the rigid school schedule.
>
> (196–198)

MacDonald and Rudduck (1971) argue that it is the responsibility of a curriculum development team to take acount of barriers: 'the system is "given" and it is for a development team to find out how the system works in order to cope effectively with its characteristics.' (148) But they note the team's difficulty in handling authority and avoiding the 'corrosive effects of dependency'. Great stress is laid on problems of understanding and of teacher development and autonomy, and communications and training are seen as key factors.

Hoyle (1972a) emphasizes materials, time and facility. 'If time is an important resource for innovation,' he declares, 'then those who desire educational innovation must seek to provide more of this resource.' He uses the term *facility*: 'to include all those resources – power, authority, influence, etc. – which those who wish to induce others to adopt an innovation can call upon in seeking to bring it about.' (32) The model of innovation which Hoyle has in mind may be more reformist than that of Gross and MacDonald and Rudduck, who are interested not in

> a pattern of development and diffusion in which a finished programme, by virtue of the prestige and authority of its originators, is carried intact through the diffusion chain to the classroom [but in] an alternative plan which is sensitive to the diversity of educational settings and recognizes the autonomy of decision makers at different levels of the system.
>
> (148)

Another way of conceptualizing barriers is in terms of 'gaps' as impediments to communication and understanding. Jung (1967) diagnoses gaps between teachers and the possible resources open to them, and he suggests activities to attempt to bridge them.

1. Gap between the teacher or school staff and the resource: persons who are experts;

2. Gap between the teacher or school staff and the resource: organized bodies of knowledge such as theories and research findings;
3. Gap between the teacher or school staff and the resource: innovations of other teachers and persons who work with youth;
4. Gap between the teacher or school staff and the resource: administrators in their system;
5. Gap between the teacher or school staff and the resource: other youth socializing systems such as organized recreation, therapeutic agencies, or families;
6. Gap between the teacher or school staff and the resource: pupils with whom they relate;
7. Gap between one teacher's way of trying to help a child and the resource: another person's different way of trying to help the same child;
8. Gap between the teacher's application of skills and the resource: the teacher's own potential – the skills which the teacher has, but is not applying for some reason.

(*Adapted from* Jung 1967, 91)

One gap, not mentioned by Jung, is that some of his 'resources' are seen by many teachers not as resources at all but as sources of direction or even as burdens.

Indeed, one of the problems which emerges is that of climate. On the one hand, there is a suggestion that those concerned with research and development projects should communicate with much greater clarity. On the other, is the problem that in practice, clarity and precision of definition often appear to communicate certainty and hence prescription. Thus, in my own experience, the clarity of the definition of the role of neutral chairman tended to make people see the project as authoritarian. It was difficult to communicate the message: this appears to us to be an intelligent line of experiment in teaching. In the absence of a research climate, uncertainty and provisonality is associated with vagueness, whereas research requires tentative precision.

Dalin (1973), in drawing together the implications of a series of studies commissioned by the Centre for Educational Research and Innovation of O.E.C.D., offers a general summary of the barriers to innovation disclosed by the studies under four heads.

Of the first of these, *value conflicts*, he writes:

> Major innovations will always be based on changes in educational, social, political or economic objectives. These changes reflect changes in values and thereby value conflicts in society. Any groups interested in education necessarily have more or less clearly expressed opinions about the changes in values implied by the innovations. For a large number of people these value conflicts are not clearly understood and are only

vaguely felt. Many reactions, therefore, may well be unclear and only vaguely communicated and therefore only partly understood by the decision-makers.

(236)

In Britain this problem of value conflicts often expresses itself as ambivalence between desire for consensus and desire for diversity. If diversity is to have real meaning, it must imply diversity of values, yet there is habitual pressure towards consensus. In a decentralized system it is presumably desirable to have value divergence within each school. This is perhaps more readily accepted in some university departments where different views of the discipline within the department may be seen as a strength. For example, a psychology department may represent different positions in psychology ranging from the extreme behaviourist to the Freudian and Jungian. One barrier to innovation may be that schools adopt a more positive posture – I have called it above one of rectitude or moralism – in the interests of pupil control; and such a posture is a barrier to innovation in a system where lip-service is paid to divergence. Value divergence is difficult for an institution to maintain, since it demands a loyalty to the spirit of inquiry.

Dalin's second barrier is *power conflicts*, of which he writes:

> Major innovations also imply a redistribution of power. The reactions from teacher groups, as well as from researchers, administrators, parents or students can best be understood in many instances as resistance due to unfavourable changes in the power distribution. . . . One cannot overlook these problems or even manipulate them.

(236–237)

This is certainly borne out in experience. All significant changes threaten the distribution of power. At one level they may create new administrative structures – for example new departments or the grouping of previously autonomous departmental heads under a 'faculty head'. At another, they shift the balance of power and status anong former equals – different voices begin to carry weight at staff and departmental meetings. These changes in power distribution are naturally and inevitably resisted. And, as Dalin comments, they cannot be manipulated by the developer, but must be negotiated in the management of schools themselves.

Dalin's third barrier, *practical conflicts*, is a barrier we must preserve.

> A number of innovations introduced into a system cannot prove their quality. They are simply not good enough and therefore do not serve

> to replace the old practice, or they are only a part of the answer and do not take other considerations into account. . . . Nearly all institutions studied have experienced resistance, especially from teachers, on these grounds which are perfectly valid.
>
> (237)

This barrier is, in itself, highly desirable. It is the filter of professional judgement on the basis of experience. But there are two reservations which I think should be expressed. First, it should be judgement *on experience*: new ideas can too easily be rejected without being tested. Second, ideas in themselves quite worthwhile may suffer from the research and development team botching the job of helping the teachers to implement them experimentally. Resistance 'can *develop* among organizational members who are positively oriented to change *after an innovation has been introduced* into the organization as a consequence of frustrations they experience in attempting to implement it'. (Gross, Giacquinta and Bernstein 1971, 198) In short, the difficulty in overcoming barriers may lead to rejection of the innovation, and though this is sensible in itself, rejection of the innovation may wrongly lead to rejection of the ideas it represents.

Dalin's final category of barriers is *psychological conflicts*. 'In conventional language, the term "barriers to change" is used to refer to the inability of human beings to change from one situation which is well known to one which is unknown.' (237)

Rather surprisingly, I think, he comments:

> The case studies seem to point out that this type of resistance is rare. On the other hand, if individuals or interest groups feel that they can benefit from a certain change they will have few difficulties with the change. Changes therefore not accompanied by incentives or, even worse, not changing old incentives that are counter-active to the new situation, will necessarily produce 'psychological barriers' which can raise serious problems for the implentation of innovations.
>
> (237)

It seems to me that the problem of incentives raised here is a real one, but that the judgement that discomfort about change is rare is hard to justify. It is difficult to advance 'beyond the stable state' (Schon 1971) and our capacity to do so probably depends on our developing routines for change and development and experiment which are themselves well-known and therefore reassuring. It is this that a research tradition offers.

The problem of barriers is interwoven with that of responsibility for action towards the betterment of the present situation. Dalin comments that 'negative reactions towards innovations are treated as "barriers" by the managerial group' (236) but he does not identify the managerial group. It is part of my thesis that research and development *projects* in curriculum and teaching should not see themselves as engineering change. In so far as it is their job to promote change, they should be concerned to make intelligent, but provisional, lines of development accessible to those whose responsibility it is to make decisions about educational practice. Accordingly, the crucial barrier for them is communication.

Responsibility lies with local authorities, schools and teachers. Among the personnel who carry that responsibility there will be those who incline to system maintenance and those who are dedicated to bettering the situation. The balance of power between them will depend upon either criteria or appointment or the way people respond to their gradual assessment of their power and how it can be used after they have been appointed. Those who are professionally concerned with research and development can do no more than collaborate with those in the action setting who want to improve things and perhaps make improvement a more attractive and practicable policy, as compared with system maintenance, to those teachers and administrators who do not have a determined policy commitment.

If this characterization is correct, then the 'barriers' are obstacles to the alliance of those who, having direct power in the system, wish to pursue policies of improvement, and those who have the power through research and development to support these actors. One is the army, the other the weapon designers, as it were. The issue is the utilization of knowledge by power.

And since, as Dalin has it, ' "barriers" cannot simply be treated any longer as *side effects* but rather as indications of the basic problems that may be inherent in the process itself', the whole process of the utilization and dissemination of knowledge and the implementation of innovation invites our attention.

Schon (1971) distinguishes three models for the dissemination of innovation.

The centre-periphery model rests, according to Schon, on three basic elements:

1. The innovation to be diffused exists, fully realized in its essentials, prior to its diffusion.
2. Diffusion is the movement of an innovation from a centre out to its ultimate users.
3. Directed diffusion is a centrally managed process of dissemination, training, and provision of resources and incentives.

He is concerned with the process of dissemination in general, not simply in education, and he draws instances from agriculture, medicine and industry. In his view,

> The effectiveness of a centre-periphery system depends first upon the level of resources and energy at the centre, then upon the number of points at the periphery, the length of the radii or spokes through which diffusion takes place, and the energy required to gain a new adoption. (82)

Schon also notes two variants of the centre-periphery model:

> **'Johnny Appleseed'** Here the primary centre is a kind of bard who roams his territory spreading a new message. Into this category fall the travelling scholars, saints and artisans of the Middle Ages; Voltaire and Thomas Paine; and contemporary bards of radical activism like Saul Alinsky.
> **The 'magnet' model** The 'magnet' attracts agents of diffusion to it, as universities have long since done. With the flowering of science and medicine in the universities of nineteenth century Germany, for example, students flocked to Germany from all parts of the world and then returned to their own country to teach and practise what they had learned. The United States, Britain and the Soviet Union play magnet, particularly in technology and economics, to developing nations. (83)

Schon calls his second model 'the proliferation of centres', and regards it as an elaboration of the centre-periphery pattern, in which there are secondary as well as primary centres. 'Secondary centres engage in the diffusion of innovations; primary centres support and manage secondary centres. . . . The limits to the reach and effectiveness of the new system depend now on the primary centre's ability to generate support and manage the new centres.' (85) In a system such as this the primary centre is concerned to manage the secondary centres' relations to their clients.

> The model of the proliferation of centres makes of the primary centre a trainer of trainers. The central message includes not only the content of the innovation to be diffused, but a pre-established method for its diffusion. The primary centre now specializes in training, deployment, support, monitoring and management. (85–86)

As I have said, Schon is not primarily concerned with innovation in education. His examples of the proliferation of centres model are the Roman army, industrial expansion, the communist movement, imperialism, and the Coca Cola Company. But the model is probably closest to the facts of curriculum innovation in England and Wales. In encouraging the setting up of teachers' centres, for example, the Schools Council could be seen as concerned to set up a nation-wide chain of secondary centres. In this case, however, unlike for example that of the Coca Cola Company, the projects, as primary centres, were temporary systems with a limited life. Accordingly, the teachers' centres were associated administratively, not with the primary centres, but with enduring structures in the receiving system, the local authorities. This gives much greater power to the secondary centres. And from their point of view it is primary centres – projects – which proliferate and disappear.

This seems to me to be a strong argument for the research model I have proposed in this book. Secondary centres must have a tradition which is not determined by individual and transient projects, but which is capable of responding to many primary initiatives. Such a tradition must either be on the model of a consumer association helping clients with a choice between projects as products, or it must be on the model of a research centre helping clients to work out lines of development which will become autonomous and organic. The second alternative is more difficult to achieve in practice; but seems to me to offer much greater potential. However, it must be admitted that in opting for such a title as *Choosing a Curriculum for the Young School Leaver* instead of *Developing a Curriculum for the Young School Leaver*, the Schools' Council appears to be adopting the notion of a choice of products.

Schon attempts to diagnose the sources of failure in the proliferation of centres model, and these can be clearly related to the position in curriculum.

The first is *the limits of infrastructure.*

> When the network of communications of money, men, information and materials is inadequate to the demands imposed on it, the system must either retrench or fail . . . the need for rapid central response, or for a more differentiated response to widely varying regional conditions, may overtax the available infrastructures.
>
> (91)

Certainly, projects can be hard pressed to meet the demands of local centres, while local centres complain of the flood of paper from the Schools Council. But the adoption of a common research tradition would make local centres more independent of projects and would also provide for a simpler, because more consistent, response to the offerings of the Schools Council and its projects.

This is true also for Schon's second source of failure, *constraints on the resources of the centre* in the face of increasing demands for leadership and management laid upon the primary centre. Many of these demands are pressing precisely because the secondary centres rely on primary centres, rather than on a public research tradition, to support their responses; and because the primary centres have to define themselves to the secondary centres without a context of tradition on which to rely.

The third of Schon's sources of failure, the lack of motivation of the agent of diffusion in the secondary centre, is also associated with his lack of identification with a research tradition. He sees himself as an agent rather than as a critical colleague.

Finally, the problem of regional diversity and the rigidity of central doctrine is well on the way to solution once the central doctrine is seen as a research hypothesis to be tested, adapted and developed in the unique situations of the region and the individual school.

Given the criticism of 'movements' which I mounted in the last chapter, it is interesting that Schon appears to see a good deal of potential in the movement as a medium for the diffusion of innovation.

He characterizes a movement as having neither a clearly established centre nor a stable, centrally established message. 'The movement must be seen as a loosely connected, shifting and evolving whole in which centres come and go and messages emerge, rise and fall.' (112) It expresses itself largely through informal networks and is, he claims, 'survival prone because of its fluidity and its apparent lack of structure'. (113)

The examples of movements offered by Schon are largely political or social: civil rights, black power, peace, disarmament and student revolt. And he claims that 'The withdrawal of President Johnson established the effectiveness of the movement.' (111)

I believe that the movement in Schon's sense has the defects I ascribed to movements. Within limits it is a good model in the areas of political and social policy. It is powerful. And of course education is a branch of political and social policy. However, my argument throughout this book has been that a central problem in the improvement of education is the gap between accepted policy and practice. Policy is too often out of touch with reality. The problem is that the movement's learning capacity is largely instrumental. The direction of the movement is assumed and its learning is learning of tactics. Within its structure there is no systematic basis for the critical development of either the message or its practical implementation in classrooms.

The desideratum in educational innovation is less that we improve our tactics in advancing our cause than that we improve our capacity to criticize our practice in the light of our beliefs, and our beliefs in the light of our practice. It is this that points to the need for a research tradition which can temper the confidence of movements.

Schon is concerned rather generally with the climate and dynamics of innovation. Havelock, though he surveys work in other areas, is primarily concerned with education, and his *Planning for Innovation through Dissemination and Utilization of Knowledge* is regarded as the 'educational change agent's' *vade-mecum*. It is a large volume which is based on an industrious survey of published work in the field, on which certain conclusions are built.

Havelock groups the principal models used by most authors concerned with dissemination and utilization under three heads: 1) research, development and diffusion; 2) social interaction; and 3) problem solving.

The research, development and diffusion model has been characteristic of farming, where innovations must be disseminated to a large number of units – farms. It is sometimes called 'the agricultural model' (even in curriculum literature) and it is often accepted as a pattern for dissemination and implementation in medicine and in education, where, as in agriculture, ideas have to reach geographically dispersed users.

The R, D and D system posits an orderly translation of knowledge from research to development to diffusion and finally to adoption. Havelock comments:

> Although consumer needs may be implicit in this approach, they do not enter the picture as prime motivations for the generation of new knowledge. Research does not begin as a set of answers to specific human problems. . . . In development basic theories and data are used to generate ideas which are then turned into prototypes which have to be tested and redesigned and retested before they represent anything that is truly useful to the bulk of humanity.
>
> (Havelock 1973, 2–42)

This pattern is the one adopted, with variations, in the first wave of curriculum development through the use of the objectives model and the emphasis on the production of classroom materials and teacher handbooks. The main point of divergence from a research model is in the assumption that it is products embodying solutions, rather than the hypotheses or ideas behind those products, which are being tested. The main concern is getting the product 'right' and then marketing it.

In the social interaction model the focus shifts to the diffusion of ideas. It stresses not the marketing of products but the flow of messages from person to person. Within it the two-step theory of the flow of knowledge is important, with its suggestion that ideas are mediated to the general public through opinion leaders. There is a stronger empirical base for the diffusion process than there is in the R, D and D model, for it is based on studies of how innovations have actually taken place. But again there is an assumption that the message carries conviction rather than evokes critical reaction and modification.

Both the R, D and D model and the social interaction model are what are termed 'centre-periphery' models, at least as they are usually conceived. A centre is seen as having a product or message which is to be diffused throughout the system. There has been a good deal of criticism of centre-periphery patterns of innovation on the grounds that they imply a degree of centralization of ideas which is not acceptable and that they fail to take account of local variations and local needs.

The problem-solver model does something to meet such criticisms by starting from the problems and needs which are defined by the client – the school or teacher – or diagnosed by a 'change agent' by direct study of the client's situation. Stress is laid on close collaboration between the client and the 'change agent'. As Havelock has it, 'the problem solvers may also be outside specialists but they will act in a two-way reciprocal and collaborative manner if they are to be effective'. (2–41)

In spite of this shift towards a client-centred approach, there remains an emphasis on solutions. A more research-oriented approach would accept that solutions are evolved gradually by the continuous evaluative study of a particular line of development. This argues that schools must have their own learning systems. The barrier to the acceptance of this seems to be an underestimate of the capacity of teachers to learn research and development procedures in the context of one innovation and transfer that learning to new problems. There is a continual emphasis on the use of expertise by schools to solve specific problems rather than to generate their own expertise in problem solving.

There is less tendency in Britain than in the United States to build theory and models for the utilization and dissemination of knowledge, but the emphasis in patterns of curriculum development has reflected a parallel experience. At first the emphasis was on the production of new materials and new courses. Later developments in thinking were reactions to the shortcomings diagnosed in the course of practical experience.

In 1968 the Schools Council defined the roles of research and development in these terms:

> The Council only finances educational research when it can foresee a return in terms of help to teachers in devising a curriculum for the pupils with whom they are concerned. . . . Research therefore merges naturally with 'development', which can be defined as the rendering of the results of the research into a form which will be of practical use to teachers.
>
> (Nisbet 1973, 73)

This position underlies the division between the research programme and the development programme in the Council; and in spite of the reference to teachers 'devising a curriculum for the pupils with whom they are concerned', the notion of 'the rendering of the results of the research into a form which will be of practical use to teachers' points to curricula as products. Devising a curriculum is more a matter of choice than school-based development.

Like other agencies, however, the Council became aware of problems in this pattern of curriculum development. Often the curricula did not 'take' in the schools.

Two lines of response emerged. One was concerned with the role of the teacher. The other laid emphasis on the need for dissemination and training.

The Council has always wanted the work which it has sponsored to relate closely to the reality of the schools. This emphasis expressed itself initially in the employment of seconded teachers on curriculum projects. But I do not think this works in the way that is intended. First, teachers working on projects give too much weight to *their own* past experience, which is not as generalizable as they often assume. Second, teachers commonly change radically and rapidly on taking up an appointment with a project; they become curriculum developers!

Hence there developed a desire to involve serving teachers in curriculum development without seconding them to projects. The earliest example of the attempt to work this pattern in a wholehearted way was the North-West Regional Curriculum Development Project. It did good work, but had, I think, serious shortcomings.

First, it imposed the objectives model on the teacher groups. The result was to weed out those who could not accept the model, and thus to diminish the worth of the project to the constituency of teachers they represented.

Second, it emphasized the teachers' producing materials, rather than servicing the teacher groups with production teams. But the actual production of materials is probably the least rewarding aspect of curriculum development in terms of personal professional development. Research participation and the study of one's own classroom are the educative part of the process and teachers producing materials have less time for that.

Finally, the teachers may have been pushed into a more directive role than they or the director desired.

> The director of the North-West Regional Curriculum Development Project sees this process as contributing to the professional development of teachers as much as, if not more than, to the development of materials or of the curriculum itself. But the materials, as the immediately tangible product, may assume greater importance in the minds of financing authorities and teachers, some of whom see the project as having a more directive role.
>
> (Schools Council 1973a, 19)

In effect, the North-West Regional Project attempted to find a pattern of professional self-education through involvement in curriculum development, just as the Humanities Project attempted professional self-development through involvement in research into teaching methods. Both found it hard to maintain the teacher-centred and research-centred pattern against their social context, which emphasized material products and recommended solutions.

The setting up of teachers' centres on the initiative of the Schools Council was both a step to provide teachers with a basis for local development and a move towards the proliferation of centres for the dissemination of national projects. But the Council's new emphasis on dissemination is signalled by the report of its own working party. (Schools Council 1974) This report recommends the strengthening of information services, the preparation of training materials and the mounting of training programmes and after-care support.

I think the Council working party's response in general an intelligent, practical and creative one, given the assumption that projects are about products and recommendations; and it is clear that for some time at least this assumption will for the most part be justified. Hence the injunction to projects to sell themselves positively.

However, I believe that long-term improvement of education through the utilization of research and development hinges on the creation of different expectations in the system and the design of new styles of project in harmony with those expectations.

The different expectations will be generated only as schools come to see themselves as research and development institutions rather than clients of research and development agencies. Against that background assumption a project will see itself as helping schools to undertake research and development in a problem area and to report this work in a way that supports similar work in other schools. Then 'dissemination is about the transfer of experience from a small number of schools to a larger number of schools'. (Rudduck 1975) And the experience is that of a research procedure, which can help to evolve better ways of teaching.

Skilbeck (1971, 27) declares that 'it ought not to be too readily assumed that the full personal commitment of a perceptive, intelligent teacher to ongoing classroom processes results in curriculum development that is inferior to those changes which result from advance planning and calculation'. I entirely agree and indeed would go farther in doubting the effectiveness of preplanned change as opposed to change evolving from process. He goes on to comment: 'These two types of approach may be crudely polarized as the intuitive and the rational.'

We should not opt for either pole but rather for research as the means towards a 'disciplined intuition', fusing creativeness and self-criticism.

Research in curriculum and teaching, which involves the close study of schools and classrooms, is the basis of sound development, and the growth of a research tradition in the schools is its foundation. Full-time research workers and teachers need to collaborate towards this end. Communication is less effective than community in the utilization of knowledge.

BIBLIOGRAPHY

Abercrombie, M. L. Johnson (1960) *The Anatomy of Judgement*. London: Hutchinson (Pelican Books, 1969).

Adelman, Clem and Walker, Rob (1973) Flanders' system for the analysis of classroom interaction – a study of failure in research. Centre for Applied Research in Education, University of East Anglia, mimeographed paper.

Adelman, Clem and Walker, Rob (1974) Stop-frame cinematography with synchronized sound: a technique for recording in school classrooms. *Journal of the Society of Motion Picture and Television Engineers*, 83, 3, 189–191.

Airasian, Peter W. (1967) *An Application of a Modified Version of John Carroll's Model of School Learning*. University of Chicago, unpublished Master's thesis. (Abstract in Block (1971) 99.)

Allen, Bryan (1968) *Headship in the 1970's*. Oxford: Blackwell.

Amidon, Edmund J. and Hough, John B. (1967) *Interaction Analysis: Theory, Research and Application*. Reading, Mass.: Addison-Wesley.

Amidon, Edmund J. and Hunter, Elizabeth (1966) *Improving Teaching: Analysing Verbal Interaction in the Classroom*. New York: Holt, Rinehart and Winston.

Archambault, Reginald D. (editor) (1965) *Philosophical Analysis and Education*. London: Routledge and Kegan Paul.

Arnold, Matthew (1908) *Reports on Elementary Schools 1852–1882*. New edition. London: Wyman and Sons for His Majesty's Stationery Office.

A.S.C.D./N.E.A. (1966) *The Way Teaching Is*. Washington D.C.: Association for Supervision and Curriculum Development and National Education Association.

Atkin, J. Myron (1968a) Research styles in science education. *Journal of Research in Science Teaching* 5, 338–345.

Atkin, J. Myron (1968b) Behavioral objectives in curriculum design: a cautionary note. *The Science Teacher*, 35, 27–30.

Atkin, J. Myron (1969) On looking gift horses in the mouth: the federal government and the schools. *The Educational Forum*, November, 9–20.

Bagley, Christopher and Verma, Gajendra K. (1972) Some effects of teaching designed to promote understanding of racial issues in adolescence. *Journal of Moral Education*, 1, 231–238.

Bales, R. F. (1950) *Interaction Process Analysis: A Method for the Study of Small Groups*. Reading, Mass.: Addison-Wesley.

Banks, J. A. (1972) *The Sociology of Social Movements*. London: Macmillan.

Banks, L. J. (1969) Curriculum developments in Britain 1963–8. *Journal of Curriculum Studies*. 1, 247–259.

Beishon, John and Peters, Geoff. (editors) (1972). *Systems Behaviour*. London: Harper and Row for the Open University Press.

Bellack, Arno *et al.* (1966) *The Language of the Classroom*. New York: Teachers' College Press, Columbia University.

Berger, Peter L. and Luckmann, Thomas (1966) *The Social Construction of Reality*. New York: Doubleday. (Penguin Books, 1971.)

Bernbaum, Gerald (1973) Countesthorpe College, United Kingdom. 7–88 in C.E.R.I. (1973c).

Bernstein, Basil (1971) *Class, Codes and Control. Volume I: Theoretical Studies towards a Sociology of Language*. London: Routledge and Kegan Paul, 1971. (Paladin Books, 1973).

Bertalanffy, Ludwig von (1962) General system theory – a critical review. *General Systems*, 7, 1–20 (reprinted 29–49 in Beishon and Peters (1972)).

Birley, Derek (1972) *Planning and Education*. London: Routledge and Kegan Paul.

Block, James H. (editor) (1971) *Mastery Learning: Theory and Practice*. New York: Holt, Rinehart and Winston.

Bloom, Benjamin S. *et al.* (1956) *Taxonomy of Educational Objectives. I: Cognitive Domain*. London: Longmans.

Bloom, Benjamin S. (1963) The role of the educational sciences in curriculum development. Mimeographed paper.

Bloom, Benjamin S. (1970) Toward a theory of testing which includes measurement – evaluation – assessment. 25–50 in Wittrock and Wiley (1970).

Bloom, Benjamin S. (1971) Mastery learning. 47–63 in Block (1971).

Bloom, Benjamin S., Hastings, J. T. and Madaus, G. F. (1971) *Handbook on Formative and Summative Evaluation*. New York: McGraw-Hill.

Boyd, William (1921) *The History of Western Education*. London: Adam and Charles Black (Fifth Edition 1950).

Bobbitt, Franklin (1918) *The Curriculum*. Boston: Houghton Mifflin.

Bobbitt, Franklin (1924) *How to Make a Curriculum*. Boston: Houghton Mifflin.

Bramwell, R. D. (1961) *Elementary School Work 1900–1925*. Newcastle-upon-Tyne: University of Durham Institute of Education. (Shortened form of an unpublished Ph.D. thesis.)

Brenckert, Stig, Nyström, Astrid and Sellergren, Ulf (1972) *Goal Description: a summary of five goal description projects in the educational development work of the National Swedish Board of Education*. Stockholm: National Swedish Board of Education.

Bruner, Jerome S. (1960) *The Process of Education*. Cambridge, Mass.: Harvard University Press. (Vintage Books 1963.)

Bruner, Jerome S. (1966) *Toward a Theory of Instruction.* Cambridge, Mass.: The Belknap Press of Harvard University Press.

Burgess, Anthony (1962) *A Clockwork Orange.* London: Heinemann.

Burnham, Peter S. (1968). The deputy head. 169–196 in Allen (1968).

Butcher, H. J. and Rudd, E. (editors) (1972) *Contemporary Problems in Research in Higher Education.* London: McGraw-Hill.

Carlson, R. O. (editor) (1965) *Change Processes in the Public School.* Eugene, Oregon: Centre for the Advanced Study of Education.

Caston, Geoffrey (1971) The Schools Council in context. *Journal of Curriculum Studies,* 3, 1, 50–64.

Cave, Ronald G. (1971) *An Introduction to Curriculum Development.* London: Ward Lock Educational.

Cave, Ronald G. (1974) In-service education after the White Paper – an L.E.A. Inspector's viewpoint. *Cambridge Journal of Education,* 4, 2, 52–59.

C.E.R.I. (1973a) Centre for Educational Research and Innovation, O.E.C.D. *Case Studies of Educational Innovation: I At the Central Level.* Paris: Organisation for Economic Co-operation and Development.

C.E.R.I. (1973b) Centre for Educational Research and Innovation, O.E.C.D. *Case Studies of Educational Innovation: II At the Regional Level.* Paris: Organisation for Economic Co-operation and Development.

C.E.R.I. (1973c) Centre for Educational Research and Innovation, O.E.C.D. *Case Studies of Educational Innovation: III At the School Level.* Paris: Organisation for Economic Co-operation and Development.

C.E.R.I. (1973) see Dalin (1973).

Checkland, P. B. (1971) A systems map of the universe. *Journal of Systems Engineering,* 2, 2, Winter 1971 (reprinted 50–55 in Beishon and Peters (1972)).

Collins, Geoffrey (1971) The role of the local authority adviser and his relationship with the teachers' centre warden. Paper read at a Schools Council Conference.

Comenius, John Amos (1631) *Janua Linguarum Reserata.* Published Laszno. English translation (without acknowledgement to Comenius) 1632.

Comenius, John Amos (?1632) *The Great Didactic.* Translated into English by M. W. Keatinge. New York: Russell and Russell, 1967. (Reprint of second revised edition, 1910.)

Comenius, John Amos (1658) *Orbis Sensualium Pictus.* English translation in the following year. Facsimile, Oxford University Press, 1968.

Cook, H. Caldwell (1919) The Play Way. London: Heinemann.

Cooper, Donald and Ebbutt, Dave (1974) Participation in action research as an in-service experience. *Cambridge Journal of Education* 4, 65–71

Cremin, Lawrence A. (1961) *The Transformation of the School.* New York: Alfred A. Knopf.

Cronbach, Lee (1963) Course improvement through evaluation. *Teachers' College Record*, 64, 672–683.

Dale, Alan (1973) The teacher and curriculum development. Unpublished paper delivered at the North of England Conference.

Dalin, Per (1969) The management of innovation in education. Report for C.E.R.I./O.E.C.D. workshop held at St. John's College, Cambridge.

Dalin, Per (1973) *Case Studies of Educational Innovation IV Strategies for Innovation in Education*. Centre for Educational Research and Innovation, O.E.C.D. (author's name not given). Paris: Organisation for Economic Co-operation and Development.

Department of Education and Science (1970) *Output Budgeting for the Department of Education and Science*. Education planning paper No. 1.

Dewey, John (1910) *How We Think*. Boston: Heath.

Eash, Maurice J. Transactional evaluation of classroom practice. 286–295 in Rippey (1973b).

Eisner, Elliott W. (1967a) Franklin Bobbitt and the 'science' of curriculum making. *The School Review*, 75, 29–47.

Eisner, Elliott W. (1967b) Educational objectives: help or hindrance. *The School Review*, 75, 250–260.

Eisner, Elliott W. (1969) Instructional and expressive educational objectives: their formulation and use in curriculum 1–18 in Popham, Eisner, Sullivan and Tylor (1969).

Elam, Stanley (editor) (1964) *Education and the Structure of Knowledge*. Chicago: Rand McNally for Phi Delta Kappa.

Elliott, John and Adelman, Clem (1973a) Reflecting where the action is: the design of the Ford Teaching Project. *Education for Teaching*, 92, 8–20.

Elliott, John and Adelman, Clem (1973b) Supporting teachers' research in the classroom. *New Era*, 54, 210–213, 215.

Epstein, Charlotte (1972) *Affective Subjects in the Classroom: Exploring Race, Sex and Drugs*. Scranton, Penn.: Intext Educational Publishers.

Esland, Geoffrey M. (1971) Teaching and learning as the organization of knowledge. 70–115 in Young (1971c).

Feyereisen, Kathryn V., Fiorno, A. John and Nowak, Arlene T. (1970) *Supervision and Curriculum Renewal: A Systems Approach*. New York: Appleton-Century-Crofts Meredith Corporation.

Flanders, Ned A. (1970) *Analyzing Teaching Behaviour*. Reading, Mass.: Addison Wesley.

Ford, G. W. and Pugno, Lawrence (editors) (1964) *The Structure of Knowledge and the Curriculum*. Chicago: Rand McNally.

Frank, Nathaniel H. (1966) The cooperative program in teacher education. 179–181 in Martin and Pinck (1966).

Frymier, Jack R. and Hawn, Horace C. (1970) *Curriculum Improvement for Better Schools*. Worthington, Ohio: Charles A. Jones Publishing Co.

Gage, N. L. (editor) (1963) *Handbook of Research on Teaching*. Chicago: Rand McNally.

Gagné, Robert (1965) *The Conditions of Learning*. Second edition. London: Holt, Rinehart and Winston, 1970.

Gagné, Robert M. (1967) Curriculum research and the promotion of learning. 19–38 in Stake (1967b).

Glaser, Robert (1970) Evaluation of instruction and changing educational models. 70–86 in Wittrock and Wiley (1970).

Glass, Gene V. (1970) Comments on Professor Bloom's paper. 56–61 in Wittrock and Wiley (1970).

Golembiewski, Robert T. (1962) *The Small Group*. Chicago: University of Chicago Press.

Goodlad, John (1960) Curriculum: the state of the field. *Review of Educational Research*, 30, 185–198.

Griffin, A. F. (1942) A philosophical approach to the subject-matter preparation of teachers of history. Unpublished doctoral dissertation. Ohio State University. Summarized in Metcalf (1963).

Gronlund, Norman E. (1970) *Stating Behavioural Objectives for Classroom Instruction*. London: Collier-Macmillan.

Gross, Neal, Giacquinta, Joseph B. and Bernstein, Marilyn (1971) *Implementing Organizational Innovations: a Sociological Analysis of Planned Change*. New York: Harper and Row.

Gusfield, Joseph R. (1968) Social Movements II: The study of social movements. 445–452 in Sills (1968).

Halsey, A. H. (editor) (1972) *Educational Priority. I. EPA Problems and Policies*. Report of a research project sponsored by the Department of Education and Science and the Social Science Research Council. London: Her Majesty's Stationery Office.

Halsey, Philip (1971) Role of research and development projects in curriculum development: an address. 61–74 in Maclure (1973).

Hamilton, David (1973) At classroom level. Unpublished Ph.D. thesis. Edinburgh University.

Hamilton, David and Delamont, Sarah (1974) Classroom research: a cautionary tale. *Research in Education*, 11, 1–15.

Hamingson, Donald (editor) (1973) *Towards Judgement: the Publications of the Evaluation Unit of the Humanities Curriculum Project 1970–1972*. Norwich: Centre for Applied Research in Education, Occasional Publications No. 1.

Hanley, Janet P., Whitla, Dean K., Moo, Eunice W. and Walter, Arlene S. (1970) *Curiosity, Competence, Community: Man: a course of study, An Evaluation*. 2 vols. Cambridge, Mass.: Educational Development Center Inc.

Hargreaves, David (1966) *Social Relations in a Secondary School*. London: Routledge and Kegan Paul.

Harlen, Wynne (1973a) The effectiveness of procedures and instruments for use in formative curriculum evaluation. Unpublished Ph.D. thesis. Bristol University.

Harlen, Wynne (1973b) *Evaluation and Science 5–13*. A report to the Schools

Council on the development of Science 5–13 curriculum materials and their formative evaluation. Draft edition. Schools Council Publications.

Harris, C. W. (1963) Some issues in evaluation. *The Speech Teacher*, 12, 191–199.

Hastings, J. Thomas (1969) The kith and kin of educational measurers. *Journal of Educational Measurement*, 6, 3, 127–130.

Havelock, Ronald G. (1973) in collaboration with Alan Guskin, Mark Frohman, Mary Havelock, Marjorie Hill, and Janet Huber. *Planning for Innovation through Dissemination and Utilization of Knowledge*. 4th printing. Ann Arbor, Michigan: Center for Research on Utilization of Scientific Knowledge.

Heberle, Rudolf (1951) *Social Movements: an Introduction to Political Sociology*. New York: Appleton-Century-Crofts.

Henry, J. (1955a) Culture, education and communications theory. 188–207 in Spindler (1955).

Henry, J. (1955b) Docility, or giving the teacher what she wants. *Journal of Social Issues*, 2, 33–41.

Henry, J. (1957) Attitude organisation in elementary school classrooms. *American Journal of Orthopsychiatry*, 27, 117–133.

Henry, J. (1959) The problem of sponteneity, initiative and creativity in suburban classrooms. *American Journal of Orthopsychiatry*, 29, 266–279.

Henry, J. (1960) A cross-cultural outline of education. *Current Anthropology*, 1, 4.

Henry, J. (1963) *Culture against Man*. New York: Random House. (Penguin edition, 1972.)

Herron, Marshall (1971) On teacher perception and curricular innovation. *Curriculum Theory Network, Monograph Supplement*.

Hirst, Paul H. (1965) Liberal education and the nature of knowledge. 113–138 in Archambault (1965).

Hirst, Paul H. and Peters, R. S. (1970) *The Logic of Education*. London: Routledge and Kegan Paul.

Hogben, D. (1972) The behavioural objectives approach: some problems and some dangers. *Journal of Curriculum Studies*, 4, 1, 42–50.

Holland, James G. and Skinner, B. F. (1961) *The Analysis of Behaviour: a Program for Self-Instruction*. New York: McGraw Hill.

Hooper, Richard (editor) (1971) *The Curriculum: Context, Design and Development*. Edinburgh: Oliver and Boyd in association with the Open University Press.

House, Ernest R. (editor) (1973a) *School Evaluation: the Politics and Process*. Berkeley, Cal.: McCutchan Publishing Corporation.

House, Ernest R. (1973b) The conscience of educational evaluation. 125–136 in House (1973a).

Hoyle, Eric (1972a) Creativity in the school. Unpublished paper given at O.E.C.D. Workshop on Creativity of the School at Estoril, Portugal.

Hoyle, Eric (1972b) Educational innovation and the role of the teacher. *Forum*, 14 42–44.

Hoyle, Eric (1972c) *Facing the Difficulties.* Unit 13, Open University Second Level Course: The Curriculum: Context, Design and Development (*Problems of Curriculum Innovation I*, Units 13–15.) Bletchley: The Open University Press.

Hoyle, Eric (1972d) *Problems: a Theoretical Overview.* Unit 17, Open University Second Level Course: The Curriculum: Context, Design and Development. (*Problems of Curriculum Innovation II*) Bletchley: The Open University.

Humanities Curriculum Project (1970) *The Humanities Project: an introduction.* London: Heinemann Educational Books.

I.L.E.A. (1973) Report of Course No. 124 – Evaluation of the Humanities Curriculum Project of the Schools Council and the Nuffield Foundation. Inner London Education Authority mimeographed paper.

Inlow, Gail M. (1966) *The Emergent in Curriculum.* New York: John Wiley.

Institute of Race Relations (1973) Paper for a conference of the project on problems and effects of teaching about race relations in the Centre for Applied Research in Education (unpublished).

Jackson, Philip W. (1964) The conceptualization of teaching. *Psychology in the Schools*, I, 232–243.

Jackson, Philip W. (1965) Teacher–pupil communication in the elementary classroom: an observational study. Paper read at American Educational meeting in Chicago.

Jackson, Philip W. (1966) The way teaching is. 7–27 in A.S.C.D./N.E.A. (1966).

Jackson, Philip W. (1968) *Life in Classrooms.* New York: Holt, Rinehart and Winston.

Johnson, Harry M. (1961) *Sociology: a systematic introduction.* London: Routledge and Kegan Paul (Harcourt Brace 1960).

Johnson, Mauritz Jr. (1967). Definitions and models in curriculum theory. *Educational Theory* 17, 127–140.

Jung, Charles C. (1967) The trainer change-agent role within a school system. 89–105 in Watson (1967).

Kansas (1958) *Kansas Curriculum Guide for Elementary Schools*, quoted in Oliver (1965).

Kast, F. E. and Rosenzweig, J. E. (1970) The modern view: a systems approach from *Organisation and Management: a Systems Approach.* New York: McGraw Hill. 14–28 in Beishon and Peters (1972).

Kerr, John F. (editor) (1968a) *Changing the Curriculum.* London: University of London Press.

Kerr, John F. (1968b) The problem of curriculum reform 13–38 in Kerr (1968a).

Kibler, Robert J., Barker, Larry L. and Miles, David T. (1970) *Behavioural Objectives and Instruction.* Boston: Allyn and Bacon.

King, Arthur R. Jr. and Brownell, John A. (1966) *The Curriculum and the Disciplines of Knowledge*. New York: John Wiley.

King, Ronald (1969) *Values and Involvement in a Grammar School*. London: Routledge and Kegan Paul.

Kliebard, Herbert M. (1966) The observation of classroom behaviour in A.S.C.D./N.E.A. (1966).

Kliebard, Herbert M. (1968) Curriculuar objectives and evaluation: a reassessment. *The High School Journal*, 241–247.

Kounin, J. S. (1970) *Discipline and Group Management in the Classroom*. New York: Holt, Rinehart and Winston.

Kounin, J. S., Friesen, W. V. and Norton, A. E. (1966) Managing emotionally disturbed children in regular classrooms. *Journal of Educational Psychology*, 57, 1, 1–13.

Kounin, J. S. and Gump, P. V. (1958) The ripple effect in discipline. *Elementary School Journal*, 59, 158–162

Kounin, J. S., Gump, P. V. and Ryan, J. J. (1961) Explorations in classroom management. *Journal of Teacher Education*, 12, 235–246.

Krathwohl, D. R. *et al.* (1964) *Taxonomy of Educational Objectives. II Affective Domain*. London: Longmans.

Lacey, C. (1970) *Hightown Grammar: the School as a Social System*. Manchester: Manchester University Press.

Larsson, Inger (1973) Individualized mathematics teaching: results from the I.M.U. Project in Sweden. *Studia Psychologica et Paedagogica*. Series Altera XXI. Lund: C. W. K. Gleerup.

Lawton, Denis (1973) *Social Change, Educational Theory and Curriculum Planning*. London: University of London Press.

Link, Frances R. (1972) The unfinished curriculum, from a working draft of *Seminars for Leadership Personnel* by Frances R. Link, with the assistance of Holly Gunner. Cambridge, Mass. and Washington, D.C. Educational Development Center and Curriculum Development Associates.

Loubser, Jan. J., Spiers, Herbert and Moody, Carolyn. York County Board of Education. 213–312 in C.E.R.I. (1973b).

MacDonald, Barry (1971a) Briefing decision makers. Internal paper, Evaluation Unit of the Humanities Curriculum Project, later reprinted in Hamingson (1973), House (1973) and Schools Council (1974a).

MacDonald, Barry (1971b) The evaluation of the Humanities Curriculum Project: a holistic approach. *Theory into Practice*, 10, 163–167.

MacDonald, Barry (1973a) Innovation and incompetence 89–92 in Hamingson (1973).

MacDonald, Barry (1973b) Educational evaluation of the National Development Programme in Computer Assisted Learning. A proposal prepared for consideration by the Programme Committee of the National Programme.

MacDonald, Barry (1975) Evaluation and the control of education. To be published in Schools Council (1975).

MacDonald, Barry and Parlett, Malcolm (1973) Rethinking evaluation: notes from the Cambridge Conference. *Cambridge Journal of Education*, 3, 1973, 74–82.

MacDonald, Barry and Rudduck, Jėan (1971) Curriculum research and development projects: barriers to success. *British Journal of Educational Psycholology*, 41, 148–154.

McGuffy, William Holmes (1879) *McGuffy's Sixth Eclectic Reader*. 1879 edition. Reprint: New York: New American Library of World Literature, Signet Classics, 1963.

Maclure, J. Stuart (1973) *Curriculum Development: an International Training Seminar, Norwich, United Kingdom, July 1971* Paris: Organisation for Economic Co-operation and Development, Centre for Educational Research and Innovation. C.E.R.I./G.C.D./73.03.

Maclure, J. Stuart and Becher, Tony (1974) *The State of the Art of Curriculum Development: a Study of a Sample of O.E.C.D. Member Countries*. To be published by O.E.C.D./C.E.R.I., autumn, 1974.

Mager, R. F. (1962) *Preparing Instructional Objectives*. Palo Alto: Fearon.

Man: A Course of Study (1970) *Evaluation Strategies*. Based on research and evaluation carried out by Dean Whitla, Janet P. Hanley, Eunice W. Moo and Arlene Walter in the Educational Development Center. Washington, D.C.: Curriculum Development Associates.

Mann, John S. (1969) Curriculum criticism. *Teachers' College Record*, 71, 27–40.

Mannheim, Karl (1936) *Ideology and Utopia: an Introduction to the Sociology of Knowledge*. London: Routledge and Kegan Paul.

Marklund, Sixten (1972) Introduction. 5–9 in Brenckert, Nyström and Sellergren (1972).

Martin, W. T. and Pinck, Dan C. (editors) (1966) *Curriculum Improvement and Innovation: a Partnership of Students, School Teachers and Research Scholars*. Cambridge, Mass.: Robert Bentley.

Metcalf, Lawrence E. (1963) Research on teaching the social studies. 929–965 in Gage (1963).

Midwinter, Eric (1973) *Patterns of Community Education*. London: Ward Lock Educational.

Miles, Matthew B. (editor) (1964) *Innovation in Education*. New York: Teachers' College Press, Columbia University.

Miles, Matthew B. (1965) Planned change and organizational health: figure and ground. In Carlson (1965).

Miles, Matthew B. (1967) Some properties of schools as social systems. 1–29 in Watson (1967).

Miller, H. J. (1967) A study of the effectiveness of a variety of teaching techniques for reducing colour prejudice in a male student sample (aged 15–21). Unpublished MA thesis, University of London.

Miller, H. J. (1969) The effectiveness of teaching techniques for reducing colour prejudice. *Liberal Education*, 16, 25–31.

Mills, Theodore M. and Rosenberg, Stan (1970) *Readings on the Sociology of Small Groups*. Englewood Cliffs, N.J.: Prentice-Hall.

Mønsterplan (1971) *Mønsterplan for Grunnskolen*. Oslo: Aschehoug. Midlertidig utgave (Provisional edition).

Musgrave, P. W. (1968) *The School as an Organisation*. London: Macmillan.

Musgrove, Frank (1968) The contribution of sociology to the study of the curriculum. 96–109 in Kerr (1968).

Musgrove, Frank (1971) *Patterns of Power and Authority in English Education*. London: Methuen.

Musgrove, Frank and Taylor, Philip (1969) *Society and the Teacher's Role*. London: Routledge and Kegan Paul.

Neagley, Ross L. and Evans, N. Dean (1967) *Handbook for Effective Curriculum Development*. Englewood Cliffs, N.J.: Prentice-Hall.

Nisbet, John (1973) The Schools Council, United Kingdom. 7–76 in C.E.R.I. (1973a)

Nisbet, Stanley (1957) *Purpose in the Curriculum*. London: University of London Press.

Nuthall, G. A. and Lawrence, P. J. (1965) *Thinking in the Classroom: the Development of a Method of Analysis*. Auckland: New Zealand Council for Educational Research.

Oliver, Donald W. and Shaver, James P. (1966) *Teaching Public Issues in the High School*. Boston: Houghton Mifflin.

Oliver, Albert I. (1965) What is the meaning of 'curriculum'? from *Curriculum Improvement* by Albert I. Oliver. 3–9 in Short and Marconnit (1968).

Owen, J. G. (1973) *The Management of Curriculum Development*. Cambridge: Cambridge University Press.

Owens, Thomas R. (1973) Educational evaluation by adversary proceeding. 295–305 in House (1973a).

Parkinson, J. P. and MacDonald, Barry (1972) Teaching race neutrally. *Race*, 13, 299–313.

Parkhurst, Helen (1922) *Education on the Dalton Plan*. London: G. Bell and Sons.

Parlett, Malcolm (1972) Evaluating innovations in teaching in Butcher, H. J. and Rudd, E. (1972).

Parlett, Malcolm and Hamilton, David (1972) Evaluation as illumination: a new approach to the study of innovatory programmes. Occasional Paper of the Centre for Research in the Educational Sciences, University of Edinburgh. Mimeographed. October, 1972.

Parlett, Malcolm R. and King, John G. (1971) *Concentrated Study: a Pedagogic Innovation Observed*. London: Society for Research into Higher Education.

Parsons, Talcott (1952) *The Social System*. London: Tavistock.

Pepper, Ron (1972) In-service training and the Thomas Calton school, Peckham. 14–17 in Hoyle (1972d).

Peters, Richard S. (1959) *Authority, Responsibility and Education*. London: Allen and Unwin.

Peters, Richard S. (1966) *Ethics and Education*. London: George Allen and Unwin.

Phenix, Philip H. (1962) The disciplines as curriculum content. 133–137 in Short and Marconnit (1968) (originally in *Curriculum Crossroads*, edited by A. Harry Passow. New York: Teachers' College Press, 1962).

Phenix, Philip H. (1964a) The architectonics of knowledge. 44–74 in Elam (1964).

Phenix, Philip H. (1964b) *Realms of Meaning*. New York: McGraw-Hill Book Company.

Phi Delta Kappa (1971) *Educational Evaluation and Decision Making*. Written by P.D.K. National Study Committee on Evaluation (Daniel L. Stufflebeam, Walter J. Foley, William J. Gephart, Egon G. Guba, Robert L. Hammond, Howard O. Merriman and Malcolm M. Provus) Itasca, Ill.: F. E. Peacock Publishers.

Popham, W. James (1967) *Educational Criterion Measures*. Inglewood, Cal.: Southwest Regional Laboratory for Educational Research and Development.

Popham, W. James (1968) Probing the validity of arguments against behavioural goals. A symposium presentation at the Annual American Educational Research Association. Meeting, Chicago, 7–10 February, 1968, 115–124 in Kibler, Barker and Miles (1970).

Popham, W. James (1969) Objectives and instruction. 32–52 in Popham, Eisner, Sullivan and Tyler (1969).

Popham, W. James (1971) Must all objectives be behavioural? Mimeographed paper. University of California, Los Angeles.

Popham, W. James and Baker, Eva L. (1970) *Systematic Instruction*. Englewood Cliffs, N. J.: Prentice-Hall.

Popham, W. James, Eisner, Elliot W., Sullivan, Howard J. and Tyler, Louise L. (1969) *Instructional Objectives*. American Educational Research Association Monograph Series on Curriculum Evaluation. No. 3 Chicago: Rand McNally.

Popper, Karl R. (1963) *Conjectures and Refutations*. London: Routledge and Kegan Paul. (4th edition 1972).

Pressey, Sidney L. (1927) A machine for automatic teaching of drill material. *School and Society*, 25, 549–552.

Raths, James D. (1971) Teaching without specific objectives. *Educational Leadership*. April, 714–720.

Richardson, Elizabeth (1967) *Group Study for Teachers*. London: Routledge and Kegan Paul.

Richardson, Elizabeth (1973) *The Teacher, the School and the Task of Management*. London: Heinemann Educational Books.

Richmond, P. G. (1970) *An Introduction to Piaget*. London: Routledge and Kegal Paul.

Richmond, W. Kenneth (1965) *Teachers and Machines: an Introduction to the Theory and Practice of Programmed Learning.*

Richmond, W. Kenneth (1971) *The School Curriculum.* London: Methuen.

Rippey, Robert M. (1973a) The nature of transactional evaluation. 8–13 in Rippey (1973b).

Rippey, Robert M. (editor) (1973b) *Studies in Transactional Evaluation.* Berkeley, Cal.: McCutchan Publishing Corporation.

Rippey, Robert M. (1973c) What is transactional evaluation? 3–7 in Rippey (1973b).

Rousseau, Jean-Jacques (1762) *Emile* (translated by B. Foxley). London: Dent (Everyman's Library) 1911.

Rowe, Michael (1973) The cyclical structure of evaluatory schemes. *New Era*, 54, 216–218.

Rudduck, Jean (1973) Dissemination in practice. *Cambridge Journal of Education*, 3, 143–158.

Rudduck, Jean (1975) *The Dissemination of Innovation: An Account of the Dissemination of one National Curriculum Project.* To be published by the Schools Council in 1975.

Schon, Donald A. (1971) *Beyond the Stable State.* London: Temple Smith.

Schools Council, The (1965) *Raising the School Leaving Age.* Working Paper No. 2. London: Her Majesty's Stationery Office.

Schools Council, The (1967) *Curriculum Development: Teachers' Groups and Centres.* Working Paper No. 10. London: Her Majesty's Stationery Office.

Schools Council, The (1968) *Enquiry 1. Young School Leavers.* Report of a survey among young people, parents and teachers by Roma Morton-Williams and Stewart Finch. Assisted by Chris Poll, John Raven, Jane Ritchie and Evelyn Hobbs. Government Social Survey. London: Her Majesty's Stationery Office.

Schools Council, The (1971) *Choosing a Curriculum for the Young School Leaver.* Working Paper No. 33. London: Methuen for the Schools Council.

Schools Council, The (1973a) *Pattern and Variation in Curriculum Development Projects: a Study of the Schools Council's Approach to Curriculum Development.* Schools Council Research Studies. London: Macmillan for the Schools Council.

Schools Council, The (1973b) *Evaluation in Curriculum Development: Twelve Case Studies.* Schools Council Research Series. London: Macmillan for the Schools Council.

Schools Council, The (1974) *Dissemination and In Service Training: Report of the Schools Council Working Party on Dissemination (1972–1973)* Schools Council Pamphlet 14. London: The Schools Council.

Schools Council, The (1975a) *Curriculum Evaluation: the State of the Art.* (Title provisional) To be published by Macmillan for the Schools Council.

Schools Council, The (1975b) *Report of the Working Party on the Whole Curriculum of the Secondary School.* To be published by the Schools Council.

Schwab, Joseph J. (1964) Structure of the disciplines: meanings and significances. 1–30 in Ford and Pugno (1964).

Schwab, Joseph J. (1970) *The Practical: A Language for Curriculum.* Schools for the 70s: auxiliary series. Washington, D.C.: National Education Association Centre for the Study of Instruction.

Science 5–13 (1972) *With Objectives in Mind: Guide to* Science 5–13. London: Macdonald Educational for the Schools Council.

Scriven, Michael (1967) The methodology of evaluation. 39–89 in Stake (1967b).

Scriven, Michael (1973) Goal-free evaluation. 319–328 in House (1973a).

Shipman, Marten (1968) *The Sociology of the School.* London: Longmans.

Shipman, Marten (1973). The impact of a curriculum project. *Journal of Curriculum Studies*, 5, 47–56.

Shipman, Marten, Bolam, David and Jenkins, David (1974) *Inside a Curriculum Project.* London: Methuen.

Short, Edmund C. and Marconnit, George D. (editors) (1968) *Contemporary Thought on Public School Curriculum: Readings.* Dubuque, Iowa: Wm. C. Brown Co.

Sills, David L. (editor) (1968) *International Encyclopaedia of the Social Sciences.* New York: Macmillan.

Skilbeck, Malcolm (1971) Strategies of curriculum change. 27–37 in Walton (1971).

Simon, Anita and Boyer, E. G. (editors) (1970) *Mirrors for Behaviour II.* Volumes A and B. Philadelphia, Penn: Classroom Interaction Newsletter in association with Research for Better Schools. (There was an earlier 1967 edition, less complete. A special 14 volume anthology of original materials by the authors of the 79 systems recorded 'has been placed in selected educational libraries throughout the world.)

Skinner, B. F. (1953) *Science and Human Behaviour.* New York: Free Press.

Skinner, B. F. (1968) *The Technology of Teaching.* New York: Appleton Century Crofts.

Skinner, B. F. (1971) *Beyond Freedom and Dignity.* New York: Alfred Knopf.

Smith, B. O. and Meux, Milton (1962) *A Study of the Logic of Teaching.* Urbana, Ill.: University of Illinois College of Education, Bureau of Educational Research.

Smith, B. O., Meux, Milton, Coombs, Jerrold, Nuthall, Graham and Precians, Robert (1967) *A Study of the Strategies of Teaching.* Urbana, Ill.: University of Illinois College of Education, Bureau of Educational Research.

Smith, L. M. and Geoffrey W. (1968) *The Complexities of an Urban Classroom: an Analysis toward a General Theory of Teaching.* New York: Holt, Rinehart & Winston.

Sparrow, F. H. (1973) The role of the evaluator. 1–3 in Schools Council (1973b).

Spindler, G. (editor) (1955) *Education and Anthropology*. Stanford, Cal.: Stanford University Press.

Stake, Robert E. (1967a) The countenance of educational evaluation. *Teachers' College Record*, 68, 523–540.

Stake, Robert E. (editor) (1967b) *Perspectives of Curriculum Evaluation*. American Educational Research Association. Monograph Series on Curriculum Evaluation No. 1. Chicago: Rand McNally.

Stake, Robert E. (1970) Comment on Professor Glaser's paper. 86–91 in Wittrock and Wiley (1970).

Stake, Robert E. (1971) Testing hazards in performance contracting. *Phi Delta Kappan*, June, 583–589.

Stake, Robert E. (1972) Responsive Evaluation. Mimeographed. Urbana-Champaign: Centre for Instructional Research and Curriculum Evaluation, University of Illinois.

Stake, R. E. (1974) Responsive Evaluation (revised) in *New Trends in Evaluation*, Institute of Education, University of Göteborg, No. 35.

Stark, Werner (1958) *The Sociology of Knowledge*. London: Routledge and Kegan Paul.

Stark, Werner (1962) *The Fundamental Forms of Social Thought*. London: Routledge and Kegan Paul.

Stenhouse, Lawrence (1961) Hartvig Nissen's impressions of the Scottish educational system in the mid-nineteenth century. *British Journal of Educational Studies*, 9, 143–154.

Stenhouse, Lawrence (1963) A cultural approach to the sociology of the curriculum. *Pedagogisk Forskning* (*Scandinavian Journal of Educational Research*) 120–134.

Stenhouse, Lawrence (1967) *Culture and Education*. London: Nelson.

Stenhouse, Lawrence (1968) The Humanities Curriculum Project. *Journal of Curriculum Studies*, 1, 26–33.

Stenhouse, Lawrence (1970) Some limitations of the use of objectives in curriculum research and planning. *Paedagogica Europaea*, 6, 73–83.

Stenhouse, Lawrence (1971a) The Humanities Curriculum Project: the rationale. *Theory into Practice*, 10, 154–162.

Stenhouse, Lawrence (1971b) Pupils into students. *Dialogue* (Schools Council Newsletter) 5, 10–12.

Stufflebeam, Daniel L. (editor) (1971) *Educational Evaluation and Decision Making*. Itasca, Ill.: F. E. Peacock for Phi Delta Kappan National Study Committee on Evaluation.

Taba, Hilda (1962) *Curriculum Development: Theory and Practice*. New York: Harcourt Brace and World.

Thelen, Herbert (1954) *Dynamics of Groups at Work*. Chicago: University of Chicago Press.

Thurlow, John (1973) Eliciting pupils' interpretations in the primary school. *New Era*, 54, 214–215.

Tylor, E. B. (1871) *Primitive Culture*. London: John Murray.

Tyler, Ralph W. (1949) *Basic Principles of Curriculum and Instruction*. Chicago: University of Chicago Press.

Verma, Gajendra K. and Bagley, Christopher (1973) Changing racial attitudes in adolescents: an experimental English study. *International Journal of Psychology*, 8, 55–58.

Verma, Gajendra K. and MacDonald, Barry (1971) Teaching race in schools: some effects on the attitudinal and sociometric patterns of adolescents. *Race*, 13, 187–202.

Walker, Robert (1971) The social setting of the classroom: a review of observational studies and research. Unpublished M.Phil thesis. University of London, Chelsea College of Science and Technology.

Walker, Robert (1972) The sociology of education and life in school classrooms. *International Review of Education*, 18, 32–43.

Walker, Rob and Adelman, Clem (1972) Towards a sociography of classrooms. Final report, Social Science Research Council Grant HR996–1: The long-term observation of classroom events using stop-frame cinematography.

Waller, Willard (1932) *The Sociology of Teaching*. New York: John Wiley and Son. (Reprint, 1965).

Walton, Jack (editor) (1971) *Curriculum Organization and Design*. London: Ward Lock Educational.

Wastnedge, Ron (1972) Whatever happened to Nuffield Junior Science? 35–40 in Hoyle (1972).

Watson, Goodwin (editor) (1967) *Change in School Systems*. Washington, D.C.: National Training Laboratories. National Education Association for Co-operative Project for Educational Development.

Weiss, Robert S. and Rein, Martin (1969) The evaluation of broad aim programmes: a cautionary tale and a moral. *Annals of the American Academy of Political and Social Science*. 385, 133–142.

Westbury, Ian (1970) Curriculum evaluation. *Review of Educational Research*, 40, 239–260.

White, John (1969) The curriculum mongers: education in reverse. *New Society*, March 6, 359–361. Reprinted 273–280 in Hooper (1971).

White, John (1973) *Towards a Compulsory Curriculum*. London: Routledge and Kegan Paul.

Wild, R. D. (1973) Teacher participation in research. Unpublished conference paper, S.S.R.C. and Gulbenkian Project on Problems and Effects of Teaching about Race Relations, Centre for Applied Research in Education, University of East Anglia.

Wiley, David E. (1970) Design and analysis of evaluation studies. 259–269 in Wittrock and Wiley (1970).

Willower, Donald J. (1965) Hypotheses on the school as a social system. *Educational Administration Quarterly*, 1, 40–51.

Willower, Donald J., Eidell, Terry L. and Hoy, Wayne K. (1967) *The School and Pupil Control Ideology*. Penn State Studies No. 4. The Pennsylvania State University Press.

Wittrock, M. C. (1970) The evaluation of instruction: cause-and-effect relations in naturalistic data. 3–21 in Wittrock and Wiley (1970)

Wittrock, M. C. and Wiley, David E. (1970) *The Evaluation of Instruction: Issues and Problems*. New York: Holt, Rinehart and Winston.

Young, Michael F. D. (1971a) An approach to the study of curricula as socially organized knowledge. 19–46 in Young (1971c).

Young, Michael F. D. (1972b) Knowledge and control. Introduction 1–17 in Young (1972c).

Young, Michael F. D. (editor) (1972c) *Knowledge and Control*. London: Collier-Macmillan.

INDEX

WITHDRAWN